Hospitality, Tourism, and Lifestyle Concepts: Implications for Quality Management and Customer Satisfaction

Hospitality, Tourism, and Lifestyle Concepts: Implications for Quality Management and Customer Satisfaction has been co-published simultaneously as *Journal of Quality Assurance in Hospitality & Tourism,* Volume 5, Numbers 2/3/4 2004.

GW00640693

The *Journal of Quality Assurance in Hospitality & Tourism*™ Monographic "Separates"

Executive Editor: Sungsoo Pyo

Below is a list of "separates," which in serials librarianship means a special issue simultaneously published as a special journal issue or double-issue *and* as a "separate" hardbound monograph. (This is a format which we also call a "DocuSerial.")

"Separates" are published because specialized libraries or professionals may wish to purchase a specific thematic issue by itself in a format which can be separately cataloged and shelved, as opposed to purchasing the journal on an on-going basis. Faculty members may also more easily consider a "separate" for classroom adoption.

"Separates" are carefully classified separately with the major book jobbers so that the journal tie-in can be noted on new book order slips to avoid duplicate purchasing.

You may wish to visit Haworth's website at . . .

http://www.HaworthPress.com

. . . to search our online catalog for complete tables of contents of these separates and related publications.

You may also call 1-800-HAWORTH (outside US/Canada: 607-722-5857), or Fax 1-800-895-0582 (outside US/Canada: 607-771-0012), or e-mail at:

docdelivery@haworthpress.com

Hospitality, Tourism, and Lifestyle Concepts: Implications for Quality Management and Customer Satisfaction, edited by Maree Thyne and Eric Laws (Vol. 5, No, 2/3/4, 2004). *A comprehensive review of current theory and case studies of the application of lifestyle marketing to the hospitality and tourism industry.*

Current Issues and Development in Hospitality and Tourism Satisfaction, edited by John A. Williams and Muzaffer Uysal (Vol. 4, No. 3/4, 2003). *Focuses on emerging approaches that measure customer satisfaction and how to apply them to improve hospitality and tourism businesses.*

Knowledge Management in Hospitality and Tourism, edited by Ricarda B. Bouncken and Sungsoo Pyo (Vol. 3, No. 3/4, 2002). *"Of great value. . . Introduces the concepts associated with knowledge management and provides examples of these concepts through case studies and unique real-world applications. . . . A lot of great information on a fascinating topic. . . ." (Cary C. Countryman, PhD, CHE, CHTP, Director, Technology Research and Education Center, Conrad N. Hilton College of Hotel and Restaurant Management)*

Benchmarks in Hospitality and Tourism, edited by Sungsoo Pyo (Vol. 2, No. 3/4, 2001). *"A handy single volume that clearly explains the principles and current thinking about benchmarking, plus useful insights on how the techniques can be converted into profitable business operations. Includes conceptual, practical, and operational (or 'how-it-is-done') chapters." (Chris Ryan, PhD, MEd, MPhil, BSc (Econ) Hons, Professor of Tourism, The University of Waikato, Hamilton, New Zealand)*

Hospitality, Tourism, and Lifestyle Concepts: Implications for Quality Management and Customer Satisfaction

Maree Thyne
Eric Laws
Editors

Hospitality, Tourism, and Lifestyle Concepts: Implications for Quality Management and Customer Satisfaction has been co-published simultaneously as *Journal of Quality Assurance in Hospitality & Tourism*, Volume 5, Numbers 2/3/4 2004.

Routledge
Taylor & Francis Group
NEW YORK AND LONDON

First Published by

The Haworth Hospitality Press®, 10 Alice Street, Binghamton, NY 13904-1580 USA

The Haworth Hospitality Press® is an imprint of The Haworth Press, Inc., 10 Alice Street, Binghamton, NY 13904-1580 USA.

Transferred to Digital Printing 2009 by Routledge
270 Madison Ave, New York NY 10016
2 Park Square, Milton Park, Abingdon, Oxon, OX14 4RN

Hospitality, Tourism, and Lifestyle Concepts: Implications for Quality Management and Customer Satisfaction has been co-published simultaneously as *Journal of Quality Assurance in Hospitality & Tourism,* Volume 5, Numbers 2/3/4 2004.

Cover design by Jennifer Gaska

Library of Congress Cataloging-in-Publication Data

Hospitality, tourism, and lifestyle concepts: implications for quality management and customer satisfaction/Maree Thyne, Eric Laws, editors.
     p. cm.
    Includes bibliographical references and index.
    ISBN: 13: 978-0-7890-2754-2 (hard cover: alk. paper)
    ISBN: 10: 0-7890-2754-2 (hard cover: alk. paper)
    ISBN: 13: 978-0-7890-2755-9 (soft cover: alk. paper)
    ISBN: 10: 0-7890-2755-0 (soft cover: alk. paper)
  1. Hospitality industry--Management. 2. Tourism--Management. I. Thyne, Maree. II. Laws, Eric, 1945-
  TX911.3.M27H66235 2004
    647.94'068--dc22

                          2004016723

Indexing, Abstracting & Website/Internet Coverage

This section provides you with a list of major indexing & abstracting services and other tools for bibliographic access. That is to say, each service began covering this periodical during the year noted in the right column. Most Websites which are listed below have indicated that they will either post, disseminate, compile, archive, cite or alert their own Website users with research-based content from this work. (This list is as current as the copyright date of this publication.)

Abstracting, Website/Indexing Coverage . . . . Year When Coverage Began

- *CIRET (Centre International de Recherches et d'Etudes Touristiques). Computerized Touristique & General Bibliography <http://www.ciret-tourism.com>* 2000

- *EBSCOhost Electronic Journals Service (EJS) <http://www.ejournals.ebsco.com>* 2001

- *Google <http://www.google.com* 2004

- *Google Scholar <http://www.scholar.google.com>* 2004

- *Haworth Document Delivery Center* 2000

- *HTI Database (Hospitality, Tourism Index); EBSCO Publishing* 2003

- *IBZ International Bibliography of Periodical Literature <http://www.saur.de>* 2000

- *INSPEC is the leading English-language bibliographic information service providing access to the world's scientific & technical literature in physics, electrical eng., electronics, communications, control eng., computers & computing, and information tech <http://www.iee.org.uk/publish/>* 2000

(continued)

   *Exact start date to come.

Special Bibliographic Notes related to special journal issues (separates) and indexing/abstracting:

- indexing/abstracting services in this list will also cover material in any "separate" that is co-published simultaneously with Haworth's special thematic journal issue or DocuSerial. Indexing/abstracting usually covers material at the article/chapter level.
- monographic co-editions are intended for either non-subscribers or libraries which intend to purchase a second copy for their circulating collections.
- monographic co-editions are reported to all jobbers/wholesalers/approval plans. The source journal is listed as the "series" to assist the prevention of duplicate purchasing in the same manner utilized for books-in-series.
- to facilitate user/access services all indexing/abstracting services are encouraged to utilize the co-indexing entry note indicated at the bottom of the first page of each article/chapter/contribution.
- this is intended to assist a library user of any reference tool (whether print, electronic, online, or CD-ROM) to locate the monographic version if the library has purchased this version but not a subscription to the source journal.
- individual articles/chapters in any Haworth publication are also available through the Haworth Document Delivery Service (HDDS).

Hospitality, Tourism, and Lifestyle Concepts: Implications for Quality Management and Customer Satisfaction

CONTENTS

ABOUT THE EDITORS

Dr. Maree Thyne has published in a number of areas of tourism research including host community issues, social distance, tourist behavior and lifestyle segmentation. Maree has a PhD from the University of Otago, and moved to The Robert Gordon University, Aberdeen, Scotland, in 2001. Maree is currently a Senior Lecturer in the Aberdeen Business School and is a member of the Scottish Centre of Tourism, a consultancy group within the University. Maree is involved in a number of areas of tourism research, particularly with respect to tourism in Scotland. Her main current area of research is the Backpacker market in Scotland, which is addressed in an article included in this special volume.

Eric Laws has a PhD from Griffith University, Australia, an MPhil from the University of Surrey, England and an MA from Thames Polytechnic, London, England. He has written and edited over 50 refereed articles and a dozen books on aspects of tourism quality, the structure of the tourism industry and destination management. Eric has recently retired from full time teaching and research, and is now Visiting Professor in Tourism at James Cook University, Cairns, Australia. He can be contacted on e.laws@runbox.com

Hospitality, Tourism, and Lifestyle Concepts: Implications for Quality Management and Customer Satisfaction

Eric Laws
Maree Thyne

SUMMARY. This article provides an overview of the significance of the lifestyle concept for the management of service quality and customer satisfaction in the hospitality and tourism industry. It discusses aspects of its continuing evolution and outlines the contents of articles relevant to this volume, providing a brief summary of the articles collected. It concludes by identifying a number of opportunities for further research into hospitality and tourism lifestyle concepts. *[Article copies available for a fee from The Haworth Document Delivery Service: 1-800-HAWORTH. E-mail address: <docdelivery@haworthpress.com> Website: <http://www.HaworthPress. com> © 2004 by The Haworth Press, Inc. All rights reserved.]*

Eric Laws has recently retired from full time teaching and research, and is now Visiting Professor in Tourism at James Cook University, Cairns Australia (E-mail: e.laws@ runbox.com).

Maree Thyne is a Senior Lecturer in the Aberdeen Business School and is a member of the Scottish Centre of Tourism, a consultancy group within the Robert Gordon University, Garthdee II Garthdee Road, Aberdeen, AB 107QG UK (E-mail: m.thyne@rgu.ac.uk).

[Haworth co-indexing entry note]: "Hospitality, Tourism, and Lifestyle Concepts: Implications for Quality Management and Customer Satisfaction." Laws, Eric, and Maree Thyne. Co-published simultaneously in *Journal of Quality Assurance in Hospitality & Tourism* (The Haworth Hospitality Press, an imprint of The Haworth Press, Inc.) Vol. 5, No. 2/3/4, 2004, pp. 1-10; and: *Hospitality, Tourism, and Lifestyle Concepts: Implications for Quality Management and Customer Satisfaction* (ed: Maree Thyne and Eric Laws) The Haworth Hospitality Press, an imprint of The Haworth Press, Inc., 2004, pp. 1-10. Single or multiple copies of this article are available for a fee from The Haworth Document Delivery Service [1-800-HAWORTH, 9:00 a.m. - 5:00 p.m. (EST). E-mail address: docdelivery@haworthpress.com].

http://www.haworthpress.com/web/JQAHT
© 2004 by The Haworth Press, Inc. All rights reserved.
Digital Object Identifier: 10.1300/J162v05n02_01

KEYWORDS. Hospitality, tourism, lifestyle, quality management, customer satisfaction

INTRODUCTION

As the supply and demand of consumer services and products proliferated during the twentieth century it became increasingly clear to managers that they needed to focus product development and promotion on the specific needs (or wants) of selected groups of consumers. The undifferentiated competitive market place of early economic theory based on rational economic choice was no longer a valid model within which to structure an understanding of how people made purchasing decisions (see Duesenberry, 1949; Simon, 1976; Etzioni, 1978 and Lewis, Webley and Furnham, 1995 for discussions). Instead, as Mitchell et al. (2001) point out, the focus now is on understanding customers.

At the beginning of the twenty-first century, Western society was characterised by widespread enjoyment of previously unknown standards of living, including a higher disposable income allowing a wide choice of luxury goods and services, including tourism. This change in access to life choices is spreading into many societies where such freedoms were unthinkable a decade ago. (See for example Wen Pan and Laws (2001) and Zang and Hueng (2001) for a discussion of the development of the outbound Chinese tourist market.)

The demand for tourism is dependent on significant free time, knowledge of other countries and the transportation, accommodation and allied sectors of the industry facilitating leisure travel (Urry, 1990; Laws, 2003). But the demand for tourism is stimulated by individual interest in travel, and a range of activities offered at destinations which appeal to personal self-images or lifestyle concepts evoked and promoted not only by the tourism industry's advertising but by the linking of many sectors' products to various tourism locations. People have almost constant exposure to marketing and media messages combining to encourage them to adopt continually more complex and self-determined aspirations for activities and sets of possessions (Kotler and Armstrong, 1999).

At the same time, tourism has serious consequences for destination populations; it is often asserted that the traditional roots of society are under threat. Long established patterns of family life and responsibilities between the generations, adherence to the beliefs of a widely espoused (locally at least) religion and its practices, and attachment to the place where one grew up are amongst some of the key societal changes which both affect tourism demand and are affected by tourist activity. This is not a static situation; the pace of change appears to be increasing. Therefore an analysis of lifestyle issues for tourism has to take into account both the potential to better promote tourism through lifestyle research (see for example the individual papers by Dolničar; Moscardo; and Scott and Parfitt in this volume for further discussion on this point) and the consequences of tourism for the lifestyles of the industry's stakeholders (see for example the articles by Goulding, Baum and Morrison; Simpson, Bretherton and de Vere; and Tucker and Lynch).

Implicit in the foregoing discussion is a view that tourism, and indeed contemporary society are in a constant state of evolution under pressure from a variety of factors. It is therefore evident that a lifestyle marketing analysis conducted at one period to determine new market products or segments will have to be reappraised after a period of time because of changes occurring in the target population's demand preferences, development of new target groups, and supply changes in terms of new or enhanced products and newer forms of competition. Furthermore, the attacks on America in September 2001 and the subsequent defensive measures adopted by the airline industry and government agencies have undermined the tourism industry's expectation of continuing growth as the demand for travel, whether for leisure or business, evaporated and has still not fully recovered.

MARKETING AND LIFESTYLE APPROACHES

Marketing is widely regarded as the core business function concerned with matching the organisation's skills with market demand. "The organisation's task is to determine the needs, wants and interests of target markets and to deliver the desired satisfactions more effectively and efficiently than competitors, in a way that preserves or enhances the customers' and the society's well being" (Kotler, 1994:26). The purpose of marketing is to obtain (and retain) customers by ensuring that the service offered is attractive to target groups, and by influencing their decision to purchase. The contexts include the marketplace within which the firm operates, its own competitive capabilities, and consumers' attitudes towards it.

The main paradigm in theories of marketing strategy has traditionally been the managerial requirement to bring potential clients to the point where the action of purchasing a product yields satisfaction to the customer and profit to the vendor. More recently, it has been accepted that purchases are made to gain a range of benefits from use or ownership, leading to the 'market orientation' paradigm, and it is this which underlies the managerial concern to define the conditions under which clients are more or less likely to purchase future hospitality or tourism services from a particular business. Haywood (1997) and Laws (2004) have reviewed the relevance of the marketing concept for tourism. The issue is not confined to tourism: the wider context to this situation is the growth of consumer-rights awareness (Prus, 1989; McCracken, 1990), and the 'meta-context' of scepticism about the underlying values and institutions of western societies (Hughes, 1993).

One academic response to these conditions has been the development of theories relating to lifestyle as a way of understanding how people make choices about products and services (Raaij, 1986; Lawson, Tidwell, Rainbird, Loudon and Della Bitta, 1996). Managers, too, have adopted the approach, one illustration familiar to people who watch advertising for cars is that they are now seldom overtly concerned with performance features such as speed or acceleration, instead they provide imagery, music and show people enjoying the car in specific settings such as moody empty city streets, holidays spent in high risk sport in exotic environments, romantic interludes in various settings and so on. Thus, the paradigm underpinning many advertising messages is to link the product to lifestyle concepts.

Tourism and Hospitality Lifestyles

The term 'style of life' was coined over 50 years ago by Alfred Adler to refer to the goals people shape for themselves and the ways they reach them (Lawson et al. 1996). Lazer (1963) suggests that lifestyle can be viewed as a pattern of living which influences and is reflected by consumption behaviour. Craig-Lees, Joy and Browne (1995) stress that 'lifestyle' relates to how people live, how they spend their money and how they allocate their time. Thus, 'lifestyles' can also be just as relevant to the supplier (as discussed in the articles by Goulding et al.; Simpson et al.; and Tucker and Lynch). Predominantly, however, the 'lifestyles' of the consumer have been researched chiefly to provide a detailed understanding of underlying target markets to enable the development of more effective marketing strategies (as discussed in the articles by Hede et al.; Hughes; Moscardo; and Thyne et al., in this volume).

Due to the increased understanding of the effect and influence of lifestyles on consumption, there has been a heightened emphasis on 'lifestyles' in marketing, particularly in promotion strategies. This suggests the need for more research, both to better understand the nature of such links and to gain deeper insights into how people see themselves in terms of their purchase decisions. This collection of articles summarises a variety of existing lifestyles literature and researches and addresses the business and academic rationale for undertaking it (each article will be discussed in more detail later in this Introduction).

Customer Satisfaction and Lifestyle Considerations

Consideration of the question of customer satisfaction suggests that there are a number of dynamic factors at work driving change in the tourism and hospitality marketplace, as Fuchs and Weiermair (2003) point out. Effective managers are always asking questions about what makes their service successful or unsuccessful (Zeithaml, 2000). Noe (1999: Introduction) has stated that "no greater challenge exists in the marketplace than for a business to be responsible for providing satisfactory tourist and hospitality services."

Ultimately, the individual's test of his or her tourism experience is how well it has satisfied his or her own expectations, but importantly it is the sum of all of these which underpins the organisation's reputation, and its continuing success. This reinforces Grönroos (2001) who suggests both that the organisation should be designed around good service delivery, and that its management should focus on quality issues, designing the system from the perspective of its ability to satisfy consumers. Similarly, Chisnall (1984) identified the following twin roles for marketing managers:

1. Interpretation, the analysis and interpretation of behaviour in the market place, both present and projected.
2. Integration, that is, working closely with company colleagues in other functions.

Chisnall argued that marketing is not just concerned with the obvious audiences outside the company, it has an important role to play in adapting attitudes and performance by all company members, that is 'internal selling'. Cowell (1986) has defined the concept in the following way: "internal marketing means applying the philosophy and practices of marketing to people who serve the external customers so that the best possible people can be employed and retained, and they will do the best possible work." The implications of internal selling are that the firm recognises the impact of employees' detailed job decisions on client's satisfaction. This is discussed further in terms of lifestyles and lifestyle choice in the articles by Simpson et al.; and Tucker and Lynch.

It is worth emphasising the effect on tourists' satisfaction of their interactions with the staff of an airline, airport, hotel and other companies supplying facilities for their holiday. This concern with service encounters reflects other writers' views. "Since service encounters are the consumer's main source of information for conclusions regarding quality and service differentiation, no marketer can afford to leave the service encounter to chance" (Shostack, 1985). These interactive aspects of service encounters are significant at a more fundamental level when considered in the context of lifestyle research: interactions with other people are basic human activities, and occupy a large part of our time. Poor service encounter experiences affects the quality of every day life, and staff may spend their entire working day in repeated service encounters with customers who may already be dissatisfied by some incident which occurred earlier. Thus stressing the point that it is important that tourism operators are closely matched (psychologically and in terms of lifestyles) to their visitors and their visitors' expectations (reiterated in the article by Tucker and Lynch). Thus, lifestyle approaches can help conceptualise why people choose to work in the tourism and hospitality sectors, and why they choose particular places to live and work as discussed in the articles by Goulding et al. and Simpson et al. Lifestyle approaches may also be of assistance in providing a framework to analyse the effects of subsequent experiences on their chosen lifestyle self-images and this appears to the Editors to be an area ripe for further conceptual and methodological development.

Lifestyle Research Presented in This Special Edition

Collectively the articles cover four main areas of lifestyles research and its link to quality management and customer satisfaction. Two articles focus on the match between the tourism provider and the guest/tourist. Tucker and Lynch look at this in terms of the B&B market in both New Zealand and Scotland. They suggest that tourism boards and other bodies in charge of tourism promotion and marketing could conduct psychological profiling of homestay hosts, to enable potential guests to match themselves with compatible hosts. Simpson, Bretherton and de Vere investigate the nature of buyer/seller relationships which evolve in a wine tourism setting (in New Zealand) to again analyse a potential match between the two.

Goulding, Baum and Morrison analyse a similar concept; however, they focus solely on the tourism business operator/supplier. Specifically they discuss tourism businesses (within the United Kingdom) which are being chosen as lifestyle enterprises, providing a range of benefits, some of which occur due to the businesses operating on a seasonal basis. This article advocates that policies focusing on extending the seasonality of the tourism industry need to consider the lifestyle aspirations of the operators.

Another topic area covered in this special edition includes articles which utilise and describe various types of lifestyle segmentation studies undertaken to provide more detailed information on specific markets. Hede, Jago and Deery discuss the link between personal values and attending special events (specifically a major block-buster musical in Australia). Hughes discusses and analyses commonly held views about the gay market and their value to the tourism industry and he evaluates the lifestyle marketing opportunities of this segment. Moscardo describes the lifestyle segmentation of Rainforest visitors in North Eastern Australia based on travel interests, activities and desired rainforest based tourism experiences. The article links the segments uncovered with management frameworks for the specific tourism destination. Thyne, Davies and Nash outline a lifestyle segmentation study of the backpacker market in Scotland, determining that although often viewed as one target market, it actually consists of a number of underlying segments with quite distinct interests, attitudes and motivations.

The final area of lifestyle research covered in this special edition relates to methodological issues. Dolničar and Leisch compare *a priori* geographic segmentation and *a posteriori* behaviour segmentation on an Austrian visitor survey data set, providing recommendations for destination management. Scott and Parfitt compare and evaluate three case studies which have implemented three different methods of lifestyle segmentation (Roy Morgan Values Segments; brand and domain specific segmentation; and AIO segmentation). Dolničar evaluates two data-driven segmentation solutions (behaviour and benefit segmentation) which are constructed independently from the same data set (Australian surfers). All of these three studies stress the importance of matching the right lifestyle segmentation methodology with the context, aim and objectives of the research.

Taken together, the Editors expect that the articles will contribute to a better understanding of the significance of lifestyle concepts in two ways. First, the articles bring together and summarise a wide range of theoretical insights while providing description and analysis through case studies of recent application of lifestyle concepts in a variety of sectors and cultural settings. Second, the collection of articles acts as a benchmark of current knowledge, with the hope of stimulating further research into the concepts and practices of 'lifestyles.'

CONCLUDING COMMENTS

The assumptions underlying traditional marketing are that marketing activity has the primary purpose of attracting new customers and that the market consists of a large number of potential customers. In this simplified approach to marketing, the needs of all customers were regarded as very similar, and it was thought to be easy to replace any who desert with new customers so there was little concern with methods of retaining existing customers. In contrast, service marketing and contemporary approaches to marketing in other sectors emphasise the importance of developing long term relationships with their customers (Bergen and Nasr, 1998; Bloemer, de Ruyter and Wetzels, 1999; Edvardson and Standvik, 2000; Leong and Han, 2002; Raffii and Kampas, 2002).

McCarthy (1960: 288-289) commented "a firm can through long term relationships with customers get access to detailed and useful knowledge about the customer . . . develop a core of satisfied committed customers. . . . Service firms have started to identify their customers, which enables them to be more focused in their marketing." As this collection of articles demonstrates, lifestyle research, particularly when linked to the study of quality management and customer satisfaction, contributes to better understanding customers, developing long term relationships and improving the efficiency of marketing. Taken together, these articles also provide an accessible and comprehensive review of major themes in the literature and extensive bibliographies on which, the Editors hope, the study of lifestyles will be taken further by the next generation of research into tourism and hospitality.

REFERENCES

Asseal, H. (1987). *Consumer behaviour and marketing action.* Boston, Mass: Kent Publication Co.

Band, W. (1991). *Creating value for customers: Designing and implementing a total corporate strategy.* New York: John Wiley and Sons.

Berger, P. D. & Nasr, N. I. (1998). Customer lifetime value: Marketing models and applications, *Journal of Interactive Marketing*, 12 (1): 17-30.

Bloemer, J., de Ruyter, K. & Wetzels, M. (1999). Linking perceived service quality and service loyalty: A multi-dimensional perspective, *Journal of Marketing*, 33: 1082-1106.

Chisnall P. M. (1984). *Marketing, a behavioural analysis.* Maidenhead: Mc Graw Hill.

Cohen, J. B. (1982). Involvement, separating the state from its causes and effects. In Wilkie, W. L., *Consumer Behaviour.* Chichester: John Wiley & Sons.

Cowell, D. W. (1986). *The Marketing of Services.* London: Heinemann.

Craig-Lees, M., Joy, S. & Browne, B. (1995). *Consumer Behaviour.* Singapore: John Wiley and Sons.

Duesenberry, J. (1949). *Income, saving and the theory of consumer behaviour.* Cambridge, MA.: Harvard University Press.

Edvardsson, B. & Strandvik, T. (2000). Is a critical incident critical for a customer relationship? *Managing Service Quality,* 10 (2): 82-91.

Etzioni, A. (1988). *The moral dimension.* New York: Free Press.

Fodness, D. & Murray, B. (1997). Tourist Information Search, *Annals of Tourism Research,* 24 (3): 503-23.

Fornell, C. & Wernerfelt, B. (November, 1987). Defensive Marketing Strategy by Customer Complaint Management: A Theoretical Analysis, *Journal of Marketing Research,* 24: 337-46.

Garvin, D. A. (1988). *Managing Quality, the Strategic and Competitive Edge.* New York: Free Press.

Gilbert, G. R. & Parhizgari, A. M. (2000). Organizational effectiveness indicators to support service quality, *Managing Service Quality,* 10 (1): 46-52.

Grönroos, C. (1982). *Strategic Management and Marketing in the Service Sector.* London: Chartwell-Bratt.

Grönroos, C. (2001). The perceived service quality concept–a mistake? *Managing Service Quality,* 11 (3): 150-152.

Hayes, B. E. (1998). *Measuring Customer Satisfaction: Survey Design, Use, and Statistical Analysis Methods.* Milwaukee. WI: American Society for Quality.

Haywood, K. (1997). Revising and Implementing the Marketing Concept as It Applies to Tourism, *Tourism Management,* 18(3): f195-205.

Hughes, R. (1993). *Culture of complaint.* New York: Warner Books.

Laws, E. (2004). *Improving tourism and hospitality services,* CABI Publishing, Wallingford, Oxford.

Lawson, R., Tidwell, P., Rainbird, P., Loudon, D. & Della Bitta, A. (1999). *Consumer Behaviour in Australia and New Zealand.* Sydney: McGraw-Hill Inc.

Leong, J., Kim, W. and Ham, S. (2002). The effects of service recovery on repeat patronage, *Journal of Quality Assurance in Hospitality and Tourism,* 3 (1/2): 69-94.

Levitt, T. (1969). *The Marketing Mode.* New York: McGraw Hill.

Lewis, A., Webley, P. & Furnham, A. (1995). *The New economic mind, The social psychology of economic behaviour.* Hemel Hempstead: Harvester Wheatsheaf.

McCracken, G. (1990). *Culture and consumption.* Indianapolis: Indian University Press.

McCarthy, J. (1960). *Basic Marketing: A Management Approach.* Homewood, Illinois: Irwin.

Mitchell, V., Hogg, M. K., Lewis, B. R. & Littler, D. A. (April, 2001). Editorial: Understanding customers: Contributions from theory and practice, *Journal of Marketing Management*, 17 (3-4): 261.

Noe, F. (1999). *Tourist service satisfaction: Hotel, transport and recreation.* Champagne, Illinois: Sagamore

Pan, G. W. & Laws, E. (2001). Tourism Marketing Opportunities for Australia in China, *Journal of Vacation Marketing*, 8 (1): 39-48.

Pyo, S. (Ed.) 2002. *Benchmarks in Hospitality and Tourism.* Binghamton, NY: The Haworth Press, Inc.

Prus, R. C. (1989). *Pursuing Customers, An Ethnography of Marketing activities.* London: Sage.

Rafii, F. & Kampas, P. J. (November, 2002). How to identify your enemies before they destroy you, *Harvard Business Review*, pp. 115-123.

Rapert, M. & Wren, B. (1998). Service quality as a competitive opportunity, *Journal of Services Marketing*, 12 (3): 223-235.

Shostack, L. (1985). Planning the Service Encounter. In Czepiel, J. A., Soloman, M. R. & Surprenant, C. F. (Eds.). *The Service Encounter.* Mass: Lexington Books, pp. 243-253.

Simon, H. (1957). *Models of man.* New York: Wiley.

Thomas, M. (February, 1987). Coming to terms with the customer, *Personnel Management*, pp. 24-28.

Urry, J. (1990). *The Tourist Gaze.* London: Sage Publications.

Wisner, J. (1999). A study of successful quality improvement programs in the transportation industry, *Benchmarking: An International Journal*, 6 (2): 147-163.

Zeithaml, V. A. (2000). Service quality, profitability, and the economic worth of customers: What we know and what we need to learn, *Journal of Academy of Marketing Science*, 28(1): 67-85.

Zhang, H. Q. & Hueng, V. C. S. (2001). The emergence of mainland Chinese outbound travel market and its implications for tourism marketing, *Journal of Vacation Marketing*, 8(1): 7-12.

Host-Guest Dating:
The Potential
of Improving the Customer Experience
Through Host-Guest
Psychographic Matching

Hazel Tucker
Paul Lynch

SUMMARY. This article argues for the potential use of lifestyle segmentation in order to achieve psychographic matching between hosts and guests in Bed and Breakfast and homestay accommodation. The discussion draws on research conducted in home-hosted accommodation in New Zealand and Scotland that highlighted the central role that the host-guest interaction plays in guest experience and satisfaction. The idea is then developed as to the potential for tourism boards and other promotional bodies to conduct psychographic profiling on homestay hosts so that potential guests might match themselves for potential com-

Hazel Tucker is affiliated with the Department of Tourism, University of Otago, Dunedin, P.O. Box 56, New Zealand (E-mail: htucker@business.otago.ac.nz).

Paul A. Lynch is affiliated with the School of Business and Enterprise, Queen Margaret University College, Edinburgh EH12 8TS, Scotland (E-mail: plynch@ qmuc.ac.uk).

[Haworth co-indexing entry note]: "Host-Guest Dating: The Potential of Improving the Customer Experience Through Host-Guest Psychographic Matching." Tucker, Hazel, and Paul Lynch. Co-published simultaneously in *Journal of Quality Assurance in Hospitality & Tourism* (The Haworth Hospitality Press, an imprint of The Haworth Press, Inc.) Vol. 5, No. 2/3/4, 2004, pp. 11-32; and: *Hospitality, Tourism, and Lifestyle Concepts: Implications for Quality Management and Customer Satisfaction* (ed: Maree Thyne and Eric Laws) The Haworth Hospitality Press, an imprint of The Haworth Press, Inc., 2004, pp. 11-32. Single or multiple copies of this article are available for a fee from The Haworth Document Delivery Service [1-800-HAWORTH, 9:00 a.m. - 5:00 p.m. (EST). E-mail address: docdelivery@haworthpress.com].

Digital Object Identifier: 10.1300/J162v05n02_02

patibility with hosts. Whilst points of caution are noted, it is argued that such profiling could increase the possibilities of successful host-guest interaction and thus the quality of experience of both guests and hosts. *[Article copies available for a fee from The Haworth Document Delivery Service: 1-800-HAWORTH. E-mail address: <docdelivery@haworthpress.com> Website: <http://www.HaworthPress.com> © 2004 by The Haworth Press, Inc. All rights reserved.]*

KEYWORDS. Homestay, lifestyle segmentation, psychographics, host-guest interactions

INTRODUCTION

This article discusses the potential use of lifestyle segmentation in order to achieve psychographic matching between hosts and guests in small accommodation enterprises in which a home dimension is a common feature. The discussion focuses specifically on the cases of New Zealand and Scotland, looking comparatively at the nature of small tourist accommodation businesses in those contexts. The comparative discussion is based on separate studies investigating B&B and homestay accommodation conducted in New Zealand and Scotland by the authors.

The term 'homestay' accommodation is inevitably a term with specific cultural associations. For instance, in New Zealand, along with Australia, the term is associated with farmhouse accommodation, and B&B type accommodation within private homes (Ogilvie, 1989; Craig-Smith et al., 1993; Tucker, forthcoming). In a study conducted in Scotland, Lynch (2003) collectively referred to as 'homestay' or commercial home accommodation the following accommodation types: host families, cultural stays, bed and breakfasts, farmhouse stays, self-catering accommodation, guest houses, and small hotels.

The term 'lifestyle business' is often associated with such accommodation enterprises (Morrison, 2002; Dewhurst and Thomas, 2003; Shaw and Williams, forthcoming). The term refers to owner-managers' pursuit of both social as well as economic goals and is suggestive of the highly individual approach taken to running such enterprises. One discourse associated with this type of accommodation is of a negative nature and tends to revolve the idiosyncratic behaviour and rules of the hosts. This is seen most notably in Stringer (1981) and Wood (1994), and is in respect of issues pertaining to the quality of the guest experience (Bywater, 1998) and the level of social control afforded to the hosts because of the intense social exchange occurring (Tucker, forthcoming). As Heal has noted on the obligatory position of the guest, the guest is obliged 'to accept the customary parameters of his hosts' establishment, functioning as a passive recipient of goods and services defined by the latter as part of his hospitality' (1990:192).

It is argued in this article that because the host-guest relationship is central to the product experience in these types of accommodation, a psychographic matching between hosts and guests would inevitably enhance the quality of the experience of both guests and hosts. Whilst lifestyle and psychographic segmentation is usually conducted on the potential market, or in this case, the 'guests', in this article the suggested use is aimed at gaining a profile of the hosts in order that empowered guests can more fully anticipate how their homestay experience will be.

It should be noted that the authors have not conducted psychographic profiling of homestay hosts or guests themselves, but rather have conducted ethnographic-style research focusing on the nature and quality of guest and host experience within this small accommodation context. Reflection on such experiences has led to the view that the lifestyles concept would be of potential use to enhance the guest experience of this product. The discussion is therefore intended as conceptual in nature but grounded in the findings of field research.

CASE STUDIES

As a starting point in this discussion, relevant aspects of the two case studies informing the comparative discussion will now be described. This will be followed by a review of psychographics and the Values and Lifestyles adaptations. Then, the article will highlight the importance of the guests' relationship with the hosts and thus the centrality of the host in product construction. The argument will then be developed as to the potential use of lifestyle segmentation in order to achieve psychographic matching of hosts and guests.

New Zealand

In New Zealand, Bed and Breakfast (B&Bs), homestays and farm-stays represent a rapidly growing sector of the tourism industry, providing tourists with a variety of accommodation choices (Ombler, 1997). Under the general label of Bed and Breakfast, both the *New Zealand Bed and Break-*

fast (2001) guidebook and the *Charming Bed and Breakfast in New Zealand* (2002) guidebook include homestays, farm-stays, lodges, inns, and boutique accommodation. Yet, the distinctions between those establishments labelled a B&B and those as a homestay are often unclear. On average such establishments have three rooms offering mostly double accommodation. All establishments offer breakfast, usually in a shared dining area, and some also offer evening dinner, usually accompanying the hosts at the dining table.

Fieldwork conducted by Tucker in 2001-2002 investigated the host-guest relationship in Bed and Breakfast and home and farm-stay accommodation businesses in rural New Zealand. The study aimed at identifying the ways in which the experience of commercial hospitality in home-hosted accommodation is mutually satisfactory to both hosts and guests, and at identifying any areas of mismatch between the experiences of hosts and guests. This research was based principally on participant observation and in-depth interviews conducted with the hosts and guests at 30 Bed and Breakfast and homestay establishments in rural parts of the south island of New Zealand. Simultaneous to qualitative interviewing methods, participant observation was employed to focus on the interactions between hosts and guests in the accommodation businesses. Participation observation is recognised as the most appropriate method to obtain significant data on interactions and relationships as it allows the recording of behaviour, conversation and experience 'in situ' (Maanen, 1995).

The data from the participant observation and interviews was analysed by drawing out the key themes and variables relating to the host-guest relationship. The themes that emerged included: the meanings surrounding the concepts of 'host', 'guest' and 'hospitality' among tourist visitors and hosts; comparisons between the expectations and experiences of domestic tourists and international visitors; the extension of hospitality in the form of guiding and interpretation of the local area; levels and foci of satisfaction in hosts' and guests' experiences; levels and foci of dissatisfaction in hosts' and guests' experiences; potential areas of 'balance' between the experiences of commercialised hospitality. Part of the participant observation process involved the researcher staying for one night or more in the participating establishments and keeping a research diary during the stays. As with Lynch's study described below, this also afforded the researcher a guests' view of staying in the establishments and interacting with hosts and other guests in a guest role (albeit a declared guest-researcher role).

The study found that both hosts and guests see home-hosted accommodation as the buying and selling of more than 'just a bed'. In relation to the hosts, Tucker's study found that home-hosting is usually a lifestyle choice. Very infrequently did hosts cite income as the primary motivation for operating a business, but rather they talked about the social benefits such as the opportunity to meet people from a wide range of backgrounds and nationalities and to exchange knowledge and develop potentially long lasting friendships. One host noted that by offering B&B as their children were growing up, their children were exposed to ideas and cultures that they would not normally have had experience of. Hosts also frequently mentioned how good it made them feel to have been able to make a positive difference to someone's holiday in New Zealand by offering the 'personal touch'.

These findings were mirrored in the interviews with the guests. Whilst the reasons guests gave for staying in B&Bs often included wanting the accommodation to be in beautiful settings, to be peaceful, 'homely', and 'unique', the overriding reason they gave was 'to have a relationship with local people', 'to have the opportunity to talk with them', 'to get to know the lifestyle of New Zealanders' and 'to learn about their culture'. Thus, adding value to home-hosted accommodation is the way in which it allows tourists backstage into the lives of 'real' New Zealanders, as represented by homestay hosts.

However, the level to which guests can enter into this 'real life' is dictated largely by the hosts, and depends on the extent to which the hosts are prepared to interact with their guests. Moreover, the ties of obligation are impressed upon the guests throughout their stay. As the guests are in the hosts' space, as well as abiding by the general social rules that ensure the interaction will run smoothly, they are also expected to respect and submit to their hosts' way of doing things. As one host explained, 'they are aware that they are in our situation at the time so they are wanting to be like us, or accept the way we do things'. Similarly, guests are fully aware of the relationship they have entered into by staying in a homestay situation, as seen in the following interview extract: 'In someone's home you feel more conscientious about tidying up after yourself, and you have to hang around longer–you can't up and leave like in a hotel.'

As a basis for the present article, therefore, Tucker's research highlighted the pivotal role that the hosts and the politics of identity play in home-hosted accommodation. Moreover, by letting 'strangers' stay in their home, B&B hosts are taking a variety of risks and must therefore take certain measures to ensure that their guests will understand and play by the rules. The ways in which they do so strongly impacts on the guests' experience. In this regard, Tucker identified a range of host 'personality' types and the implications of these types for guests' relationships and experiences with their hosts. These are laid out in Table 1.

Of course, these types are extremes, and many hosts may be a combination of some, or even all, of these. Most guests interviewed clearly preferred the 'relaxed' and 'people people' types of hosts, although of course, a few preferred a more formal level of hospitality.

TABLE 1. Categorization of Host Types and Implications for the Host-Guest Relationship

Host Personality 'Types'	Description	Implications for Host-Guest Relationship
'People People'	Genuine interest in meeting and talking with new people. Wants to help with whatever the guests might be interested in, whether that be driving guests to the beginning point of a good walking track, or making them feel welcome to sit in the lounge watching cricket all afternoon.	Guests feel that they are receiving personal, friendly and "real" hospitality. They enjoy the chance they have to spend time chatting with their hosts and "exchanging" friendship, knowledge and culture.
'Relaxed'	Not overbearing or 'fussy.' Doesn't panic if things aren't 100% ready when guests arrive.	Allows guests to relax also, feeling they're seeing the 'real' New Zealand household. As long as a basic level of cleanliness is maintained, most guests do not worry if everything is not 'just so.'
'Perfect Host'	Wants to put on the right image to guests, so ensures everything is ready and absolutely perfect from the beginning to end of the guests' stay.	The stay is a rather formal experience, from the perfection of the room and en suite, through the welcome drink in the lounge with hosts and other guests, to the dining and breakfast experiences. Guests may find the hosts rather overbearing, and might not feel able to ask for something, such as a cup of tea or an extra towel, for fear of offending the hosts.
'House proud'	Makes clear the rules and regulations of the household, letting the guests know that the home, its contents and organization are precious and not to be tampered with.	Guests may be unable to relax, feeling nervous in case they step out of line, or spill or break something. In extreme cases, they may feel completely unwelcome in the house, feeling as though they are intruding.
'Business wo(man)'	Runs the place purely as a business, fitting as many guests in as possible, charging for everything, and not having/making time to chat with guests.	Guest feels like another tourist on the conveyor belt that passes through, and see what they are getting as a bed and breakfast service, rather than hospitality and a chance to meet New Zealanders.

Scotland

In the United Kingdom, high growth is discerned in private house/bed and breakfasts and self-catering in a rented friend's/relative's house (UKTS, 2000). The demand for private house, or 'hosted', accommodation therefore appears to be increasing in both of these contexts. In the United Kingdom, homestay has been associated traditionally with the English as a Foreign Language Sector. As a generic term, 'homestay' is used variously to refer to types of accommodation where visitors or guests pay directly or indirectly to stay in private homes. An Internet search found the term used to refer to a range of accommodation types including farm-stay accommodation, host families, some small hotels and B&Bs (Lynch, 2003). Accommodation such as guest houses, boarding houses, lodging houses whose terms are sometimes used synonymously with hotels and B&Bs are also included as homestay establishments. Not only the objective description is important, but also the associations: private homes, interaction with host/family who live on the premises, sharing of space which thereby becomes 'public'. The associations may be described as linked by the concept of the home which may be perceived to distinguish homestay establishments from other forms of accommodation. A fuller discussion of the significance of the home setting can be found in Lynch and MacWhannell (2000).

A study by Lynch (2003) investigated the guest experience of homestay hospitality from the perspective of the guest-researcher. The author stayed a total of 17 nights in a purposive sample of six commercial homestay units ranging from ungraded to three star accommodation which was low to moderately priced, and based in primary, secondary and tertiary locations. The units chosen were consistent with the personae and, as far as possible, the lifestyle of the researcher and his family, and covered a range of homestay accommodation as follows: a cultural stay, a bed and breakfast, a farmhouse bed and breakfast, self-catering accommodation, a guest house, and a small hotel. Establishments were chosen in part because marketing materials indicated in their narrative that some degree of interaction between hosts and guest could be expected, for example, 'a warm welcome'. An evening meal was always taken in each establishment, other than the self-catering property.

The methodology employed was a form of autobiographical sociology (Friedman, 1990) described by the author as sociological impressionism (Lynch, 2003). The researcher documented his covert observations of the personal experience of being a guest as soon as possible after an event or sequence, for example, being shown to the bedroom, or having a meal, occurred, using a stream-of-consciousness approach to record 'spontaneous' observations. Observations focused upon: feelings, emotions, observations of facilities, artefacts, people, conversations and events. Thus, observations were concerned with both the tangible and intangible experiences of being a guest. Ellis (1991) refers to the neglect of emotions and their experience and argues for the importance of studying how private and social experience are melded in felt emotions.

A personal diary or reflexivity journal was also maintained (Carney, 1990). The author argues (Lynch, 2000a; 2000b; 2003) that the methodology is much closer to the guest experience than previous significant studies of the homestay sector, for example, Goffman (1953), Pearce (1990) or Stringer (1981). With such an autobiographical approach, validity and reliability of the results occurred through the methodological process followed. The 'audit trail' of the procedures followed is the most visible expression of this. Reliability is achieved through highlighting the subjective process in the construction of knowledge rather than assuming that truth exists.

The study found that the politics of identity of both the host and the guest were identified as highly significant in constructing the homestay product. Politics of identity are distinguished as being of two types: 'objective' and 'subjective' (Lynch, 2003). Objective refers to aspects such as gender, social class, clothing, and occupation. Subjective refers to aspects such as warmth of welcome, solicitousness, non-verbal behaviour and degree of interaction with guest. Central to this product construction process is the subjective experience of the guest. The objective experience of the accommodation product is certainly an important part of the whole, but so too is the guest's subjective experience of staying in someone's (commercial) home. The extent to which engagement with the local people occurs, and insights into the lifestyle of people, would seem to vary according to where on the home/commercial home/hotel continuum (Lynch, 2000b; 2003; Lynch and Tucker, forthcoming) the accommodation unit is located. Thus, the greater the opportunity for engagement, the closer the accommodation is to the private home end of the continuum. It was also found that the relationship with the home setting and the hosts is clearly an important part of the subjective experience of the guest.

A categorization of host types based on the social control strategies and interaction styles of the hosts is given in Table 2. Each host categorization acts as both a personal descriptor of the guest-researcher's perception of the host as well as a summative descriptor of the host's approach to social control. Thus, in the self-catering accommodation, the host, who literally lived next door, presented herself akin to a neighbour, for example, apologizing for putting out her washing on 'your' washing line:

TABLE 2. Categorization of Host Types Based on Social Control Strategies and Interactions with Guests

Type of Accommodation	Host Categorization	Social Control Strategies and Interactions with Guests
Cultural Stay	Upper middle class/ Upper class hostess	The hostess acts like a domestic hostess as if one had gone to an upper middle class/upper class friend's house for the weekend but found the friend had gone away.
Farmstay bed-and-breakfast	Service/Jeeves-like	Taciturn host providing a formal service with minimum interaction; the interaction that does occur is invariably concerned with social control.
Self-catering	Neighbour	A notable feature being the host's distancing from personal responsibility.
Guest House	Maternal	The host takes a very maternal approach, and is solicitous of the guest's welfare.
Bed-and-Breakfast	Neurotic	The host displays inconsistency and oscillating patterns of behaviour. Is the guest welcome or not?
Small Family-run Hotel	Fawlty Towers	These hosts are reminiscent of the husband/wife categorization from the television series 'Faulty Towers' forlornly trying to maintain control and appearances.

when we arrived the washing was out next door on the washing line but also sheets on the clothes-horse in the garden in the grounds here and she (the host) *apologized for having to dry clothes on our on 'your', she said, 'clothesline'.*

In the same unit, attention was drawn to artefacts defective from the outset of the stay, a certain distancing from personal responsibility was apparent:

We advised her about the need for four light bulbs, she referred to the fact that they if you put them in at the same time they all go off at the same time . . . she was aware about the wonky table leg.

Table 2 highlights the variety of host types and is indicative of how experiences will differ from one establishment to another partly because of a fusion between host politics of identity, the social control strategies employed and the ensuing nature of the interactions with guests.

Both of the research projects described above are relevant to this article in various ways. Unlike previous homestay studies, they focused upon the lived tangible and intangible experiences of being a guest. Further, they focused upon the actuality of hospitality from a guest perspective as well as, in the case of Tucker's research, conceptions of hospitality from a host perspective. In addition, in both cases the experiences were recorded very close to the time they happened rather than being distilled some time after. Experiences of both a positive and a negative nature were identified and these were contingent on artefacts (quality and selection of furnishings and artifacts), spatial control strategies, politics of identity (personal values, behaviours, social embarrassment, the product) and the product (marketing-actuality gap). Both studies highlighted the role of the hosts and the significance of politics of identity in the host-guest relationship. This was found to contribute towards potential negative experience as it suggested that quality perceptions have a strong subjective element, as opposed to the possibility of a universal objective quality benchmark system.

DISCUSSION

Psychographic Segmentation

Against this background, the desirability of psychographic matching of host and guest is posited as one means of enhancing the probability of successful guest experiences. Psychographics is an operational technique to measure lifestyle (Arnould et al., 2002), and is described by Witt and Moutinho (1995: 316) as an attempt to gain a deep understanding of the way consumers live; it takes account of features such as daily activities, hobbies, entertainment, what they consider important such as their interests and community involvement, as well as their opinions and attitudes regarding holidays. Plog (1987) suggests that psychographics has many applications in tourism. Psychographics is often used, as is demographics, with specific situation segmentation. Witt and Moutinho (1995: 317) point out that psychographics is useful for 'marketing communication purposes' as it is 'too general to predict specific behavioural differences'. Psychographics is thus the principle technique used by consumer researchers as an operational definition and a measure of lifestyle (Gunter and Furnham, 1992).

Lifestyles are conceived of as patterns of living that both influence and reflect a person's consumption behaviour (Lawson et al., 1999). They are distinctive modes of living defined by many factors including income, employment, educational attainment, attitudes, interests and opinions. Moreover, because values and attitudes are influences on lifestyle, the categories produced by psychographics systems based on values and lifestyles will represent groups who are likely to share similar lifestyles because they have similar sets of values. Arnould et al. (2002: 273) suggest that marketers assume that consumer lifestyles reflect individuals' attempts to 'realize a desired lifestyle or idealized self-concept' and this description seems to sit well with hosts' descriptions of their lifestyle businesses, as indicated in Tucker's case study. VALS 1 and VALS 2 are examples of values-based psychographic techniques used in lifestyle marketing. Holt (1997; 1998) has pointed to the need for ethnographic research to better understand the context of consumption. Arguably, the studies which inform this article, both of which used ethnographic research in a context where previous consumer research is very limited, support Holt's contention.

Ross (1998) advises that relatively little research has been conducted to date on specific personality dimensions such as employment in the tourism and hospitality industry. Given the importance of human interaction in the service context, this omission is somewhat surprising. Swarbrooke and Horner (1999) point out that market segmentation approaches can only be done with general behaviour and motivations rather than with individual people. Therefore, it is apparent that what is proposed in this article would require further research into homestay hosts before segmentation profiles could be developed.

Successful Host-Guest Interaction

Both Tucker's and Lynch's studies found that a key common feature of all of these establishments is that there is a strong sense that a part of the product is being 'hosted', and there is thus a close level of interaction between the hosts and guests. This supports previous research by Stringer (1981) and Lynch (1999). Of course, the experience of the host-guest relationship goes both ways and is also important for the hosts in this type of more personalised accommodation. Research into motivations of homestay hosts highlights how motivations for hosting are not just economic or entrepreneurial but also educational and social/psychological (Lynch, 1998). Indeed, as indicated in Tucker's case study, when asked about their motivations for operating a home-hosted accommodation business, New Zealand homestay hosts expressed their enjoyment in 'having the company' and 'meeting different people and sharing ideas'. Therefore, integral to understanding the host motivations and experiences, also, is the quality of the interactions with their guests.

Selwyn points out that 'The basic function of hospitality is to establish a relationship or to promote an already established relationship' (2000:19). Hospitality is thus a transformation process, wherein the key transformation taking place is that from a set of strangers into friends (Tucker, 2003). Indeed, many of the homestay hosts interviewed in New Zealand by Tucker described this transformation process when discussing their guests. For example, one homestay host said in conversation, 'it gives me a great buzz that perfect strangers can come on in and I can see within an hour they feel quite relaxed'. Many hosts stated that they saw their guests as 'guests' when they first arrived but as 'friends' when they departed.

For this transformation process to take place smoothly, however, there needs to be a certain level of matching, or commonality, between hosts and guests. Interviews with hosts and guests in New Zealand found that hosts have largely positive interactions with their guests, and the same for guests with their hosts. One guest even reported discussing this very issue with his hosts the previous evening: 'We were talking last night and they were saying they've never had a guest they regret or they wouldn't have back'. He then added the thought: 'But then I think homestay is a sort of self-selecting experience as well, there is a type of person who goes to homestays as well . . . and it's a type of person who mixes in fairly rapidly'.

Occasionally, however, definite problems do arise. One host couple interviewed during Tucker's research reported turning a potential guest away at the door even though they had taken a booking for him over the telephone. Their instant disliking to him was based on his 'scruffy' appearance. Another host couple reported clashing quite severely with one set of guests: 'A young American couple came and they were staying for two nights firstly but only stayed for one night. They wrote in the book 'We were made to feel most unwelcome here'. The hosts then commented, 'You don't know whether it's you or them I suppose'.

Previously, Pearce (1990) has also identified some farm hosts being irritated with overseas guests wishing to practice their English with them because this did not fit into their perceived role. In an examination of host attitudes towards guests in host families in Scotland where the primary purpose of the stay is to learn English, however, Lynch (1999) did not identify the same role conflict, and attributed this to guests coming for a specific purpose understood by hosts. The study's findings suggested the importance of goal congruence between hosts and guests as an ingredient for a successful stay. Likewise, Ireland (1993) identified host-guest relations as showing social and physical differentiation according to the socio-economic status of hosts and guests. Lynch (1999) has also suggested that host attitudes to guests can be differentiated on the basis of life cycle factors such as age, education, number of people in household and number of children in household. Host-guest matching is already used by some organizations operating in the host family sector. Some English language schools, for example, seek to 'match' their incoming students with suitable families in order to enhance the accommodation experience which on average is of three and a half weeks duration (Lynch, 1999; Lynch and Guerin, 1996). In Islington, London, account has been taken of the location of the property, the attitude of the owner, and often, a description of the owner in order to be able to match owners and guests as part of an accommodation database (Ferguson and Gregory, 1999: 19-20).

The preceding points show that, at the least, demographic factors have been considered with a view to host-guest matching. It might be pertinent, however, given the potential for tension and conflict to take place in the host-guest relationship as already suggested, to take this further to include, although more nebulous, lifestyle and 'personality' factors. Indeed, a guest interviewed during Tucker's New Zealand research reflected on what makes a successful experience with hosts and captured precisely this point:

> *It depends on the person really ... on you ... we're very interested in people and like to know about sheep farming or whatever, you know ... I think there may well be types of tourists who don't want that ... and we're very interested in the history and the politics and we like to discuss these things with people who live here. ... I think it's personality really.*

Adding to this, also, is the 'personality' of the hosts. Many of the homestay hosts interviewed in New Zealand stated that they saw themselves as 'people people' and thus suitable to host guests. Many also suggested that their role as hosts placed them in the position of being representatives of the New Zealand people, and they felt particularly suited to the hosting role if they held some particular aspect of local knowledge, such as history or wildlife, or a 'local' skill such as home-preserve making. These issues concerning the hosts' 'hosting' identity are inevitably crucial when considering the quality of the experience in this type of accommodation.

Current Host Segmentation

Guests also usually undertake an informal process of host segmentation when deciding on which establishment to stay in. Whether they are looking through B&B books, browsing the Internet or the leaflets in the Visitors' Centre, as well as looking for appropriate facilities and setting, potential guests also consider what their hosts will be like in a particular place. Following are two quotes from Tucker's interviews with homestay guests in New Zealand, explaining what they look for when choosing a homestay from advertisements:

> *I try to get a feel for what the atmosphere would be. You know when you are walking in and you get a feeling. It's a matter of what lifestyle I want, so I don't know if that is necessarily good or bad, but it gives you an idea of how comfortable you will be.*

> *I was going through the Internet and you know those describe the people, you get the feeling they are older, and so you either go I want to be in that environment or I don't, so I probably make a judgment based on that. I can't really remember how I decided* (to stay in this B&B) *but I remember thinking 'Oh I like the sound of those people'* (the hosts).

This informal segmentation takes place on the basis of what and how the hosts write about themselves in advertising literature. Problems can clearly emerge, however, when hosts are portrayed in a way that would contradict guests' experiences of them. For instance, a farmhouse stay in Scotland was selected by Lynch for his research as the properties were described as 'all family homes to which you will be warmly welcomed' and seemingly appealing to children with the accommodation guide stating 'you can see what is going on, you can talk with the farmer and see farm activities close at hand' (Lynch, 2003). The reality was a perfunctory welcome by a rather taciturn host:

> *Mr (X) came out of, don't know if it is the main entrance or not, an entrance round the side of the building, and oh yes we shook hands in a fairly perfunctory fashion, and we introduced one another, and Y. (researcher's child), and he took us upstairs to our room, and just showed us it really, and I don't think he even said there's your room.*
>
> (Lynch, 2003)

The body language and behaviour of the host's wife suggested guests were at best a nuisance. For example, this observation whilst sitting in the lounge:

> *Mrs walked through a couple of times, she didn't say hello, shortly after arriving, she had a good old shout at the kids just outside the double doors.*

(Lynch, 2003)

Advice was given that to see animals it was best to go to an open farm down the road. In this example, the farmer's children were listed with their ages and certainly represented the most natural component of the stay although behaviour was not always the most 'decorous'. Thus:

> *Having breakfast, we came down and met A. and B. watching TV, brother C., who we hadn't seen before, came along, said "Daddy wants to see you" and B. left, at which point G. noticed that (B.) hadn't got any pants on.*

(Lynch, 2003)

The pricing of B & B and home-stay accommodation is also a way that both hosts and guests hope to attract or gauge the appropriate match. Many of the New Zealand hosts interviewed, for example, said that whilst they knew they could quite reasonably charge perhaps $20 more because of the facilities and setting their establishment offered, they would not feel comfortable doing so because they would feel pressured to become more of a 'perfect host' type of operator. They also did not feel that they would get on socially with guests who would prefer the more formal type of setting. Many guests interviewed in New Zealand had similar feelings, reading social factors from price as well as physical factors:

> *I think price is an issue, I don't like necessarily the really posh . . . like posh, really comfortable home from home, you know I'm a bit of a minimalist myself, I'm quite happy with fairly basic spartan conditions, provided it's clean and friendly.*

So, although host segmentation is not formally carried out within the industry as yet, on the basis of their studies Tucker and Lynch found that guests do conduct a type of lifestyle segmentation process in choosing their accommodation. As seen in the preceding description of the two studies, the research undertaken by the authors in Scotland and New Zealand also identified a variety of types of host.

This is precisely why there is potential for a more formal method of host-guest matching as being a useful tool in increasing the possibility of high quality stays. Lifestyle segmentation based on demographics and particularly psychographics may afford a positive opportunity to facilitate guests' ability to choose appropriate hosts and thereby enhance the quality of their own and also their hosts' experiences.

The Potential Use of Lifestyle and Psychographic Segmentation

One can envisage a system whereby, ideally, one would seek to match psychographic profiles of prospective hosts and guests. In practice, for most homestay situations currently this is not practical. It also might be perceived to take away from the nature of the homestay experience. However, rather than an emphasis upon psychographic segmentation of the market, it is suggested that emphasis should be on psychographic segmentation of the hosts in order that prospective guests might match themselves for potential compatibility and a successful guest experience. The suggestion is put forward here, then, as to the possibility of using psychographic and lifestyle profiling in order to provide additional information on the host (and, if appropriate, the family) in promotional media of homestay accommodation establishments. The use of business Websites lends itself to such an approach and, arguably, is especially suitable for homestay accommodation. Essential features of a business Website would ideally include details of the facilities and services, a virtual tour of the property, plus a customer-friendly psychographic profile of the host(s) with accompanying photographs. Given that part of a successful homestay experience is engaging with the setting and to an extent the lifestyle of the host, marketing methods that encourage self-selection by the guests seem especially suitable. An additional advantage of such an approach is that the development of psychographic profiles through a standardised questionnaire can be facilitated readily by a tourist board or business consortium responsible for marketing. Whilst guests also try to undertake such a selection based largely upon the facilities, location, aesthetic appeal and so on, such a host-profile selection process might well become an added value element in the homestay experience.

To an extent, this type of approach is already happening. Thus, in the farmhouse stay example cited earlier, the accommodation was selected from a guide whose cover featured a young boy about two years old holding a walking stick/shepherd's crook with a lamb beside a farm gate and the legs of a male adult in jeans (Lynch, 2003). Guidance was given that 'all farms and crofts are being worked full or part-time by the family you stay with. This means that you can see what is going on, you can talk with the farmer.' The bed and breakfast chosen listed the names and ages of the host's children, and described the type of farm. Further information was given on the accommodation. The booking agent recommended the farmer as he was a 'chef'. Thus, through promotion, to an extent one already sees information being provided which is assisting with an undeveloped form of psychographic matching. The irony here is that, as previously described, the stay was not the most successful and might have been avoided if additional factually accurate information had been provided.

One should also recognize the significance of virtual tours of such homestay properties. In a fascinating study, Marcus (1995) interviewed private homeowners and concluded that the home is a reflection of self, so that in effect one can 'read' the household residents through their interior décor and artifacts. In a commercial home setting, Lynch (2000b; 2003) observed personal artifacts were found which provided insights into the lives of the householders in their absence, although this varied to a degree on the basis of the size of the accommodation and frequency of receiving guests. In this context then, one might recognize that in providing a virtual tour of properties, hosts are not just exhibiting the property, they are also revealing information about themselves which assists in the guest decision on whether to stay. In effect, such information starts to build a psychographic profile of themselves for the guests. One Scottish Thistle awards winning Website promoting guest houses not only provides photos of the hosts and their dogs, but also of some of the guests (*http://www.gems.scot.info/specgraphics/special.htm*). The Website conveys information, through photographs, text, and a video presentation, about the nature of the stays on offer, for example, sociable hosts, potentially high levels of host-guest interaction, interests in gardening, photography, local history, shows some of the household artefacts and describes their personal and historical significance. Insights are given into the type of hospitableness [*sic*] to expect, the family history, the type of cooking on offer, a sense of the hosts' relationship with the locality. Such detailed psychographic information about the hosts and their lifestyle is conveyed discreetly but highly effectively. It might be argued that such Website personalization is part of a growing trend of particular relevance and highly appropriate to the individual characteristics of homestay properties. Given that such businesses are often described as 'lifestyle' it seems to make perfect sense to describe that lifestyle for the benefit of potential guests.

One might also wish to speculate on the extent to which ethical issues arise. There is a body of literature (for example, Goffman, 1959; Hochschild, 1983; Crang, 1997) concerned with service work from the perspective of performance or aesthetic labour. Arguably, such an approach as suggested and identified accentuates the host, if not as a performer, certainly as an object of fascination. Concerns might rightly raise themselves with regard to extension of such an approach to include psychographic profiles of host children! In addition, given that the psychographics profile would in essence be a marketing tool, it would lend itself to potential manipulation and distortion for the purposes of commercial gain. Might it encourage hosts to perform to their particular profile rather than 'be themselves'?

Further criticism might be levelled at the method of psychographic measurement itself. In particular, a major criticism of the lifestyles concept is that it may oversimplify individuals' personalities and behaviours and does not account for the complexity of human tendencies and behavioural inconsistencies (Doswell, 1997). Another difficulty would be in finding suitable descriptors for host clusters that could be easily conveyed to potential guests when browsing promotional literature. For this reason there is a need to focus upon elaboration of objective facets, for example, hobbies and interests. Whilst cluster descriptors are fully understood amongst the circles of marketing personnel who develop and use them, they would need to be adapted so as to be useable for the purposes put forward in this article, for potential guests to identify appropriate hosts.

Furthermore, it might be argued that as the host-guest experience becomes less intense with the larger the homestay unit and the greater the volume of guests, such psychographic profiles of hosts will become less valuable. In addition, whilst the politics of identity of the host is an important ingredient in the homestay experience, it ignores other aspects such as the way that space is managed and the social control strategies in place which arguably make a large contribution to the homestay experience (Lynch, 1999; 2003).

Stringer (1981) raises understandable concerns about the dangers of, in effect, McDonaldising (Ritzer, 2000) the uniqueness of bed and breakfast experiences through inappropriate interventions. To an extent this might be seen to have already happened in relation to the homestay sector, through accommodation grading schemes which seek to encourage particular models of accommodation and which are based on hotel, as opposed to home, models of accommodation (Lynch and Tucker, forthcoming). On the other hand, psychographic profiling of hosts seeks to emphasise the individuality and uniqueness of the homestay product of which the host is one essential part.

CONCLUSION

Based on Tucker and Lynch's case study research in New Zealand and Scotland respectively, it has been argued in this article that quality and experience in homestay accommodation is largely hinged upon the success of the interaction between hosts and guests. Because the host-guest relationship is central to the product experience, it becomes important as to the particular personalities that come together in what can often be quite intense interaction. Whilst an informal matching is conducted by certain measures taken by hosts and guests currently, it has been suggested in this article that a more formal process of lifestyle segmentation would be of potential use by tourism boards and quality grading schemes in order that guests can be matched, or rather match themselves, with suitable potential hosts. Such information would allow potential guests to anticipate the nature of the lifestyle of the hosts and whether they would fit in on a temporary basis. Such matching would be achieved through the provision of more holistic information on the hosts and their properties, and on the types of guests received. The process would undoubtedly be rather like that of dating, and reading up the personal columns, hence the title of this article; an element of good fortune is required if the date will be successful or otherwise.

An interesting further study would be to conduct a survey on guest satisfaction before and then following the implementation of such a scheme by a local tourism board. That would determine what difference successful matching had made to the 'dates' that hosts and guests embark upon. So, whilst care should be taken to avoid the potential pitfalls as outlined here, the conclusion of this discussion is that the lifestyles concept and psychographic profiling of the host could have some value in potentially enhancing the quality of homestay experiences for both the guests and the hosts concerned.

REFERENCES

Arnould, E., Price, L. and Zinkhan, G. (2002). *Consumers*. London: McGraw-Hill.
Bywater, M. (1998). The Guests are Sad and Desolate, The Owner is a Sociopath, Welcome Back to the Great British Hotel. *The Observer*, 4 (October), p. 31.

Carney, T.F. (1990). *Collaborative Inquiry Methodology*. Ontario: Division for Instructional Development, University of Windsor.

Charming Bed & Breakfast in New Zealand (2002). Dunedin: Travelwise Publications.

Craig-Smith, S., Cody, N. and Middleton, S. (1993). *How to Be Successful at Home Hosting and Farm Tourism*. Queensland: Gatton College, The University of Queensland.

Crang, P. (1997). 'Performing the Tourism Product.' In Rojek, C. and Urry, J. (eds.) *Touring Cultures: Transformations of Travel and Theory*, pp. 137-154. London: Routledge.

Dewhurst, H. and Thomas, R. (Forthcoming, 2003). 'Encouraging Sustainable Business Practices in a Non-Regulatory Environment: A Case Study of Small Tourism Firms in a UK National Park.' *Journal of Sustainable Tourism*, 11(5).

Doswell, R. (1997). *Tourism: How Effective Management Makes the Difference*. Oxford: Reed International and Professional Publishing Ltd.

Douglas, M. (1991). 'The Idea of a Home: A Kind of Space.' *Social Research*, 59(1), 287-307.

Ellis, C. (1991). 'Sociological Introspection and Emotional Experience.' *Symbolic Interaction* 14(1), 23-50.

Ferguson, D. and Gregory, T. (1999). *The Participation of Local Communities in Tourism: A Study of Bed and Breakfasts in Private Homes in London*. London: Tourism Concern.

Franklin, A.S. (1991). 'Owner-occupation, Privatism and Ontological Security: A Critical Reformulation'. In Madigan, R. and Munro, M. 'Gender, House and 'Home': Social Meanings and Domestic Architecture in Britain'. *The Journal of Architectural and Planning Research*, 8(2), 116-132.

Friedman, L. (1990). 'Autobiographical Sociology'. *The American Sociologist*, 21(1), 60-66.

Gems of Midlothian–Bed & Breakfast and Guest House Accommodation. (http://www.gems.scot.info/specgraphics/special.htm accessed 15 October 2003).

Goffman, E. (1953). *Communication conduct in an island community*. Unpublished doctoral dissertation, Chicago, University of Chicago.

Goffman, E. (1959). *The Presentation of Self in Everyday Life*. Middlesex: Penguin.

Gunter, B. and Furnham, A. (1992). *Consumer Profiles: An Introduction to Psychographics*. London: Routledge.

Hall, M. and Page, S. (2002). *The Geography of Tourism and Recreation* (2nd ed). London: Routledge.

Heal, F. (1990). *Hospitality in Early Modern England*. Chicago: Clarendon Press.

Hochschild, A.R. (1983). *The Managed Heart: Commercialisation of Human Feeling*. London: University of California Press.

Holt, D.B. (1997). 'Poststructuralist Lifestyle Analysis: Conceptualising the Social Patterning of Consumption in Postmodernity'. *Journal of Consumer Research*, 23(4), 326-350.

Holt, D.B. (1998). 'Does Cultural Capital Structure American Consumption?' *Journal of Consumer Research*, 25(1), 1-25.

Ireland, M. (1993). 'Gender and Class Relations in Tourism Employment'. *Annals of Tourism Research*, 20(4), 666-684.

Lawson, R., Thyne, M., Young, T. and Juric, B. (1999). 'Developing travel lifestyles: a New Zealand example'. In Pizam, A. and Mansfield, Y. (eds.), *Consumer Behaviour in Travel and Tourism*, pp. 449-479. New York: The Haworth Hospitality Press, Inc.

Lynch, P.A. (1998). 'Female Entrepreneurs in the Host Family Sector: Key Motivations and Socio-Economic Variables'. *International Journal of Hospitality Management* 17(3), 319-342.

Lynch, P.A. (1999). 'Host Attitudes towards Guests in the Homestay Sector'. *Tourism and Hospitality Research: The Surrey Quarterly Review,* 1(2), 119-144

Lynch, P.A. (2000a). 'Setting and It's Significance in the Homestay Sector Explorations'. In Roper, A. and Guerrier, Y. (eds.) *A Decade of Hospitality Management Research*, pp. 101-120. Oxford: Butterworth Heinemann.

Lynch, P.A. (2000b). Homing in on Home Hospitality. *The Hospitality Review*, 6, 48-54.

Lynch (2003). *Conceptual relationships between hospitality, space and social control in the homestay sector.* Unpublished doctoral dissertation, Queen Margaret University College, Edinburgh.

Lynch, P.A. and Guerin, S. (1996). *Host Family Accommodation in Edinburgh.* Edinburgh: Department of Hospitality Management, Queen Margaret College.

Lynch, P.A. and MacWhannell, D. (2000). 'Home and Commercialised Hospitality'. In Lashley, C. and Morrison, A. (eds.), *In Search of Hospitality: Theoretical Perspectives and Debates*, pp. 100-114. Oxford: Butterworth Heinemann.

Lynch, P. and Tucker, H. (Forthcoming). 'Quality Homes, Quality People: The Challenge of Quality Grading and Assurance in Small Accommodation Enterprises'. In Thomas, R. (ed.) *Small Firms in Tourism: International Perspectives*. Oxford: Pergamon.

Marcus, C.C. (1995). *House as a Mirror of Self.* Berkley: Conari Press.

Morrison, A. (2002). 'Small Hospitality Businesses: Enduring or Endangered?' *Journal of Hospitality and Tourism Management*, 9(1), 1-11.

New Zealand Bed and Breakfast (2001). Wellington: Moonshine Press.

Ogilvie, B. (1989). *1990 Home-stay Australia: A Guide to Accommodation and Travel, Homes, Farms, Outback, Sydney's Good Accommodation and Travel Guide.* Bathurst: Pty Ltd.

Ombler, K. (1997). 'Motels vs Private Lodging . . . Same Game . . . Different Rules'. *Hospitality* 33(6), 6-10.

Pearce, P. L. (1990). 'Farm Tourism in New Zealand: A Social Situation Analysis'. *Annals of Tourism Research*, 17(3), 337-352.

Plog, S. (1987). 'The Uses and Demands for Psychographic Research'. In Brent-Ritchie, J.R. and Goeldner, C.R. (eds.), *Travel, Tourism and Hospitality Research*, pp. 209-218. New York: J. Wiley and Sons.

Ritzer, G. (2000). *The McDonaldization of Society.* London: Pine Forge Press.

Ross, G. (1998). *The Psychology of Tourism.* Melbourne: Hospitality Press.

Selwyn, T. (2000). 'An Anthropology of Hospitality'. In Lashley, C. and Morrison, A. (eds.), *In Search of Hospitality: Theoretical Perspectives and Debates*, pp.18-36. Oxford: Butterworth-Heinemann.

Shaw, G. and Williams, A.M. (Forthcoming). 'From Lifestyle Consumption to Lifestyle Production: Changing Patterns of Tourism Entrepreneurship'. In Thomas, R. (ed.), *Small firms in Tourism: International Perspectives.* Oxford: Pergammon.

Stringer, P.F. (1981). 'Hosts and Guests: The Bed-and-Breakfast Phenomenon'. *Annals of Tourism Research* 8(3), 357-376.

Swarbrooke, J. and Horner, S. (1999). *Consumer Behaviour in Tourism.* Oxford: Butterworth-Heinemann.

Tucker, H. (2003) *Living with Tourism: Negotiating Identities in a Turkish Village.* London: Routledge.

Tucker, H. (Forthcoming). ''Let Me Be': The Host-Guest Relationship and Its Implications in Rural Tourism'. In Hall, D., Roberts, L. and Mitchell, M. (eds.), *New Directions in Rural Tourism.* Aldershot: Ashgate.

UKTS (2000). *The UK Tourist: Key Trends 1990-99.* English Tourism Council, Northern Ireland Tourist Board, Scottish Tourist Board and Wales Tourist Board.

Witt, S.F. and Mountinho, L. (1995). *Tourism Marketing and Management Handbook.* Harlow: Pearson Education Ltd.

Wood, R.C. (1994). Hotel Culture and Social Control. *Annals of Tourism Research,* 21(1), 65-80.

Segmentation of Special Event Attendees Using Personal Values: Relationships with Satisfaction and Behavioural Intentions

Anne-Marie Hede
Leo Jago
Margaret Deery

SUMMARY. This article presents the findings from research undertaken within a conceptual framework that included personal values, satisfaction and post-consumption behavioural intentions. The findings of a quantitative study (n = 354) conducted at a theatre-event indicate that attendees who were more inclined to place importance on their 'connectedness' with others were generally more satisfied with their attendance overall and with most of the attributes of the special event that were measured. Similar results were also found for attendees' post-con-

---

Anne-Marie Hede is a lecturer (Marketing) at the Bowater School of Management and Marketing, Faculty of Business and Law, Deakin University, Burwood, Victoria 3125, Australia.

Leo Jago is Professor of Tourism, and Margaret Deery is Associate Professor of Tourism at the Centre for Hospitality and Tourism Research, Victoria University, Melbourne, Australia.

[Haworth co-indexing entry note]: "Segmentation of Special Event Attendees Using Personal Values: Relationships with Satisfaction and Behavioural Intentions." Hede, Anne-Marie, Leo Jago, and Margaret Deery. Co-published simultaneously in *Journal of Quality Assurance in Hospitality & Tourism* (The Haworth Hospitality Press, an imprint of The Haworth Press, Inc.) Vol. 5, No. 2/3/4, 2004, pp. 33-55; and: *Hospitality, Tourism, and Lifestyle Concepts: Implications for Quality Management and Customer Satisfaction* (ed: Maree Thyne and Eric Laws) The Haworth Hospitality Press, an imprint of The Haworth Press, Inc., 2004, pp. 33-55. Single or multiple copies of this article are available for a fee from The Haworth Document Delivery Service [1-800-HAWORTH, 9:00 a.m. - 5:00 p.m. (EST). E-mail address: docdelivery@haworthpress.com].

Digital Object Identifier: 10.1300/J162v05n02_03

sumption behavioural intentions; however, other personal value systems, such as that associated with hedonism, also emerged as important. These results can be used by managers and marketers of special events to enhance the special event experience and contribute to the industry's sustainability. *[Article copies available for a fee from The Haworth Document Delivery Service: 1-800-HAWORTH. E-mail address: <docdelivery@haworth press.com> Website: <http://www.HaworthPress.com> © 2004 by The Haw orth Press, Inc. All rights reserved.]*

KEYWORDS. Personal values, satisfaction, segmentation, special events

BACKGROUND

While Laser (1963) is generally considered to be the originator of the lifestyle segmentation, Heath (1995) indicated that the first psychographic study was not conducted until 1965. Lifestyle segmentation is based on identifying groups of similar consumers based on their attitudes, opinions and interests, or psychographics (Plummer, 1974) and Kamakura and Wedel (1995) noted that since its introduction, lifestyle segmentation has become quite popular in marketing management. Information is gathered on consumers based on a range of variables such as their demographics, product and media use, and leisure interests, and, in some cases, attitudes about a specific topic (e.g., environmental issues) (Heath, 1995). Within the context of tourism, lifestyle segmentation has been used by a number of national and state tourism organisations globally. Muller and Cleaver (2001) noted that the New Zealand, Canadian and Australian tourist authorities are, for example, employing such an approach to their segmentation of markets. These organisations base their marketing activities on targeting specific lifestyle segments to improve visitation, and more importantly, visitor yield.

The collection of lifestyle data is most often expensive. It is also time-consuming for researchers, and respondents alike, given the large numbers of attitudes, opinions and interests that are often surveyed (Kamakura and Wedel, 1995). Kamakura and Wedel further indicated that, in many instances, lifestyle data is collected in conjunction with other data, hence, there is often a trade-off between quality and quantity. Gonzales and Bello (2002) more recently supported this claim when investigating the construct of lifestyle in tourism.

Marketing research has indicated that attitudes and behaviour stem more specifically from personal values (Homer and Kahle, 1988). More recently, Blamey (1997) noted that personal values are relevant across different situations and their limited number makes them economical measures in the field of psychographics and marketing. Some researchers, including Fall (2001) and Muller (1991; 1995; 2000), have investigated personal values within the context of tourism. Fall (2001), for example, highlighted the role of personal values in marketing communications and found that travellers' hedonic and achievement personal values influenced the use of interpersonal media sources. Muller (1995) investigated the role of personal values within the context of destination marketing in relation to tourists' beliefs about the security, recreational and avoidance aspects of a visit to a destination. Personal values may then provide researchers with a more parsimonious method of segmenting consumer markets than lifestyles.

Much of the contemporary literature in the field of business acknowledges the importance of satisfaction as a post-consumption assessment of the service or product purchased. Pizam and Ellis (1999), for example, stated that consumer satisfaction is essential for corporate survival, while Sivadas (2000) and Disney (1999) emphasised the relationship between satisfaction and loyalty. It is also suggested that satisfied consumers are more likely to contribute to developing the reputation of the organisation (Baker et al., 2000).

Very little research has explored the relationship between personal values and satisfaction. Given the theory surrounding the two concepts, it would seem that there may be some relationship between them and that exploration in this area is warranted. The aim of this study was to investigate whether links exist between consumers' systems of personal values and their levels of satisfaction. The study was undertaken within the context of tourism, specifically at special events. This article provides a background to special events and the concepts of personal values and satisfaction. A model is then presented which provided the framework for this study. The research methodology is then described; finally, the results are presented and then discussed within the context of special events and tourism more generally.

LITERATURE REVIEW

Research Context: Special Events

Special events play an important role in many modern cultures. In western cultures, special events are often used to develop a positive image of the destination and thereby attract tourists. At their core, special events provide attendees with an opportunity to escape from the routines of their daily lives (Getz, 1997; Jago, 1997). As a "onetime or infrequently occurring event of limited duration," special events can, therefore, play an important role for attendees by providing them with an opportunity for leisure, social and cultural experiences, beyond everyday experiences (Getz, 1997; Jago, 1997).

As an area of tourism research, special events research has progressed substantially in recent years (Hede, Jago and Deery, 2002). Research has contributed to the development of typologies of special events. In his typology of events, Ritchie (1984) included political, cultural, sporting, historical, commercial and carnival/festival-based events. More recently, Jago (1997) developed a conceptual framework of special events, which included minor and major special events and festivals. Major events were further classified into those events that could be considered as mega-events (for example, the Olympic Games) and hallmark events (for example, The Boston Marathon or the Grand Prix in Monaco).

Considerable research has also been undertaken to understand what motivates people to attend special events (see, for example, Backman, Backman, Muzaffer and Mohr Sunshine) and on the economic impacts of special events (see, for example, Burns, Hatch and Mules (1986); Crompton and McKay (1994); and Gratton, Dobson and Shibli (2000)). Over the past few years, however, there has been a noticeable increase in research that has evaluated special events from a social perspective (see, for example, Fredline and Faulkner (2000); Green and Chalip (1998); Delamere, Wankel and Hinch (2001)). Whilst this trend has encouraged a more holistic approach to the evaluation of special events, little focus has been afforded to investigating the effects of attendance from the attendee's perspective. One area, in particular, which is under-developed, is that of attendee satisfaction within this context of special events. This article seeks to address this research gap in special event research.

Personal Values

Personal values are "enduring beliefs that a particular mode of behaviour or end-state of existence is preferable to opposite modes of behaviour or end-states" (Rokeach, 1973:5). It is generally thought that personal values, which are few in number, assist individuals to form their attitudes, and ultimately the behaviour that they choose. Kamakura and Novak (1992) suggested that because of the role that personal values play in the formation of attitudes and behaviour, they provide a greater understanding of consumers and can provide considerable predictive power in relation to an individual's behaviour. Personal values have been studied in a number of consumption scenarios, including that of frequency programs (Long and Schiffman, 2000); healthcare; retail outlets (Erdem, Oumilli, and Tuncalp, 1999); special events (Jago, 1997); and ski destinations (Klenosky, Gengler, and Mulvey, 1993).

The theory of personal values stems from the motivational literature, where motives and the drivers of behaviour have been extensively studied using Maslow's theory of motivation. In parallel with this theory, the theory of personal values incorporates the notion that personal values are ordered hierarchically and underlying the plethora of personal values are personal value domains. Schwartz and Bilsky (1990), for example, identified enjoyment, security, achievement, self-direction, restricted conformity, prosocial and maturity personal value domains, and used items from the Rokeach Value Survey (RVS) to develop a scale that has subsequently been tested cross-culturally. Subsequent research on personal values indicates the existence of internally and externally focused personal value domains using various instruments that measure personal values, see, for example, Madrigal (1995); Thrane (2000); and Fall and Knutson (2001).

The most commonly used quantitative measures of personal values are the RVS Rokeach (1979); the List of Values (LOV) (Khale, 1983) and Veroff, Douvan and Kulka (1981). All of these instruments are in the public domain and have been used extensively in research on personal values. Daghfous et al. (1999) stated that there is some agreement amongst researchers on the LOV's superiority in relation to the RVS. Criticism has, however, been leveled at quantitative measures of personal values as it has often been found that respondents find it difficult to differentiate between personal values based on the level of importance they ascribe to them. McCarty and Shrum (2000) proposed a method to assist in overcoming this issue that familiarises respondents with the list of personal values being used before they are asked to rate their importance of them. These authors, using both the LOV and the RVS, demonstrated that this approach to the collection of data on personal values improves the interpretability of the results obtained. In their study, the LOV outperformed the RVS in terms of its interpretability of results.

The LOV consists of nine personal values, namely a sense of belonging, sense of accomplishment, fun and enjoyment, warm relationships, excitement, being well-respected, security, self-respect and self-fulfill-ment. Seven- or nine-point Likert scales are generally used for data collection. Studies using the LOV, in a number of consumption scenarios and cultures, have identified intrinsically oriented and extrinsically oriented personal value domains (see for example, Thrane (1997a); Jago (1997); and Fall and Knutson (2001)). The intrinsically oriented personal value domain is generally associated with achievement-based personal values, such as *to have a sense of accomplishment* or *to have security*. The extrinsically oriented personal value domain is, on the other hand, generally associated with how individuals relate to others. *To be in warm relationships* and *to be well-respected*, for example, are often found to be associated with this personal value domain. In some studies, a hedonistic personal value domain, comprising *to have fun and enjoyment* and *to have excitement*, has emerged. Some criticism, however, has been directed at the LOV in terms of its validity across cultures and its use in consumption scenarios. Many of the results obtained using the LOV in western cultures have been consistent, however, hence its use in these contexts seems to be appropriate.

Satisfaction

Satisfaction is a complex concept that is rooted in social psychology and consumer behaviour theory, specifically adaptation theory and opponent-process theory (Oliver, 1980). Satisfaction is a post-consumption evaluative judgement and is considered to be attitude-like (Hunt, 1977). Later, however, Oliver (1981) proposed that expectancy disconfirmation was a more appropriate paradigm in which to understand satisfaction, and stated that satisfaction was the complex emotional response following the consumption experience. As such, satisfaction cannot be formed vicariously.

The expectancy disconfirmation paradigm is commonly understood to consist of two processes: the formation of expectations; and the comparison of those expectations to some form of comparison standard (Oliver and DeSarbo, 1988; Van Montfort, Masurel, and Van Rijn, 2000). The result is a better-than or worse-than judgment. The better-than judgment represents positive disconfirmation and the worse-than judgment represents negative disconfirmation. Confirmation occurs when the judgment is as expected. The expectancy disconfirmation paradigm has been used extensively in the literature and has played an important role in the development of the understanding of the satisfaction since its introduction and use in satisfaction research (Halstead, 1999).

Notwithstanding the influence of the expectancy disconfirmation process, other processes are believed to determine satisfaction responses. Oliver and DeSarbo (1988:503) suggested that consumers are sensitive to a number of processes, including assimilation, equity, and attribution and identified that disconfirmation and (attribute) performance "may operate in tandem, and that individuals can respond separately to the two concepts even though they appear to be related from a definitional standpoint." Halstead (1999) cautioned that the continued measurement of pre-choice expectations as the sole comparison standard will limit the usefulness and predictability of satisfaction models.

Jones and Suh (2000) highlighted that there has been little attention given to the empirical investigation of both transaction-specific and overall satisfaction concurrently in the literature. In the case of services, Oliver (1996) and Bitner (1997) suggested that overall satisfaction is more likely to be an aggregated impression of a number of events based on multiple expectancy disconfirmations, rather than of a single occurrence. Similarly, de Ruyter and Bloemer (1999:323) suggested that consumers make fast evaluative satisfaction judgments, based on singular occurrences, and/or as an "aggregated impression of a number of events."

A number of concepts have been proposed as antecedents of satisfaction. Quality of performance and service quality have been linked to satisfaction across a range of consumption scenarios (see, for example, Oh and Parks, 1997 or Gummesson, 1998). As part of the expectancy disconfirmation model, expectations are considered to be key antecedents of both satisfaction and quality (McGuire, 1999). The links between these concepts highlight the importance of enhancing consumers' perceptions of the links between satisfaction and quality assurance.

Why Is Consumer Satisfaction Important?

For most organisations, a primary benefit of satisfying customers is likely to be higher levels of profitability and Anderson and Mittal (2000) and Keiningham, Goddard, Vavra and Iaci (1999) recently provided empirical support for this relationship. This relationship, however, is not likely to be one that is direct and is likely mediated by a number of outcomes, such as positive word of mouth and repurchase intent. Links between satisfaction and positive word of mouth have dated back decades. Cronin and Taylor (1992) concluded that customer satisfaction affected repurchase intent significantly.

Given the notion that satisfaction is 'attitude-like' it seems that there may be some connection then between it and personal values. This study explored the relationships between personal values and satisfaction and post-consumption behavioural intentions and was based on the conceptual framework presented in Figure 1. In this framework, personal values are viewed as the drivers of attitudes and behaviour, as well as the concept that distinguishes individuals from each other. Based on the current understanding of satisfaction, satisfaction with the attributes (attribute satisfaction) is included in the model as an antecedent to overall satisfaction. These concepts are then related to intentions to revisit and recommend the special event and the special event destination. In this study, the focus of investigation was on the relationship between personal values and each of the other concepts in the model.

RESEARCH QUESTION

The research question posed here is: *Are there differences between personal values-based segments of special event attendees in terms of their satisfaction with the special event and their resulting behavioural intentions?*

Research Site

The special event for this study was a block-buster musical held in a major Australian metropolitan destination and was related to contemporary popular culture, commercial in nature, was a major special event for the destination, and could be considered as a part of the developing hallmark of the destination. As such, the special event exhibited a number of attributes that make it difficult to classify into one type of special event. For the purposes of this article, the special event will be referred to as a major theatre-event as this term encompasses many of its attributes.

FIGURE 1. A Model of Personal Values, Satisfaction and Behavioural Intentions

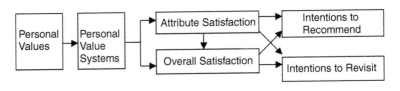

Research Approach

Although consideration was given to a qualitative approach for this research, a quantitative research approach was deemed to be the most appropriate to obtain the type of data required. It was hoped that the results of this study could be generalised to the population and, therefore, adequate sampling was necessary. The research methodology was also suitable given the nature of the concepts being examined and the nature of the research problem.

Research Instrument

Personal values were measured with the LOV using a seven-point scale and the item sequence technique proposed by McCarty and Shrum (2000). Post-consumption variables, namely, satisfaction with the attributes of the special event, the special event overall and recommending behaviour in relation to the special event were also measured. A panel of experienced consumers of theatre-events was consulted and a list of theatre-event attributes was developed so that respondents to the survey could indicate their level of satisfaction with them. The list comprised satisfaction with the following attributes of costumes, storyline, stage work, vision from the seats, value for money, quality of the acting and the singing, service at the theatre and the ambience of the theatre. Each of the satisfaction responses was measured on a 10-point scale to accommodate differentiation amongst the responses, as this is not always obtained in satisfaction surveys. A seven-point scale was used to measure post-consumption behavioural intentions. Data was also obtained on respondents' demographics to provide descriptive analysis of the sample.

Data Collection

The data were collected using a 'two-staged' approach to data collection (Pol and Pak, 1994) over a ten-month period. *In situ* random sample intercept surveys were conducted at the conclusion of selected performances of the theatre-event where contact names and telephone numbers were collected from attendees. Intercepted respondents were then contacted randomly to participate in Stage Two of the data collection process, which involved follow-up telephone interviews. It was understood that attendees would be keen to leave the theatre precinct at the conclusion of performances, thus the two-staged approach was primarily used to optimise response rates to the survey. Further to this, the approach to data collection minimised the interruption to attendees at the special event so that this would not detract from the theatre-experience.

Response Rates

The response rate to the *in situ* survey was 43%. When later contacted, almost 90% of those attendees intercepted, who had agreed to a telephone interview, also agreed to participate in the telephone survey. The resulting sample size was 354.

RESULTS

Descriptive Analysis and Results

Results of the descriptive analysis indicate that the sample comprised a large proportion (83%) of females, 83% in the 25-64-year age group; 77% married or in a defacto relationship; 67% working either full or part-time; and 77% with an annual household income less than AU$104,000. These results are not entirely dissimilar to the results of other studies on special events (see, for example, Crompton and McKay, 1994 or Hede, Jago and Deery, 2003), or more generally in studies on performing arts audiences (see, for example, Osborne, Wheeler and Elliot, 1999).

The skewness and kurtosis statistics indicated that the satisfaction data and the personal values data were both negatively skewed and bunched in sections of the scales. Satisfaction data is often distributed in this way and this can sometimes be attributed to respondent and/or interviewer bias (Rossi, Giulla and Allenby, 2001). Steps were taken, using Blom's (1958) proportionate estimate algorithm, to remedy this statistical problem and enable multivariate data analysis to be used. Blom's algorithm re-positions the levels of the scale, based on the derived frequencies and a normal distribution. Effectively, scales are 'stretched' to reflect a normal distribution of the data. Transformations are widely used in data analyses and can be data driven, as is the case for this study, or theoretically driven, for example, when factor analysis is used (Hair, Anderson, Taitham, and Black, 1995).

Multivariate Data Analysis and Results

So that the research question could be investigated, multivariate data analyses was used and a staged approach to this analysis was required.

Stage One involved factor analysis of the personal values data; Stage Two involved segmenting the sample based on the results of the factor analysis; and Stage Three involved testing for differences between the derived segments in relation to their satisfaction responses and their post-consumption behavioural intentions that were of interest in this study.

Stage One. The results of the principal components analysis, using varimax rotation, are presented in Table 1. As can be seen from Table 1, the factor-solution comprised three underlying factors, or personal value domains. In this study, the three factors have been described as the 'extrinsic', 'hedonistic' and 'achievement-based' personal value domains. The Cronbach's alphas for these three factors were 0.70, 0.65 and 0.70 respectively. Combined, the three factors, each with an eigenvalue over one, explained a total of 61% of the variance. The personal values loading most significantly on the extrinsic personal value domain were *to have a sense of belonging, to be well-respected, to be in warm relationships* and *to have security.* The hedonistic personal value domain represents the personal values *to have fun and enjoyment* and *to have excitement* and the achievement- based personal value domain represented the personal values *to be self-fulfilled* and *to have a sense of accomplishment.*

Stage Two. This stage of the data analysis involved segmenting the sample, based on systems of personal values. As the LOV has demonstrated high levels of validity and reliability, the cluster variate used as the

TABLE 1. Results of Factor Analysis of the Personal Value Variables

	Extrinsic	Hedonistic	Achievement
To have a sense of belonging	.75		
To be well-respected	.70		
To be in warm relationships	.65		
To have security	.61		
To have self-respect	.46		
To have excitement		.85	
To have fun and enjoyment		.83	
To be self-fulfilled			.86
To have sense of accomplishment			.74
Eigenvalue	3.1	1.4	1.1
Cronbach's alpha	.70	.65	.70
Percentage of variance explained	34.0	15.7	11.3

basis of an exploratory hierarchical cluster analysis of sample comprised the summated scores for each of the derived factors. Hair, Taitham, Anderson and Black (1995) stated that the use of summated factor scores is appropriate when validated instruments have been employed.

The Wards cluster algorithm was used for this study in an exploratory hierarchal cluster analysis. Based on the research problem, a five-cluster solution was deemed to be the most appropriate for this study. When selecting the most appropriate number of clusters for the K-means analysis, the five-cluster solution appeared to provide the most 'reasonable and distinctive solution' of the eight solutions that were analysed. Naylor and Klesier (2002:348) employed this approach to the selection of the number of the clusters in their study that employed lifestyle variables as a means of segmenting a sample of health resort. A K-means cluster analysis (confirmatory) was then conducted using the centroids of the five clusters derived from the exploratory hierarchical analysis as the original cluster centres. The results of this cluster analysis, or segmentation, of the sample, are presented in Table 2.

As can be seen from Table 2, the resulting five-cluster solution comprised Drifters (75 respondents); Playful Achievers (52 respondents); Dynamos (100 respondents); Hedonists (55 respondents); and the Temperate Networkers (72 respondents). The maximum score for each of the summated scales is presented in the final column of the table as a point of reference for the reader. These clusters will be described in terms of the cluster variate later in the article.

TABLE 2. Final K-Mean Scores and Mean Distance of the Cases from the Centroid for the Five-Cluster Solution

	Drifters n = 75	Hedonists n = 55	Playful Achievers n = 52	Temperate Networkers n = 72	Dynamos n = 100	Max. score on the scale
Extrinsic personal value domain	123.8	140.2	124.3	230.51	230.2	281.4
Hedonistic personal value domain	84.3	232.9	170.4	116.9	267.5	296.0
Achievement personal value domain	95.4	81.2	242.9	203.2	240.3	299.8
Mean distance of cases from the cluster center	79.2	76.6	75.1	79.9	72.8	

The mean distances from the centroids for each of the clusters are very similar to each other ranging from 72.8 to 79.9. Members of the Dynamos, however, are less dispersed in the cluster 'space' than members of the Hedonists or Playful Achievers. The Drifters and Temperate Networkers both contain a similar number of respondents and are similarly dispersed in the cluster spaces. These levels of dispersion provide an indication of the levels of homogeneity within the clusters and in comparative terms, The Dynamos has the highest level of homogeneity; the Drifters and the Temperate Networkers have a moderate level of homogeneity; and the Playful Achievers and Hedonists have the lowest level of homogeneity of all the clusters.

When using the Ward's method for clustering, the squared Euclidean distance is the measure of distance between the clusters that should be used (Hair et al., 1995). The distance between the clusters assists the researcher to identify the proximity of each of the clusters in relation to all the other clusters. The squared Euclidean distance results (non-standardised) are presented in Table 3 and a diagram (Figure 2) has been developed to represent these results visually. It should be noted that Figure 2 is not to scale, but provides a good indication of the distances between the clusters.

The Dynamos (100 respondents) is the largest cluster in terms of the number of members it contains and, as has been mentioned, is also the most homogenous of the five derived clusters. Members of this cluster place a high level of importance on all the personal value domains that were used in this study. Generally, members of this cluster want to have positive experiences in their lives by having meaningful relationships, fun, and a sense of achievement. These goals are almost equally important to them and each of the levels of importance they place on them is intense.

FIGURE 2. Visual Representation of Distances Between Final Five Clusters

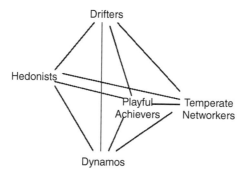

TABLE 3. Distances Between Final Cluster Centers (Squared Euclidean Distances)

Cluster	Drifters	Hedonists	Playful Achievers	Temperate Networkers
Hedonists	150.2			
Playful Achievers	170.8	174.0		
Temperate Networkers	155.1	191.0	125.4	
Dynamos	256.7	186.1	143.8	155.2

As mentioned earlier, the Drifters (75 respondents) is a moderately homogenous cluster compared to the other four clusters. Members of the Drifters are quite the opposite of members of the Dynamos. This is evidenced in the levels of importance they placed on each of the personal domains and the distance between the two clusters. Although members of the Drifters do not place very much importance on the three personal value domains used here, they do, however, place slightly more importance on their connectedness with others, but his is only marginally so. In this study, members of this cluster are relatively aimless in terms of the personal value domains measured here.

Members of the Temperate Networkers cluster (72 respondents) are not so concerned with having fun times in their lives as they are about having meaningful relationships. Members of this cluster also want a sense of achievement. Life is possibly quite serious for this cluster. Members of Temperate Networkers are quite similar to members of Playful Achievers (52 respondents) and the clusters are in close proximity to each other (see Figure 2). Members of the Playful Achievers aim to achieve in their lives and life has got to be interesting for them. Members of the Playful Achievers are not, however, overly concerned with building relationships. They possibly harness opportunities, seek novelty, without considering their relationships and networks. They are self-focussed and are self-gratifying.

Of all the clusters, the Hedonists (55 respondents) cluster is possibly the most simple in its interpretation. The Hedonists very much want to have fun and enjoyment and excitement in their lives. They are not, however, very concerned with having meaningful relationships and are even less predisposed to gaining a sense achievement in their lives. The term 'live for today' comes to mind when thinking about this cluster.

Stage Three. The third, and final, stage of the data analysis involved describing the clusters in terms their demographic profiles, their satisfaction responses and behavioural intentions. Pearson's chi-square analysis and

Analysis of Variance (ANOVA) were conducted to identify statistically significant differences between the clusters based on these variables.

Of the demographics used to profile the clusters, only age was found to impact significantly on the cluster profiles (p < .05, df = 12, α = 32.51). The Hedonists comprised a larger proportion of younger members (25-44 years) and the Temperate Networkers comprised a larger proportion of middle-aged (45-64 years) members than what was expected based on chi-square analysis. Hence, the profiles of the clusters were generally very similar to the profile of the entire sample, based on this analysis.

Table 4 presents the results of the ANOVA tests using the clusters as the independent variable and satisfaction variables and the behavioural intentions attributes and the clusters as the dependent variables. As can be seen from Table 4, no statistically significant differences (p > .05) were identified between the clusters based on their satisfaction with the vision from the seats, but statistically significant differences (p < .05) were identified between the clusters in terms of the other seven attributes of the theatre-event that were measured here.

TABLE 4. Results of the ANOVA Tests–Satisfaction Variables

Satisfaction with the...	Sig.	F Statistic df = 4	Lowest		Level of satisfaction		Highest
Storyline	.000	5.937	Drifters	Hedonists	Playful Achievers	Temperate Networkers	Dynamos
Stagework	.003	4.087	Drifters	Playful Achievers	Hedonists	Temperate Networkers	Dynamos
Costumes	.003	4.117	Drifters	Playful Achievers	Hedonists	Temperate Networkers	Dynamos
Acting and singing	.005	3.823	Drifters	Playful Achievers	Hedonists	Temperate Networkers	Dynamos
Ambience of the theatre	.003	4.014	Drifters	Playful Achievers	Hedonists	Temperate Networkers	Dynamos
Service at the theatre	.002	4.452	Drifters	Playful Achievers	Hedonists	Temperate Networkers	Dynamos
Value for money	.007	3.602	Drifters	Playful Achievers	Hedonists	Dynamos	Temperate Networkers
Vision	.188	1.547	Drifters	Playful Achievers	Hedonists	Temperate Networkers	Dynamos
Theatre-event overall	.130	3.202	Drifters	Playful Achievers	Hedonists	Temperate Networkers	Dynamos
Destination	.321	1.183	Drifters	Playful Achievers	Dynamos	Hedonists	Temperate Networkers

Tukey post hoc tests were used to identify the specific differences between the clusters. Statistically significant differences were identified between the Drifters and the Dynamos in relation to their satisfaction for all seven of the theatre-event attributes. The post hoc tests also indicated that the Drifters were very much less satisfied with the attributes of the theatre-event than were the Dynamos. A further source of the statistically significant differences were identified between the Drifters and the Temperate Networkers. The satisfaction levels of the Temperate Networkers for the storyline, stage work, service at the theatre and the value for money were much higher than that of the Drifters.

The Temperate Networkers also demonstrated a statistically significant difference from the Dynamos based on their levels of satisfaction with the value for money. The Temperate Networkers were more satisfied with this aspect of the theatre-event than were the Dynamos. The Hedonists demonstrated a statistically significant difference from the Dynamos based on their levels of satisfaction with the storyline and the theatre and its ambience. The Playful Achievers did not demonstrate any statistically significant differences with any of the other clusters based on their satisfaction with the attributes of the theatre-event measured here. Table 4 also highlights that no statistically significant differences ($p > .05$) were identified between the clusters based on their levels of satisfaction with the special event overall and the special event destination. Although the differences between the clusters, based on their level of satisfaction with the theatre-event overall and the destination, were not found to be statistically significant, the patterns in the levels of satisfaction that the clusters demonstrated were fairly consistent with the other satisfaction variables measured here.

Statistically significant differences ($p < .05$) were also identified between the clusters based on their intentions to attend the theatre-event again; attend more theatre-events and to recommend the host destination to others. These results are presented in Table 5. In terms of intentions to re-attend the theatre-event, statistically significant differences ($p < .05$) were identified between the Dynamos and the Drifters, Hedonists and the Playful Achievers. Tukey's post hoc test further indicated that the Dynamos and the Temperate Networkers were an homogenous subset of the sample. In terms of intentions to attend more theatre-events in the future and the host destination, statistically significant differences ($p < .05$) were identified between the Drifters and the Dynamos.

TABLE 5. Results of the ANOVA Tests–Level of Satisfaction

Intentions to...	Sig.	F Statistic Df = 4	Lowest ← Level of satisfaction → Highest				
Attend the theatre-event again	.000	6.571	Playful Achievers	Hedonists	Drifters	Temperate Networkers	Dynamos
Attend more theatre-events	.005	3.830	Drifters	Temperate Networkers	Hedonists	Playful Achievers	Dynamos
Recommend the host destination	.013	3.273	Drifters	Hedonists	Playful Achievers	Temperate Networkers	Dynamos
Recommend the theatre-event to friends	.166	1.633	Drifters	Playful Achievers	Hedonists	Temperate Networkers	Dynamos

DISCUSSION

The results of the factor analysis of the personal values data provide further support for the validity and reliability of the LOV. The three-factor solution was intuitively appealing and provided a sound basis for segmentation of the sample. The final cluster solution comprised segments that were sufficiently different from each other, and also demonstrated acceptable levels of intra-cluster homogeneity, providing opportunities to develop the theatre-event that will more likely meet their needs.

The ANOVA tests identified statistically significant differences across the clusters for seven of eight attributes of the theatre-event measured here and when the results were analysed, patterns in the satisfaction responses became evident. Each of the clusters demonstrated fairly consistent responses along the satisfaction continuum. The Drifters were most often the least satisfied of the clusters and the Dynamos most often the most satisfied of the clusters. The Playful Achievers, Hedonists and Temperate Networkers were generally 'placed' between the Drifters and the Dynamos on the satisfaction continuum. These results appear to provide convergent validity for the derived cluster solution, which was based on the personal value domains, particularly for the way in which the clusters are juxtaposed in relation to each other in Figure 2. Despite the fact that no statistically significant differences were found in the levels of overall satisfaction with the theatre-event between the clusters, similar response patterns emerged in these data.

The statistically significant differences between the Drifters and the Dynamos and the Drifters and the Temperate Networkers appear to be attributable to the different levels of importance they placed on the Extrinsic personal value domain. These results indicate that the extrinsic personal value domain is an important factor in the formation satisfaction responses in this context. At the outset of this research, it was thought that the hedonistic personal value domain was going to play a dominant role in the personal value systems of the attendees at theatre-events and that this would impact on satisfaction. The results here, however, indicate that this was not the case.

Managerial Implications of the Results

Information in relation to how the segments responded to the product on offer is useful in developing and refining the product and for developing the market segments. Managers may wish to focus their attention on the Dynamos and the Temperate Networkers as, combined, these two clusters represent almost half of the sample. Further to this, these clusters most often reported very positive satisfaction responses and behavioural intentions in relation to the special event and the special event destination.

Developing theatre-event products that enable members of the Dynamos and Temperate Networkers to gain a sense of belonging and nurturing their personal relationships is prudent. Enabling these segments to also attain a sense of accomplishment and be in control should similarly be considered when developing products for them. These markets may particularly appreciate access to reserved seating, for example, or a tour of the theatre with a group of friends or even an opportunity to 'mingle' with the cast after the performance. Hence, 'hospitality packages' could be offered to them. Ticketing strategies that provide an opportunity to attend the theatre-event in a preview period and again later in the season with a group of their friends may also appeal to these segments.

The Playful Achievers is an interesting segment and may be one that is worthy of developing. This segment demonstrated the greatest levels of variability in their behavioural intentions; members of this segment are the least likely to attend the same theatre-event again, yet they are very likely, however, to attend more theatre-events in the future. Playful Achievers are not as likely to recommend attendance at the theatre-event as the Dynamos and Temperate Networkers, but should be considered seriously in terms of their continued attendance at theatre-events. Promoters of theatre-events wanting to attract Playful

Achievers may benefit from offering this segment the opportunity to purchase tickets, perhaps to preview performances, to a series of theatre-events at discounted prices. As this segment is likely to be price sensitive, which is supported by the relatively low levels of satisfaction members this segment afforded to the attribute 'value for money', this marketing strategy may be useful in developing a segment of loyal theatre-event attendees.

Obtaining further information about the segments, in terms of their lifestyles, will enhance the value of this segmentation analysis of the consumers of this special event. By doing this, programs can be designed that meet the needs of the segments more effectively.

CONCLUSION

Aspects of the model, presented in Figure 1, were supported, but the results here indicate that the model can be refined. Personal values seem to be related to attribute-satisfaction, but not to overall satisfaction. Personal values appear to have impacted on the evaluations of the special event, and post-consumption behavioural intentions specifically related to the special event and this type of product, but not on recommending behaviour in this context. As such, a more parsimonious model might omit overall satisfaction and recommending behaviour and focus on those concepts related to consumption of special events.

The differences across the five clusters, in terms of their satisfaction responses, were fairly consistent and these results provide some support for the notion that personal values and satisfaction are conceptually related to each other. Personal values assisted in segmenting and profiling special event attendees that would otherwise not be achieved if only demographics were used. The derived clusters in this study are useful for practioners in the field aiming to incorporate a lifestyle approach to their marketing. Similarly, the derived clusters, based on systems of personal values, shed further light on how consumers may be better understood using their personal value systems as a point of differentiation. A greater understanding was gained of respondents' satisfaction responses and their post-consumption behavioural intentions when the attributes of the personal values segments were used. This study also highlighted the problems associated with satisfaction data, which are not often reported on yet must seemingly occur often in social research. The results of the factor analysis of the personal values data, using the

LOV, provided further support for personal values theory and demonstrated the application of the theory within the context of special events.

Limitations of the Research and Further Research

The type of special event studied may have impacted on the results obtained here. Further research is required to investigate the personal value systems of attendees at different types of special events, such as community or sporting events. Profiling of attendees at sporting events, for example, may uncover different personal value segments that require different products and services to satisfy their needs. Further validation of the link between personal values and satisfaction, which was tested in this study, is, however, required. This will contribute to the development of theory and provide a greater understanding of the role of personal values in consumer behaviour. Further to this, because of the growing interest in the segmentation of markets using personal values within the context of tourism and leisure, it may be useful to conduct further research on personal values to develop a more encompassing measure of them in this context for future research.

REFERENCES

Anderson, E., and Mittal, V. (2000). Strengthening the satisfaction-profit chain. *Journal of Service Research*, *3*(2), 107-120.

Backman, K. F., Backman, S. J., Muzaffer, U., and Mohr Sunshine, K. (1995). Event tourism: An examination of motivations and activities. *Festival Management and Event Tourism*, *3*(1), 26-24.

Baker, D. A., and Crompton, J. L. (2000). Quality, satisfaction and behavioural intentions. *Annals of Tourism Research*, *27*(3), 785-804.

Bitner, M. J., Faranda, W. T., Hubbert, A. R., and Zeithaml, V. A. (1997). Customer contributions and roles in service delivery. *International Journal of Service Industry Management*, *08*(3), 193-205.

Blamey, R. K., and Braithwaite, V. A. (1997). A social values segmentation of the ecotourism market. *Journal of Sustainable Tourism*, *5*(1), 29-45.

Blom, G. (1958). *Statistical Estimates and Transformed Beta Variables*. New York: John Wiley and Sons.

Burns, J. P. A., Hatch, J. H., and Mules, T. (1986). The Adelaide Grand Prix: The impact of a special event. Adelaide, The Centre for South Australian Economics.

Crompton, J. and McKay, S. (1994). Measuring the economic impacts of festivals and events: Some myths, applications and ethical dilemmas. *Festival Management and Event Tourism* 2(1): 33-43.

Crompton, J., and McKay, K. (1997). Motivations of visitors attending festival events. *Annals of Tourism Research*, *24*(2), 426-439.

Cronin, J. J., and Taylor, S. A. (1992). Measuring service quality: A re-examination and extension. *Journal of Marketing, 56*(3), 55-68.

Daghfous, N., Petrof, J., and Pons, F. (1999). Values and adoption of innovations: A cross cultural study. *Journal of Consumer Marketing, 16*(4), 314-331.

de Ruyter, K., and Bloemer, J. (1999). Customer loyalty in extended service settings. The interaction between satisfaction, value attainment and positive mood. *International Journal of Service Industry Management, 10*(3), 320-336.

Delamere, T. A. (2001). Development of a scale to measure resident attitudes towards the social impacts of community festivals. Part II: Verification of the scale. *Event Management: An International Journal, 7*(1), 25-38.

Delamere, T. A., Wankel, L. M., and Hinch, T. (2001). Development of a scale to measure resident attitudes towards the social impacts of community festivals. Part I: Item generation and purification of the measure. *Event Management: An International Journal, 7*(1), 11-24.

Delpy Neirotti, L. (2001). Motivation to attend the Summer Olympic Games. *Journal of Travel Research, 39*(3), 327-331.

Disney, D. (1999). Customer satisfaction and loyalty: The critical elements of service quality. *Total Quality Management, 10*(Jul.), 491-497.

Erdem, O., Oumilli, A. B., and Tuncalp, S. (1999). Consumer values and the importance of store attributes. *International Journal of Retail Distribution and Management, 27*(4), 137-144.

Fall, L. T., and Knutson, B. (2001). Personal values and media usefulness of mature travellers. *Journal of Hospitality and Leisure Marketing, 8*(3/4), 97-112.

Fredline, E., and Faulkner, B. (2000). *Community perceptions of the impacts of events.* article presented at the Events Beyond 2000: Setting the Agenda, Sydney.

Getz, D. (1997). *Event management and event tourism.* New York: Cognizant Communication Corporation.

Gratton, C., Dobson, N,, and Shibli, S. (2000). The economic importance of major sports events: A case study of six events. *Managing Leisure 5:* 14-28.

Green, C., and Chalip, L. (1998). Sport tourism as the celebration of subculture. *Annals of Tourism Research, 25*(2), 275-291.

Gummesson, E. (1998). Productivity, quality and relationship marketing in service operations. *International Journal of Contemporary Hospitality Management 10*(1): 4-15.

Hair, J. F., Anderson, R. E., Taitham, R. L., and Black, W. C. (1995). *Multivariate data analysis with readings.* Englewood Cliffs: Prentice Hall.

Halstead, D. (1999). The use of comparison standards in customer satisfaction research and management: A review and proposed typology. *Journal of Marketing Theory and Practice, 7*(3), 13-26.

Heath, R. P. (1995). Psychographics: Q'est-ce que c'est. *American Demographcis.* Nov. 74-79.

Hede, A-M., Jago, K. L. and Deery, M. A. (2003). Recommending behaviour at special events: The roles of attribute satisfaction, expectancy disconfirmation and overall satisfaction. article presented at the *Australian and New Zealand Marketing Association Conference*, Melbourne.

Homer, P. M., and Kahle, L. R. (1988). A structural equation test of the value-atti-tude-behaviour hierarchy. *Journal of Personality and Social Psychology, 54*(4), 638-646.

Hunt, H. Keith. (1977). CS/D-overview and future research directions. In H. K. Hunt (Ed.), *Conceptualisation of consumer satisfaction and dissatisfaction* (pp. 455-488). Cambridge: Marketing Science Institute.

Jago, L. K. (1997). *Special events and tourism behavior: A conceptualisation and an empirical analysis from a values perspective.* Unpublished Doctor of Philosophy, Victoria University, Melbourne.

Jones, M., and Suh, J. (2000). Transaction-specific satisfaction and overall satisfac-tion: An empirical analysis. *Journal of Services Marketing, 14*(2), 147-159.

Kahle, L. R. (1983). *Social Values and Social Change: Adaptation to life in America.* New York: Preager.

Kamakura, W. A., and Novak, T. (1992). Value-system segmentation: Exploring the meaning of LOV. *Journal of Consumer Research, 19*(June), 119-132.

Keiningham, T. L., Goddard, M. K. M., Vavra, T. G., and Iaci, A. J. (1999). Customer delight and the bottom line. *Marketing Management, 8*(3), 57-63.

Klenosky, D. B., Gengler, C. E., and Mulvey, M. (1993). Understanding the factors in-fluencing ski destination on choice: A means-end analytic approach. *Journal of Lei-sure Research, 25*(4), 362-379.

Long, M. M., and Schiffman, L. G. (2000). Consumption values and relationships: Segmenting the market for frequency programs. *Journal of Consumer Marketing, 17*(3), 214-232.

Madrigal, R. (1995). Personal values, traveller personality type and leisure travel style. *Journal of Leisure Research 27*(2): 125-142.

Maslow, A. H. (1954). *Motivation and personality.* New York: Harper.

McCarty, J. A., and Shrum, L. J. (2000). The measurement of personal values in survey research: A test of alternative rating procedures. *Public Opinion Quarterly, 64*(3), 271-298.

McGuire, L. (1999). *Australian Services: Marketing and Management.* Mc Millan, Melbourne.

Muller, T. E. (1991). Using personal values to define segments in an international tour-ism market. *International Marketing Review, 8*(1), 57-70.

Muller, T. E. (1995). How personal values govern the post-visit attitudes on interna-tional tourists. *Journal of Hospitality and Leisure Marketing, 3*(2), 3-24.

Muller, T. E. (2000). Targeting the CANZUS baby boomers explorer and adventurer segments. *School of Marketing and Management, 6*(2), 154-169.

Oh, H. and Parks, S. C. (1997). Customer satisfaction and service quality: A critical re-view of the literature and research implications for the hospitality industry. *Hospi-tality Research Journal 20*(3): 35-64.

Oliver, R., L. (1996). *Satisfaction: A Behavioural Perspective on the Consumer.* N.Y. New York: McGraw-Gill.

Oliver, R. L. (1980). A cognitive model of the antecedents and consequences of satis-faction decisions. *Journal of Marketing Research, 17*(4), 460.

Oliver, R. L. (1981). Measurement and evaluation of satisfaction processes in retail set-tings. *Journal of Retailing, 57*(3), 25-46.

Oliver, R. L., and DeSarbo, W. S. (1988). Response determinants in satisfaction judgments. *Journal of Consumer Research, 14*(4), 495-507.

Osborne, D., Wheeler, J, and Elliot, D. (1999). *Selling the performing arts. Identifying and expanding audience for music, dance and theatre.* Australia Council. Surry Hills

Pizam, A., and Ellis, T. (1999). Customer satisfaction and its measurement in hospitality enterprises. *International Journal of Contemporary Hospitality Management, 11*(7), 326-339.

Pol, L. G., and Pak, S. (1994). The use of a two-stage survey design in collecting from those who have attended periodic or special events. *Journal of the Market Research Society, 36*(4), 315-325.

Ritchie, B. (1984). Assessing the impact of hallmark events: Conceptual and research issues. *Journal of Travel Research, 23*(1), 2-11.

Rokeach, M. (1973). *The Nature of Human Values.* New York: Free Press.

Rokeach, M. (1979). From Individual to Institutional Values: With Special Reference to the Values of Science. In M. Rokeach (Ed.), *Societal, Institutional and Organizational Values* (Vol. 47-70). New York: The Free Press.

Rossi, P. E., Giulla, Z., and Allenby, G. M. (2001). Overcoming scale usage heterogeneity: A Bayesian hierarchical approach. *Journal of American Statistical Association, 96*(453), 20-31.

Schwartz, S. H., and Bilsky, W. (1990). Towards a theory of the universal content and structure of values: Extensions and cross-cultural replications. *Journal of Personality and Social Psychology, 58*(5), 872-891.

Sivadas, E., and Baker-Prewitt, J. L. (2000). An examination of the relationship between service quality, customer satisfaction, and store loyalty. *International Journal of Retail and Distribution Management, 28*(2), 73-82.

Thrane, C. (1997a). Vacation motives and personal value systems. *Journal of Vacation Marketing, 3*(3), 234-244.

Van Montfort, K., Masurel, E., and Van Rijn, I. (2000). Service satisfaction: An empirical analysis of consumer satisfaction in financial services. *The Service Industries Journal, 20*(3), 80-94.

Veroff, J., Douvan, E., and Kulka, R. (1981). *The Inner American.* New York: Basic Books.

Woodside, A. G., Frey, L., and Daly, R. T. (1989). Linking service quality, customer satisfaction, and behavioural intention. *Journal of Health Care Management, 9*(December), 5-17.

A Gay Tourism Market:
Reality or Illusion, Benefit or Burden?

Howard L. Hughes

SUMMARY. There is a commonly held view that gay men, in particular, are frequent and intensive holiday-makers. This is explained by reference to distinctive characteristics relating to income and leisure time and to distinctive values and attitudes. Gay men's travel patterns are believed to be unique and such as to offer good prospects to those, such as tour operators and hoteliers, willing to target this market. The evidence for these beliefs is examined in this article. Many of the assertions are based on limited-coverage survey samples; recent US evidence suggests that the very positive views of the economic status and distinct purchasing patterns of gays are exaggerated. It is, nonetheless, apparent that there is a market segment that it is 'economic' to target but which is unlikely to be representative of gay men. It is apparent that existing surveys are incomplete and are an inappropriate basis for targeting the gay consumer. The article also includes a discussion of marketing approaches to which, it is claimed, gay men are responsive. Whilst the targeting of the gay tourism market does have the effect of validating gay lifestyles, the article includes discussion of other more negative issues that may flow from the perpetuation of the 'myth' of the affluent, care-free gay con-

---

Howard L. Hughes is Professor in the Tourism Management Department, Manchester Metropolitan University, Old Hall Lane, Manchester, England M146 HR (E-mail: H.Hughes@mmu.ac.uk).

[Haworth co-indexing entry note]: "A Gay Tourism Market: Reality or Illusion, Benefit or Burden?" Hughes, Howard L. Co-published simultaneously in *Journal of Quality Assurance in Hospitality & Tourism* (The Haworth Hospitality Press, an imprint of The Haworth Press, Inc.) Vol. 5, No. 2/3/4, 2004, pp. 57-74; and: *Hospitality, Tourism, and Lifestyle Concepts: Implications for Quality Management and Customer Satisfaction* (ed: Maree Thyne and Eric Laws) The Haworth Hospitality Press, an imprint of The Haworth Press, Inc., 2004, pp. 57-74. Single or multiple copies of this article are available for a fee from The Haworth Document Delivery Service [1-800-HAWORTH, 9:00 a.m.-5:00 p.m. (EST). E-mail address: docdelivery@haworthpress.com].

http://www.haworthpress.com/web/JQAHT
Digital Object Identifier: 10.1300/J162v05n02_04   *57*

sumer. These include issues such as the generation of a false sense of liberation and distraction from the pursuit of more fundamental aspects of equality. Lifestyle marketing in the context of the gay tourism market has wider and significant implications than those that are usually of direct concern to the marketer; they reach to the core of the nature of homosexuality and its acceptance in society. *[Article copies available for a fee from The Haworth Document Delivery Service: 1-800-HAWORTH. E-mail address: <docdelivery@haworthpress.com> Website: <http://www.Haworth Press.com> © 2004 by The Haworth Press, Inc. All rights reserved.]*

KEYWORDS. Gay tourism, homosexuals and holidays, market segmentation, lifestyle marketing

INTRODUCTION

There is an undoubted interest by tour operators, travel agents, accommodation providers, airlines and destinations in a 'gay holiday market'. In the UK, there are a number of tour operators, such as Man Around (also trading as Sensations) and Respect offering foreign holidays to the British market and an increasing number of destinations, such as London and Manchester, which have targeted domestic and overseas gay markets. The International Gay and Lesbian Travel Association (IGLTA) is a US-based organisation with a membership of over 1200 (mainly US) tour operators, travel agents, etc., with a purpose of 'growing and enhancing its members' gay and lesbian tourism business' (www.iglta.com). Its membership is international and includes major airlines such as American and British Midland as well as city visitor bureaus such as those of Vienna and Vancouver.

Gay men and lesbians have been referred to as 'an emerging lifestyle segment' (Fugate 1993: 46), implying the existence of a distinct lifestyle that might enable marketers to target gay men and lesbians effectively and economically. The essence of lifestyle marketing is that people's purchase decisions are as much influenced by perceptions of what those purchases say about who one is in society as by demographic and economic characteristics. The influences on lifestyle are many (including culture, ethnicity) but it could be that sexual orientation is one of them. Gays and lesbians may buy into a distinguishing way of life reflected in a particular profile of purchases and leisure activities. The reasoning behind this is believed by some to lie in the discrimination, exclusion and rejection by society and the consequent desire to formulate alternative identities that are self-affirming (see, for example, MAPS 1998).

With respect to tourism, this distinctiveness is seen as a widespread belief that gay men have distinct travel preferences, buying habits and motivations and, not only that, these are generally regarded to be particularly favourable: high likelihood of taking a holiday, frequent holiday-taking and high spend. Thomas Roth, president of a US market research company specialising in the gay and lesbian travel market has said that 'travel in the case of the gay and lesbian community is more or less a lifestyle issue. . . . We'll give up coffee before we'll give up travel' (Roth and Luongo 2002: 131). A recent article in a UK hospitality trade journal, pointing out the unexploited market opportunities, referred to gays and lesbians as being a market segment 'that is more inclined to travel and spend money (on leisure activities) than the straight community' (Golding 2003: 26). (The term 'straight' is in common usage to refer to heterosexuals.)

Targeting the gay market may be considered as a particular instance of lifestyle marketing. This article is a commentary on existing work on gay tourism. A number of existing (secondary) sources are examined with the aim of determining just how realistic it is to assume that homosexuals are an attractive market to target for holidays. The evidence relating to these assertions about tourism is examined and analysed as are studies relating to 'the gay market' generally. A further aim is to evaluate the effects of this marketing of tourism to gays and, in particular, to identify implications which may be beyond those of direct relevance to the marketer. These wider aspects of marketing are often disregarded though may be of particular relevance in achievement of more socially responsible marketing. At the least, marketers should be aware of the wider consequences of their activities.

This article focuses on the case of homosexual men with little reference to lesbians. This is, in part, because of the relatively limited amount of research that exists with regard to lesbians and tourism. (Pritchard, Morgan and Sedgley's 2002 article on Manchester's Gay Village is concerned primarily with its significance as leisure space for lesbians rather than as tourism space per se or with the tourism experiences of lesbians.) Research which does exist suggests that motivations and behaviour differ from those of males; as a consequence, the discussion in this article is, for clarity, largely confined to males. The term 'gay' is used throughout this article; it is in common usage for referring to male homosexuals though it is confusingly often used as an alternative to the term 'homosexual' to include females also. The term, unless otherwise indicated, is usually used in this article to refer to male homosexuals, however defined. Homosexuality is itself an ill-defined term but broadly refers to an emotional and physical attraction to persons of the same sex. The article also focuses primarily on the UK experience.

LITERATURE REVIEW

Gay Tourism

Similar features of market behaviour are identified in a number of studies relating to gay tourism. In the case of the USA, gay tourism has been regarded as 'a rapidly growing and profitable sector' (Holcomb and Luongo 1996: 711) and, in the case of the UK, 'an expanding and lucrative niche market' (Clift and Forrest 1999: 615). This view was shared by the British Tourist Authority (BTA, now VisitBritain; Wood 1999). It has been estimated to amount to over 10% of the US travel industry in terms of spend (Community Marketing Inc. 2003). This sector was considered to be particularly resistant to recession and other influences that might ordinarily have adverse effects on the tourism market (Holcomb and Luongo 1996; Community Marketing Inc. 2003). Gays were considered to be more likely than others to take a holiday and also to take more holidays per year than others (Community Marketing Inc 2003). In a UK survey over two-thirds of gays took an additional holiday, compared with just under half of the population as a whole (MAPS 1998). A later UK survey showed that 72% of gays took a holiday compared with 61% for the population as a whole and 24% took 3 or more holidays compared with 11% for whole population (Mintel 2000). US gays were much more likely to take an international holiday than were the rest of the US population (72% compared with 9%) (Community Marketing Inc. 2003).

Studies have also identified the importance of gay-friendliness and gay space in the choice of holiday destination. The most popular holiday destinations identified in Clift and Forrest's study included USA (40.7% had visited in the previous five years), Amsterdam (46.6%), Gran Canaria (31.5%), Ibiza (23%) and Sitges (14.4%) (Clift and Forrest 1999). The BTA's research confirmed that US gay travellers wished to experience Britain's tourist assets much as any other traveller did but they also placed a premium on gay-friendliness (Wood 1999; see also Community Marketing Inc. 2003). Clift and Forrest (1999) observed that in 'planning a holiday', gay men rated rest and relaxation, comfort and good food as the most important factors. These were no different from what the responses of heterosexuals might be expected to be though it was also important to be able to socialise with other gay men in gay space. Gay space is generally characterised as a concentration of bars and clubs but also cafes, shops, residences and public space (Hindle 1994). This gay space is unevenly spread geographically and therefore 'some places that are popular for the travelling public in general . . . may not be considered as desirable by some gay travellers' (Ivy 2001: 352). In Clift and Forrest's survey a relatively low proportion of gay men identified opportunities to have sex on holiday as important in planning a holiday. In the Mintel study, the existence of gay venues at the holiday destination was important for about half of UK gays. There was a definite determination not to visit countries perceived to be homophobic: over two-thirds of men would not go to such a place. Although there was a definite requirement for gay space, only a very small proportion (about 4%) required a 'gay-themed' or gay-centric holiday. The proportion of British gays and lesbians taking city breaks was greater than that for the population as a whole (Mintel 2000). This may be due to the fact that cities have some form of gay space or because of the intrinsic attractions of cities including arts and culture in which gays may have a particular interest generated by comparatively high levels of education (Roth and Luongo 2002). The recent 'gay tourism' campaign of the UK city of Manchester was based on a combination of significant gay space and the cultural resources of a large city (Hughes 2003).

Many of these studies also suggest that gays are particularly brand loyal and react positively to companies who market themselves at gays and who 'give back' to the gay community (Wood 1999; Mintel 2000; Stuber 2002). The two main UK gay tour operators report high levels of repeat business (Russell 2001). Mintel (2000) reported that 38% of gays were more inclined to book with gay-friendly companies but only 3% of respondents had used a gay travel agent or tour operator (probably more a reflection of the structure of supply than of consumer preference). Most gays in the UK used mainstream tour operators.

These characteristics of gay tourism are explained in a number of ways. The BTA regarded typical US gay/lesbian travellers as trendsetters with high disposable income, of a high socio-economic class and known for conspicuous consumption. They were 'more highly educated than the average with an appreciation of arts and culture' (Wood 1999: A107; see also VisitBritain market advice at www.tourismtrade.org.uk). A US study (Community Marketing Inc. 2003) confirmed many of these characteristics: above-average incomes, high educational achievement and employment in professional or executive positions with high levels of passport ownership (at 80% compared with about 29% for the rest of the US population. The BTA reported figures of 48% and 13% respectively: Wood 1999). The Mintel study reported above-average levels of income among respondents and an above-average proportion of them in the 'upper' socio-economic groups.

In addition to these economic factors, tourism studies have referred to gays and lesbians as early adopters, hedonists and aesthetes (Stuber 2002), 'early innovators of new products and services . . . ; trend-setter in fields such as fashion or music' (Russell 2001: 38), people who 'spend their personal disposable incomes differently and appear to maintain a more youthful lifestyle for longer' (Mintel 2000: 1) and as being individualistic, style-conscious, 'flexible thinkers' and having 'leading edge taste' (MAPS 1998: 16, 23). There is a common view that gays have more discretionary income and have more free time than comparable homosexuals. These are, in part, accounted for by low family commitments but also by high educational achievement and the nature of supposedly typical occupations such as professional, managerial and service occupations. These characteristics combined with attitudinal and behavioural attributes appear to make gays a lucrative market to target; they are 'the marketing department's dream consumer' (MAPS 1998: 5).

Sound Evidence?

It is clearly important to examine the basis for these assertions about the gay tourism market and to determine the reliability of the material. Holcomb and Luongo (1996) carried out little original research and their article was largely based on estimates of others. They observed the apparent growth in destinations and provision and commented on the underlying influences on gay holiday making but these and the assertions of growth and financial opportunities were made with little obvious substantiation.

With respect to the UK, the report by Market Assessment Publications (MAPS) attempted to identify the detail of a number of dimensions of the 'pink pound', including holidays. (This term 'pink pound' is in common usage to refer to the supposedly distinctive purchasing patterns of the gay market and its particularly lucrative prospects). MAPS set out to collect original data through its own NOP surveys as well as pulling together data from existing sources such as surveys in the Pink article. Their own survey was of just over 1000 gays and lesbians contacted directly through an intermediary; the response was only 162. Despite this, MAPS felt that it did represent a random cross-section of the gay community.

Clift and Forrest's surveys of gay men's holiday patterns were undertaken with a primary aim of determining sexual behaviour. They were amongst the first to attempt to identify 'holiday motivations' of gay men and to determine the more popular destinations by actually asking gay men themselves. Their surveys were directed at men in Brighton (UK) through bar and club questionnaires and also through questionnaires in local gay magazines. This resulted in a total of 562 usable responses; the researchers were aware of the limitations attached to this sampling method though they considered that it did represent a 'broader cross-section of gay men than is the case in previous related studies' (Clift and Forrest 1999: 618), a reference to sexual behaviour surveys rather than tourism surveys.

Community Marketing has, since the early 1990s, regularly published an influential survey of US gay and lesbian travellers. Their 7th annual survey (2001) was based on 3000 respondents, through e-mail newsletters and Website links, and the 8th survey (2002-03) on 1500 respondents. The organisation did acknowledge (in its 8th survey) that the results cannot be assumed to be representative and were representative only of 'active consumers' and had been validated by the fact that they have been carried out for a number of years (Community Marketing Inc. 2003; Roth and Luongo 2002).

The Mintel survey was one of the first surveys to offer comprehensive information about the UK gay travel market and was undertaken at the London Mardi Gras festival in July 2000. (This is an event that has its origins in Pride marches and has been held, irregularly, in London since the early 1970s. It is aimed at gay, lesbian, bisexual and transgendered people.) The data was derived from a sample of just under 1000 people who attended the festival. Mintel considered that those attending the festival were likely to be a more representative cross-section of the gay population than would be offered by sampling in bars and clubs. The survey was considered to be as 'robust' as possible under the circumstances. Compared with the UK population as a whole, the survey respondents were over-represented in the 20-34- age group and the AB and C1 socio-economic groups.

Some of the surveys compare characteristics and behaviour with the population as a whole (MAPS 1998; Mintel 2000; Community Marketing Inc. 2003). The issue that arises here is that like is not being compared with like. Sample surveys of the population as a whole, if appropriately undertaken, are more likely to be representative than are surveys of gays or lesbians. To make direct comparisons may well, therefore, not be justifiable.

The issue of how representative surveys are is clearly important for effective and economic marketing. Most studies recognise the limitations of their sources. There is, though, a considerable uniformity about their findings and there would seem to be a 'market segment' of gay men which is not necessarily typical of all gay men. These observations about gay men and tourism are, however, no more than part of a wider discussion about the 'gay marketing moment'.

A Wider Discourse

There has undoubtedly been an increase of interest generally in the gay market: termed the 'gay marketing moment' (Gluckman and Reed 1997b). Gays and lesbians have become an increasingly attractive target as social acceptance has increased (Penaloza 1996). The emergence and progress of gay rights' movements and the gradual progress towards equal legal rights in most Western European and North American countries have highlighted the existence of a part of the population with the possibility of distinct market characteristics and which can be approached openly. Attitudes have changed so that there is greater acceptance of homosexuality. In Britain, for instance, the proportion of the population that considered homosexuality was 'always' or 'mostly' wrong had fallen from 70% to 47% between 1985 and 2002 (still a significantly high percentage) and a third felt it was 'not wrong at all' (Evans 2002). Over 3/4 of respondents to another survey believed that gay sex should not be illegal and half agreed that same-sex couples should be allowed to marry (Yates 2002). There is increased acceptance of gays, there are a number of high-profile public figures who have been prepared to be open about their homosexuality and gay space and gay lifestyles have become more open and accepted. Visibility, self-confidence and acceptance of homosexuality have increased greatly (Wood 1999). This has coincided with a more general move to segment markets reflecting wide social and cultural changes and the adoption of lifestyle marketing (MAPS 1998). This has been accompanied by a widespread dissemination of a gay profile of affluence, high levels of education, brand-consciousness, brand-loyalty and interest in fashion and style.

Badgett (2001) has identified a number of, what she termed, 'myths' relating to the economic position of gays and lesbians. In particular she has demonstrated through a series of rigorous studies in the USA that gays and lesbians are not typically affluent and well-educated, that many do have family responsibilities and they are not typically consumption-oriented with spending patterns that are ostentatious and status-ridden.

She highlighted the weak underpinning of the early US studies that led to the generation and perpetuation of the positive profiles. She questioned why it might be expected that gays and lesbians choose to achieve higher educational qualifications and to enter mainly service, professional and managerial occupations and could find no obvious justification for this especially as many will have made choices before identifying as gay and other factors are much more influential (Badgett 1997; Badgett and King 1997). Her own studies showed that gay men earn less than heterosexuals with the same backgrounds such as education (with discrimination and fear of exposure being critical factors); lesbians' earnings were about average for females. It is possible that two-man households will have higher earnings than straight households (though even that is not shown unequivocally in studies) especially given the tendency for average female earnings to be lower than male. Two-women households are likely to have earnings and disposable income below either, especially if there are children in the household.

Regardless of incomes, it could be that gays and lesbians have tastes, product preferences and spending patterns that differ from their straight equivalents. Badgett was particularly critical of what she termed the 'gay marketing moment' and was wary of subscribing to the widely accepted view that gay and lesbian households have purchasing preferences and patterns that differ from those of equivalent straight households. No studies unequivocally show this to be the case or at least they only show a partial picture because of the inherent bias of the samples. The picture of high-spend, hedonistic, fashion-conscious, trend setting individuals will be representative of some parts of the whole gay and lesbian population but there are obvious problems when they are presented as or understood to be 'typical' (Gluckman and Reed 1997b). In some instances it has been concluded that product purchases and purchase criteria of gays were not particularly distinctive and were similar to those of equivalent heterosexuals, especially young singles.

It is simplistic and reductive to assume that sexual orientation would, by itself, be sufficient to identify a market segment. The gay market is not homogeneous (Fugate 1993; Field 1995; Stuber 2002) and is characterised by 'a host of sub-segments defined by demographic, attitudinal and ideological factors' (Pritchard and Morgan 1997: 16). 'Sexuality is cross-cut by class, race and gender in complex ways which the prevailing myths of the affluent gay consumer in the pink economy invisibilise' (Bell and Binnie 2000: 100).

A Market Segment?

Nonetheless the gay marketing moment exists and many firms consider it appropriate to target 'the gay market'. Despite the reservations about the economic and behavioural characteristics of gays and the lack of information about market size, some firms have considered it large enough, accessible and stable enough to justify targeting it even though the targeting may be at a particular 'out' and young element of the total gay population. The number of gays and lesbians is unknown; there is considerable disagreement about definitions and, in addition, some proportion of that population (however defined) will not identify as such to others. The UK government in its proposals for same-sex civil partnerships estimates that 5% of the population (over 16) in Great Britain is gay, lesbian or bisexual (Department of Trade and Industry 2003). Other estimates range between 2% and 10% depending on inclusion criteria such as same-sex sexual activity that was recent, exclusive or one-off. The gay market is regarded as stable and unlikely to change in size or buying power and, if anything, likely to expand as a consequence of growing tolerance (Fugate 1993). In the unlikely event (at least in the near future) of gays and lesbians becoming fully accepted by societies, then the market could disappear.

With respect to accessibility, there has been a significant growth in the number of articles and magazines in the UK targeted at gays and lesbians, increased 'respectability' and/or acceptance of their content and the willingness of mainstream advertisers to use them to project their message. This has involved unmodified 'mainstream' products being targeted in the simplest way such as advertising in gay magazines and articles. Some advertisers could, however, be concerned that association with the gay market alienates mainstream consumers; some articles and magazines may have put off potential advertisers by their sexual content (Fugate 1993; Wood 1999). Recent issues of the British gay magazines *Attitude* and *Gay Times* have, however, included advertisements by Ford, Diesel, Calvin Klein, Holiday Inn, the city of Vienna, the Metropolitan Police (London), Opera North, HMV and Virgin.

Advertisers who do target in the gay press or who modify their advertising to appeal directly to a non-heterosexual audience may well generate gay loyalty (Wood 1999; Mintel 2000; Pritchard and Morgan 1997).

It need not be necessary to modify the advertisements, especially as it might be uneconomic to do so, though utilisation of images such as same-sex couples and of copy in advertisements for 'mainstream' products that is directed at gays is evident in the gay media. Modifications may be minor by including iconography such as pink triangle or rainbow flag and expressions such as diversity or gay-friendly (Penaloza 1996; Stuber 2002). There is an intriguing use of 'gay imagery' and of 'ambivalent' ads such as those of Calvin Klein, in mainstream advertisements which appeal not only to the gay market but also less obviously, but as effectively, to the male and female heterosexual markets. As well as using particularly 'gay' promotional outlets, Roth has suggested that companies with a particularly 'gay' product would be advised to advertise in the mainstream media in order to capture a wider number of gays, especially those who do not read the gay press or access gay Websites (Roth and Luongo 2002).

There is a particularly good opportunity to target the gay market via the Internet as there is a high level of ownership of personal computers and of on-line access among gays (77% compared with a national average of 26%) and a higher likelihood of gay men booking holidays on-line than for the rest of the population (11% compared with 2%: Mintel 2000). Cable television and targeted direct mail can also be effective channels. These may be particularly important for their ability to confer anonymity or, at least, restricted identification as gay. Word-of-mouth is recognised as being of considerable significance, too. Promotions in gay bars and clubs may also be particularly productive.

Companies can also cultivate the gay market and loyalty by involvement in the gay and lesbian 'community': contributions to charities, sponsorship of gay and lesbian events or of activities such as the arts, 'dedicated' staff for gay and lesbian customers but also equal rights employment policies (Roth and Luongo 2002). Insincere, misdirected and misinformed attempts to cultivate this market will fail and respect, reassurance and stimulation of positive inclusive self-images are key factors (Russell 2001).

In some cases the product itself may be modified and developed to suit the particular perceived needs of the gay market. This may especially be the case where social needs are to be met and for products that are significant for gay identity-formation and identity-confirmation. The importance of the bar and similar gay space for gay identity is well recognised as is the role of the holiday (Haslop, Hill and Schmidt 1998; Hughes 1997; Pritchard, Morgan, Sedgley and Jenkins 1998). Gays go on holiday for all of the reasons that anyone else does but there may be an extra dimension of being able 'to be oneself' or of escaping 'repression' which, for instance, is still a problem in legal terms in some US states. Visiting gay communities elsewhere and places of gay historical significance can validate and strengthen gay identity (Holcomb and Luongo 1996). The significance of the holiday may, though, be threatened in many ways and gays may be particularly keen to ensure that risks are minimised (Hughes 2002). A holiday arranged by a tour operator specialising in products for the gay market may offer the reassurance that other operators are perceived not to do. Nonetheless most gays in the UK use mainstream tour operators (Mintel 2000).

There is widespread confidence, therefore, that a gay market segment exists: it is identifiable, is of adequate size, and is accessible and stable. The 'gay marketing moment' exists and continues based on the view that gay men have a distinctive lifestyle and there is an ability to undertake effective targeted lifestyle marketing. The discussion in this article suggests, though, that this 'segment' is but one 'sub-segment' of all gay men. The whole process may, too, have effects that are not wholly desirable.

Implications

Being gay has, through this marketing attention, shifted from a negative criterion of being marginalised to a more positive assertion. Gay and lesbian identity has come to be expressed through lifestyles associated with the purchase of goods and services and the establishment of gay space (Bell and Binnie 2000; Badgett 2001) and it has become increasingly possible in this way to identify as gay in a positive self-esteem sense. Gay life and identity have been determined by patterns of consumption (including body perfection, clothes and leisure activities) being used as markers of difference; this is the essence of lifestyle marketing and is no different from other members of society (Featherstone 1987). Marketing to gays and lesbians has 'legitimised' them as members of society and as distinctive people but only through the market (Penaloza 1996). In some ways the emergence of a gay identity and community owes a great deal to the attention of commercial institutions (including bars and clubs) to the supposed market potential of gays (Haslop, Hill and Schmidt 1998; Badgett 2001). The process may well have been welcomed by gays as a liberating, affirmative and profile-raising one.

There is, however, a body of opinion that sees this less favourably. Increased purchasing power and the ability to buy into a gay lifestyle may have distracted gays from more fundamental issues of sexual liberation (Whittle 1994; Field 1995; Gluckman and Reed 1997a). Consumerism may well be an opportunity to assert economic power but spending may be an expression of freedom that is illusory (Binnie 1995). This form of freedom–to consume–has been fostered and is considered acceptable by the rest of society but heterosexual society, nonetheless, restricts freedom to that dimension and determines its limits so as to restrict any threat to heterosexual hegemony (Richardson 2001). Field (1995) had a concern for the apparent lack of class-consciousness of the gay rights movements; it was her view that businesses' concern lay more with maintaining the spending of consumers through the creation of demand and continuous stimulation of new lifestyles and segments than with the liberation of gays and lesbians from 'oppression'. To that extent, capitalism was willing to allow gays and lesbians to find freedom through the purchase of goods and services, to buy themselves out to freedom, but only in that way.

This may appear to be over-stating the case given that there have been, and continue to be, advances in legal rights for gays and lesbians in many countries of Western Europe in particular. Gay rights lobbyists, however, point to the continuing need, regardless of legislation, to combat homophobia and societal disapproval. (The UK government considered that its same-sex civil partnership scheme could result in more positive attitudes to gays and lesbians. Department of Trade and Industry 2003).

Advances based on purchasing power are precarious as the gay market could be neglected as readily as it has been adopted should economic circumstances alter. There is also a risk that portraying gays and lesbians as leading privileged economic lives as earners and consumers can be counter-productive in that some will then deprecate the call for legal equality (Gluckman and Reed 1997a). In addition, an affluent, hedonistic image of gays and lesbians is generated that may be unhelpful in that it further alienates them from the rest of society (Badgett 2001). Equally the portrayal alienates many gays and lesbians themselves who do not fit into the picture of the 'typical' homosexual; it is reflective largely of white, upper middle class males (Field 1995). 'The gay moment is more of a hurdle for gay politics than a source of strength' (Gluckman and Reed 1997b: 8).

CONCLUSIONS

There are several studies that suggest that gay men are a highly desirable market to target for holiday purchase. Gays have up-scale characteristics and these, along with a distinctive approach to life, result in intensive holiday-taking. It is evident, however, that this profile applies to only a limited (and unknown) proportion of gay men. Holiday profiles of lesbians, bisexuals and transgendered people are virtually unknown. The surveys are inevitably biased towards those gays who are 'out', who are willing to identify as gay and who read particular magazines, use particular Websites or attend particular events.

Even so there is, though, a danger of 'talking-up' the potential of these identified sub-segments; business decisions may be made on the basis of misleading or misinterpreted information. There needs to be a clear awareness of reliability and of limitations. In reality, the characteristics, attitudes and lifestyles of many (if not most) gays are likely to be unknown as are their holiday propensity and frequency, destinations and decision processes.

None of this may be of any consequence for those marketers who can effectively and economically target at the identifiable gay segment. There are markets for leisure products such as bars, clubs, magazines and holidays that operate successfully with distinct offers and associated marketing. There is room for optimism insofar as progress towards legal equality and social acceptance will presumably encourage more gay men to identify as such and to purchase products that relate to sexual orientation–including holidays with specialist tour operators. Paradoxically, it may actually reduce the need to identify through the purchase of leisure goods and services.

There is an apparent preoccupation with meeting the needs of the observable market with the needs of lesbians and older gay men being neglected. The full market potential is unexplored and undeveloped and there is a limited range of holidays supplied. The beach holiday is the most popular form of holiday, as in the market as a whole, though the gay market in the USA is much more diversified than it is in the UK; it includes low volume but high value products such as cruises and adventure, sport, heritage and cultural holidays. The reluctance of many destinations and hotels (UK and overseas) to actively promote to this market may be due more to concerns about reputation than to ignorance of the market potential, but nonetheless, gays and other groups who may feel un-targeted or invisibilised may possibly appreciate a more positive approach.

For many gays it is possible that targeted marketing of holidays is of little significance. Gay men have gone, and will continue to go, on holiday regardless of 'the gay marketing moment' and the targeting of gays and provision of differentiated holidays. They have needs that are no different from those of any other holiday-maker and are content to book through mainstream agents and tour operators, travel with mainstream carriers and stay at mainstream accommodations in mainstream destinations. Existing studies do suggest that gay men do this though the full extent is not known. Nonetheless, many also have a specific requirement of gay-friendliness and gay space. Awareness of this may be restricted among mainstream suppliers who could, as a consequence, benefit from greater knowledge and understanding of the holiday needs of gay men. This applies equally to all in the supply chain from travel agent to hotelier and destination promotion bureau.

The gay marketing moment has, however, served to characterise gay men in a particular and misleading way and it is this that is a contentious issue. Lifestyle marketing has categorised gays as affluent and conspicuous consumers. In the sphere of holidays it is evident that the same categorisation has occurred and (however unintentionally) perpetuates myths and confirms stereotypes. Holiday brochures and advertisements contribute to the perception of gay men as privileged, self-indulgent and sexually active. They also perpetuate images of the idealised male body and contribute to feelings of inadequacy with consequent alienation of many gays from gay culture and community and an inability to be at ease with sexual orientation.

In addition, the ability to go on holiday, to go on several holidays a year, to travel to exotic destinations and to have more choice about timing may well be an illusion of freedom–a freedom to purchase. Although the opportunity to escape may be welcome, it may have distracted, and continue to distract, from the pursuit of more fundamental freedoms only achievable through removing anti-gay, or at least inequitable, legislation and societal disapproval at home.

Some of the implications that have been asserted in this article are, by their very nature, speculative polemic, not based on empirical study. Issues of stereotyping and consumerism's compensatory but distractive effects are not easily demonstrated. It may well be possible to determine public perceptions of gay men and alienation of some gay men from gay culture, but relating these to holidays would be problematic. None of this weakens the substantive logic of the basic theme of this article. The contribution of the article lies in highlighting the weakness of current thinking about gay men's holidays and also in identifying the wider issues that arise from targeting this market segment. The conclusion is that lifestyle marketing with respect to gay men's holidays has been a mixed blessing. It has, in effect, affirmed homosexuality; it has probably been a factor in society's acceptance of gays; it has helped create a sense of freedom and also a gay identity; and it has sustained the willingness of gays to feel comfortable with their sexual orientation. It has, however, also confirmed images of gays that nurture anti-gay feeling; it has diverted attention away from the underlying inequality of gays and has prolonged the struggle for equality in law and acceptance. Whatever the practical issues that arise in identifying and targeting a gay market for holidays, these other issues remain as important considerations.

It is apparent from the analysis in this article that a number of issues remain to be explored further. There is an obvious requirement to ensure more representative surveys of gay men and their holiday needs and patterns; this is not, however, easily resolved given the hidden nature of much of homosexuality. It is more feasible, however, to engage in more qualitative research with smaller numbers of gays. Samples are often derived through a snow-balling technique, and it is possible that this will reveal a greater range of gay men's characteristics and tourism patterns than the more public quantitative survey does. This process may identify more clearly the holiday needs of gays, other than the 'standardised' gay man of current market research, and lead to the subsequent provision of appropriate holiday products. The lack of data relating to lesbian tourism has been frequently noted and this is another obvious candidate for further research. Although not touched on in this article there are a large number of other 'gay tourism' issues that are currently unexplored. These include social and economic impact on destinations, host-guest interaction, reactions of local residents and gay men's activities and behaviour whilst on holiday. It has previously been noted how difficult it might be to substantiate empirically some of the assertions, implications and conclusions of the article but they remain, nonetheless, as issues of significance that should be considered further in future gay tourism research.

REFERENCES

Badgett, L. (1997). Beyond Biased Samples: Challenging the Myths on the Economic Status of Lesbians and Gay Men. In A. Gluckman and B. Reed (Eds.), *Homo Economics: Capitalism, Community and Lesbian and Gay Life* (pp. 65-71). London: Routledge.

Badgett, L. (2001). *Money, Myths and Change: the Economic Lives of Lesbians and Gay Men*. Chicago: University of Chicago.

Badgett, L., and King, M. (1997). Lesbian and Gay Occupational Strategies. In A. Gluckman and B. Reed (Eds.) *Homo Economics: Capitalism, Community and Lesbian and Gay Life* (pp. 73-86). London: Routledge.

Bell, D. and Binnie, J. (2000). *The Sexual Citizen: Queer Politics and Beyond*. Cambridge: Polity Press.

Binnie, J. (1995). Trading Places, Consumption, Sexuality and the Production of Queer Space. In D. Bell and G. Valentine (Eds.) *Mapping Desire: Geographies of Sexualities* (pp.182-199). London: Routledge.

Clift, S. and Forrest, S. (1999). Gay Men and Tourism: Destinations and Holiday Motivations. *Tourism Management*, 20(5), 615-625.

Community Marketing Inc. (2003). *Press Release and Executive Summary: 8th Annual Gay and Lesbian Travel Survey*. San Francisco: Community Marketing Inc. (can be accessed through www.mark8ing.com; accessed 12th May 2003).

Department of Trade and Industry (Women and Equality Unit). (2003). *Civil Partnership: a Framework for the Legal Recognition of Same-Sex Couples*. London: Department of Trade and Industry.

Evans, G. (2002). In Search of tolerance. In A. Park, J. Curtice, K. Thomson, L. Jarvis and C. Bromley (Eds.), *British Social Attitudes: the 19th Report* (pp. 213-230). London: Sage.

Featherstone, M. (1987). Lifestyle and Consumer Culture. *Theory, Culture and Society, 4, 55-70.*

Field, N. (1995). *Over the Rainbow: Money, Class and Homophobia*. London: Pluto.

Fugate, D. (1993). Evaluating the US Male Homosexual and Lesbian Population as a Viable Target Market Segment. *Journal of Consumer Marketing* 10(4), 46-57.

Gluckman, A. and Reed, B. (1997a). Introduction. In A. Gluckman and B. Reed (Eds.) *Homo Economics: Capitalism, Community and Lesbian and Gay Life* (ppxi-xxxi). London: Routledge.

Gluckman, A. and Reed, B. (1997b). The Gay Marketing Moment. In A. Gluckman and B. Reed (Eds.) *Homo Economics: Capitalism, Community and Lesbian and Gay Life* (pp. 3-9). London: Routledge.

Golding, C. (2003). The Pink Pound. *Caterer and Hotelkeeper*. 1st May, 26-28.

Haslop, C., Hill, H. and Schmidt, R. (1998). The Gay Lifestyle: Spaces for a Subculture of Consumption. *Marketing Intelligence and Planning*, 16(5), 318-326.

Hindle, P. (1994). Gay Communities and Gay Space in the City. In S. Whittle (Ed.), *The Margins of the City: Gay Men's Urban Lives* (pp. 7-25). Aldershot: Arena.

Holcomb, B. and Luongo, M. (1996). Gay Tourism in the United States. *Annals of Tourism Research*, 23(3), 711-713.

Hughes, H. (1997). Holidays and Homosexual Identity. *Tourism Management*, 18(1), 3-7.

Hughes, H. (2002). Gay Men's Holiday Destination Choice: a Case of Risk and Avoidance. *International Journal of Tourism Research*, 4(4), 299-312.

Hughes, H. (2003). Marketing Gay Tourism in Manchester: New Market for Urban Tourism or Destruction of Gay Space? *Journal of Vacation Marketing*, 9(2), 152-163.

Ivy, R. (2001). Geographical Variation in Alternative Tourism and Recreation Establishments. *Tourism Geographies*, 3(3), 338-355.

MAPS (1998). *The Pink Pound 1998: Strategic Market Report*. London: Market Assessment Publications Ltd.

Mintel (2000). *The Gay Holiday Market*. London: Mintel International Group.

Penaloza, L. (1996). We're Here, We're Queer and We're Going Shopping! A Critical Perspective on the Accommodation of Gays and Lesbians in the US Marketplace. In D Wardlow (Ed.), *Gays, Lesbians and Consumer Behavior: Theory, Practice and Research Issues in Marketing* (pp. 9-41). New York: Harrington Park Press.

Pritchard, A. and Morgan, N. (1997). The Gay Consumer: a Meaningful Market Segment? *Journal of Targeting, Measurement and Analysis for Marketing*, 6(1), 9-20.

Pritchard, A., Morgan, N., and Sedgley, D. (2002). In Search of Lesbian Space? The Experience of Manchester's Gay Village. *Leisure Studies*, 2, 105-123.

Pritchard, A., Morgan N., Sedgley, D., and Jenkins, A. (1998). Reaching Out to the Gay Market: Opportunities and Threats in an Emerging Market Segment. *Tourism Management*, 19(3), 273-282.

Richardson, D. (2001). Extending Citizenship: Cultural Citizenship and Sexuality. In N. Stevenson (Ed.), *Culture and Citizenship* (pp. 153-166). London: Sage.

Roth, T. and Luongo, M. (2002). A Place for Us 2001: Tourism Industry Opportunities in the Gay and Lesbian Market. In S. Clift, M. Luongo and C. Callister (Eds.), *Gay Tourism: Culture, Identity and Sex* (pp. 125-147). London: Continuum.

Russell, P. (2001). The World Gay Travel Market. *Travel and Tourism Analyst* no 2, 37-58.

Stuber, M. (2002). Tourism Marketing aimed at Gay Men and Lesbians: a Business Perspective. In S. Clift, M. Luongo and C. Callister (Eds.), *Gay Tourism: Culture, Identity and Sex* (pp. 88-124). London: Continuum.

Whittle, S. (1994). Consuming Differences: the Collaboration of the Gay body with the Cultural State. In S Whittle (Ed.), *The Margins of the City: Gay Men's Urban Lives* (pp. 27-41). Aldershot: Arena.

Wood, L. (1999). Think Pink! Attracting the Pink Pound. *Insights (January)*, A107-A110

Yates, R. (Ed.). (2002). Sex Uncovered. *the Observer supplement*, 27th October.

www.atc.australia.com/marketing (accessed 30th May 2003)

www.iglta.com (accessed 11th March 2003)

www.tourismtrade.org.uk/uktrade (accessed 4th June 2003)

Escaping the Jungle:
An Exploration
of the Relationships
Between Lifestyle Market Segments
and Satisfaction with a Nature Based
Tourism Experience

Gianna Moscardo

SUMMARY. One of the most challenging, but also most interesting, features of tourism and hospitality as an area of study is that there is considerable variability in the backgrounds and training of those who are involved in its management. In some commercial sectors there is a lengthy tradition of the use of marketing as an integral component of management practice, while in public management organisations, marketing concepts are either unknown or mistrusted. This lack of application of marketing is particularly apparent in the management of tourism to protected areas such as National and State Parks and forests. An ongoing challenge in this sector is to conduct research into visitors and how they choose and enjoy their nature based leisure experiences. This article will

Gianna Moscardo is affiliated with the Tourism Program at James Cook University, Townsville, QLD 4811 Australia (E-mail: gianna.moscardo@jcu.edu.au).

[Haworth co-indexing entry note]: "Escaping the Jungle: An Exploration of the Relationships Between Lifestyle Market Segments and Satisfaction with a Nature Based Tourism Experience." Moscardo, Gianna. Co-published simultaneously in *Journal of Quality Assurance in Hospitality & Tourism* (The Haworth Hospitality Press, an imprint of The Haworth Press, Inc.) Vol. 5, No. 2/3/4, 2004, pp. 75-94; and: *Hospitality, Tourism, and Lifestyle Concepts: Implications for Quality Management and Customer Satisfaction* (ed: Maree Thyne and Eric Laws) The Haworth Hospitality Press, an imprint of The Haworth Press, Inc., 2004, pp. 75-94. Single or multiple copies of this article are available for a fee from The Haworth Document Delivery Service [1-800-HAWORTH, 9:00 a.m. - 5:00 p.m. (EST). E-mail address: docdelivery@haworthpress.com].

http://www.haworthpress.com/web/JQAHT
Digital Object Identifier: 10.1300/J162v05n02_05

report on a project to improve the study and management of visitors to the Wet Tropics World Heritage Area in the North Eastern part of Australia. The study involved a travel lifestyle market segmentation of over 1200 visitors to the area based on travel interests, activities and desired rainforest based tourism experiences. The analysis identified four core types of rainforest visitor and these groups were compared and contrasted in terms of their service quality ratings and overall satisfaction. The article concludes with links to the management frameworks for this tourism destination and the value of different segmentation techniques in general. *[Article copies available for a fee from The Haworth Document Delivery Service: 1-800-HAWORTH. E-mail address: <docdelivery@haworth press.com> Website: <http://www.HaworthPress.com> © 2004 by The Haworth Press, Inc. All rights reserved.]*

KEYWORDS. Lifestyle segmentation, rainforest tourism, park management

INTRODUCTION

Natural areas such as parks and forests are attractive destinations for tourists. A core challenge for the public sector management agencies responsible for these protected natural areas is to balance the provision of access to tourists with the management of any negative impacts from this tourism. Providing visitor access to parks is desirable in a number of ways. Firstly, many protected area management agencies have as one of their goals the provision of positive natural environmental experiences to visitors. In addition, many also have the goal of using visitation to support public environmental education and enhancing general conservation attitudes. Visitation can also bring revenue to the park management and often supports tourism as a regional economic activity. But these benefits have to be balanced against the potential for visitation to result in a variety of negative impacts (Cleaver and Muller, 2002; Galloway, 2002). The challenge for park managers is to maintain a balance between the quality of the visitor experience and the quality of the visited environment.

Traditional approaches to park management, however, have focussed primarily on physical resources and often very little is known about visitors and their characteristics. In particular there have been calls for research into visitors' motivations, expectations, activity choices, perceptions of service quality and overall satisfaction. There has also been some recognition that park visitors are not a homogeneous group and that managers also need to understand the nature and consequences of critical differences between visitors (Burns, Graefe, and Titre, 2001; Crompton, Mackay and Fesenmaier, 1991; Hamilton, Crompton and More, 1991).

Several authors have proposed that to be effective, park managers must understand their visitors and must recognise the importance of providing quality experiences. Many have argued that the provision of positive experiences for visitors can result in greater support for the management agency and its actions and greater concern for the park itself on the part of the visitors. Visitors who are more concerned about the natural resource are less likely to create negative impacts (Cleaver and Muller, 2002; Cordell, Hoover, Super and Manning, 1999; Galloway, 2002; Hall and McArthur, 1993, Hammitt and Cole, 1998).

Comparisons can be drawn between this challenge for the management of park tourism and concepts in the literature of Total Quality Management (TQM). Omachonu and Ross (1994, p. 3) define TQM as "the integration of all functions and processes within an organization in order to achieve continuous improvement of the quality of goods and services." In TQM quality is defined as "fitness for use" as perceived by the users of the product or service. Alternatively, quality can be seen as meeting user expectations. Therefore users are central to the process of management and an important aspect of management practice is to understand the variety of users for a particular product or service and what they need or expect (Juran and Gryna, 1993; Omachonu and Ross, 1994; Saylor, 1992).

Park managers are responsible for decisions about:

- what uses will actually be permitted within the park,
- the location and type of facilities provided for different uses,
- the level, location and type of access provided to different areas within a park, and
- the amount and type of information provided to users (Hammitt and Cole, 1998).

Given their responsibility for balancing the needs of visitors against the needs of environmental protection, quality in park tourism could be defined as ensuring the right visitors are connected to the appropriate activities in a suitable setting. In order to achieve this balance park managers need to have an understanding of the range of visitors, particularly in terms of their motives and expectations with regard to facilities and activities. This article will report on one study conducted in the Northeast region of Australia, which focussed on understanding the different types of visitors to the World Heritage Wet Tropics rainforest in this region.

Wet Tropics World Heritage Area

The Wet Tropics World Heritage Area (WTWHA) consists of a series of rainforests located in the Far North Queensland region of Australia. These rainforests were declared a World Heritage Area in 1988 and they form an important, but not exclusive, focus for tourism in the region alongside the Great Barrier Reef. Most domestic visitors travel to the area from distant urban centres by car and access to the region by local residents for short breaks and day trips is common. International visitors mainly arrive either by air in the main urban centre of Cairns or by long distance coach or bus from southern centres. Tourist activities within the rainforest consist mainly of scenic driving to picnic areas and scenic lookouts, which are usually supported by swimming in rainforest creeks and lakes and walks of various length and difficulty. Several sites are regularly included in commercial day trip tours. The structure of tourism in the region has similarities to that in areas such as Yellowstone National Park in the United States and the Lakes District in the United Kingdom.

The tourism management plan of the Wet Tropics Management Authority (WTMA) is based on a Recreational Opportunity Spectrum (ROS) approach. The "Recreational Opportunity Spectrum" (ROS) is a planning and management framework formulated by the US Forest service for inventorying and describing recreational opportunities in a variety of settings (Clark and Stankey, 1979; Driver and Brown, 1978; Kaltenborn and Emmelin, 1991). The ROS system is based on the assumption that quality in outdoor recreation can best be achieved by providing a range of diverse recreational opportunities to meet a variety of user preferences. Using this assumption, parks are usually divided into six land management classes which range from "primitive" to "urban" type settings (Clark and Stankey, 1979; Driver and Brown, 1978). Each setting has different levels of physical alterations to the environment, remoteness, size, likely encounters with others, and types of management actions (Kaltenborn and Emmelin, 1991). The "primitive" setting assumes that visitors want to experience an area with no developed facilities, a low level of management, and few other people. At the other end of the spectrum are "urban settings" that are organised to provide high density, intensively managed experiences to its users in a developed environment (Ormsby et al., 2003).

Even where the label ROS is not used, the idea of systematically managing the numbers of visitors and the amount and type of built facilities to provide for a range of experiences is a common one in recreation management. The ROS approach to visitor management has the advantages of being easily incorporated into management plans and the use of zones to separate different forms of use. Although this type of management approach has been widely adopted by park managers, a number of problems with the system have been suggested (Hammitt and Cole, 1998). Research has indicated that visitors do not necessarily report experiential changes as they pass through different ROS settings (Yuan and McEwen, 1989) and that experience may not be as closely or directly linked to the managerial and physical setting attributes as is assumed in this model (Hammitt and Cole, 1998).

Table 1 provides a description of the site classification scheme used in the Nature Tourism Management Plan for the Wet Tropics (Wet Tropics Management Authority, 2000). As can be seen, the scheme is based upon the notion of providing experiences for six different types of visitor based on:

- the level of contact they would seek with other users,
- the amount of built infrastructure and interpretation that was desired,
- the importance of seeing famous or icon sites, and
- the nature of the activities they sought to engage in.

The ROS type system being used here can be likened to an *a priori* market segmentation scheme that divides visitors according to the assumed level of built facilities and use densities they desire and assumptions about the types of activities they seek.

Segmentation Studies of Park Visitors

As previously noted there are few segmentation studies of park visitors. Galloway (2002) reports on a psychographic segmentation of visitors to parks in Ontario, Canada, that used sensation seeking as the core differentiating variable. In both the literature review and concluding sections of this article, Galloway argues that psychographic segmentation provides a better option than socio-demographic segmentation for discriminating between visitors and understanding their expectations

TABLE 1. Site Classification Used for Tourism Management in the Wet Tropics

Site Class	Desired Experience	Strategies
Core Natural 1	Opportunities to experience the WHA and its environs in a natural state in a self-reliant manner	Maximum vehicle size 12 persons Limited infrastructure No on-site interpretation
Core Natural 2	Opportunities to see the WHA wilderness with limited interaction with the environment	Maximum vehicle size 12 persons Basic infrastructure Basic on-site interpretation
Recreation 1	Opportunities for small groups to experience the WHA and environs and recreate in a natural area	Maximum vehicle size 12 persons Limited infrastructure Basic on-site interpretation
Recreation 2	Opportunities for large numbers of people and groups to experience and recreate in the WHA and environs	Maximum vehicle size 35 persons Well developed infrastructure High on-site interpretation
Icon 1	Opportunities to experience outstanding WHA features and values in small to medium groups	Maximum vehicle size 35 persons Well-developed infrastructure High on-site interpretation
Icon 2	Opportunities for large numbers of people and groups to experience outstanding WHA features and values	Well-developed infrastructure High on-site and off-site interpretation

(Adapted from WTMA, 2000, p. 40. WHA stands for World Heritage Area.)

and satisfaction. A similar theme can be found in Moscardo, Pearce and Morrison (2001), who compared a geographic with a behavioural segmentation approach to understanding Wet Tropics visitors. They concluded that the behavioural approach fulfilled eight criteria of market segmentation effectiveness better than the geographic option. Both of these papers provide reviews that suggest that there is a growing consensus of opinion that psychological and behavioural segmentation approaches are better options for discriminating amongst visitors. These two approaches are also seen as providing a better understanding of those aspects of visitors' expectations and product preferences that are better matched to tourism management goals and options.

Lifestyle market segmentation offers a way to combine both psychological and behavioural variables into a single segmentation approach. Lifestyle segmentation can be defined simply as "the goals that people shape for themselves and the means they employ to reach them" (Lawson et al., 1999, p. 450). According to Lawson and colleagues (1999) there are two levels at which lifestyle segmentation can operate. The first level is that of general consumer patterns characterised by the use of general measures of activities, interests, and opinions (AIO). The second is within more specific product domains with measures developed to focus on the attitudes, motives, consumption situations, and activity choices relevant to understanding consumer behaviour with regard to a more specific set of products and services. Lawson and colleagues go on to describe such an approach within the context of travel behaviour by New Zealanders. This study used a series of statements on motivations and reasons for travel to identify six market segments. These segments were then profiled on activities, places visited, planning and expenditure, travel behaviours, and demographics. A similar analysis can be found in Gladwell's (1990) study of State Park Inn users in Indiana.

Aims of the Study

The Wet Tropics scheme for managing visitors, as described in Table 1, assumes that visitors can be segmented according to their motives for visiting the rainforest, their desired activities, the settings in which they choose to participate in these activities, and the style of experience they want in terms of the number of other people likely to be in the site chosen. The key word is "assumes" as the plan was developed with limited visitor use or preference information. Therefore the aims of this study were to:

- explore the relationships between rainforest travel style segments (determined using a lifestyle segmentation approach) and perceptions of the service quality and satisfaction with rainforest tourism experiences,
- compare the segments uncovered with those anticipated by the management agency, and
- consider the value of the lifestyle segmentation approach for this public sector tourism context.

METHOD

Sampling Procedure

The data for the study were collected through a survey of tourists departing the Wet Tropics region by plane, bus or other vehicle. Surveys were conducted in the domestic departure lounges of the Cairns Airport, distributed on buses departing Cairns and given to motorists and bus passengers at Cardwell. During the period of surveying, all passengers waiting in the domestic departure lounges of the Cairns airport in the hour before flight departures were approached and asked if they were a resident or a visitor. Visitors were then asked to participate in the study, and if they agreed they were given a self-completion questionnaire. The same procedure was used in the waiting lounges of the bus terminal and on the buses prior to their departure. Other travellers were targeted at Cardwell. Cardwell is a small coastal fishing village located approximately half way between the two major urban centres of Cairns and Townsville on the National Highway One. It is the only place where the highway comes to the coast and is a popular place for buses and motorists to take a refreshment break. Research assistants were stationed at the key service stations and picnic areas along the highway in the centre of the town and they approached all people who entered the chosen area during the survey times. Again a screening question was used to determine if the people approached were local residents or visitors. Visitors were defined as people staying away from home for at least one night for a purpose other than business or work. A total of 2,170 potential respondents were approached to complete the survey. Fifty-eight percent agreed to participate giving a total sample of 1, 258 questionnaires for analysis and a response rate of 58%. The sample comprised 38% car travellers who completed the survey in Cardwell, 36% air travellers who completed the survey in the Cairns Airport departure lounges, and the remainder (26%) who were surveyed in the Cairns bus terminal. The surveys were conducted in English only and thus the sample is not representative of those international visitors who did not speak English.

Questionnaire

The questionnaire consisted of five main sections. Table 2 provides a summary description of the questionnaire.

Sample

Table 3 provides a summary demographic profile of the total sample. Overall the sample was evenly split between males and females. The most common age category was 21 to 30 years, reflecting the popularity of the region for young, independent long-stay travellers, also referred to as backpackers. The largest category for usual place of residence was international, again reflecting the popularity of the destination for backpackers and other international visitors in general. Of the international visitors 71% were from Europe and 20% were from North America. Further, the majority of the respondents were travelling as part of an adult couple (46%), with 12% travelling alone, and 91% travelling without children.

TABLE 2. Summary Description of the Questionnaire

Section	Question Topics
Regional travel behaviours	Number of previous visits to the region Length of stay in the region Travel party expenditure Main form of transport within the region Places where respondents stayed overnight within the region Information sources used
Rainforest site visitation	List of all rainforest sites visited and activities participated in at each site
Rainforest travel features	23 features were rated for their importance in deciding which site/s to visit including – motivations – desired levels of facilities – desired activity opportunities – items related to the number of other people likely to be at the site. These rainforest travel style features were developed from the factors used in the Wet Tropics Tourism management plan (WTMA, 2000) to classify sites.
Satisfaction	Overall rating of satisfaction with their holiday in the region Overall rating of satisfaction with rainforest visits Likelihood of recommending the region to others Likelihood of returning to the region Quality ratings of eight features of the rainforest types
Socio-demographics	Usual place of residence Travel party details Age Gender

RESULTS AND DISCUSSION

Identifying the Segments

The first stage in the analysis followed a similar process to that described by Lawson, Thyne, Young and Juric (1999) and involved a factor analysis of the 23 rainforest travel features. A principal components analysis with a varimax rotation was used to determine any underlying dimensions in the data on rainforest travel features. According to Reisinger and Turner (2003) this type of analysis has the advantages of removing collinearity which allows for other multivariate analyses, reducing the number of variables for further analysis, which eases interpretation of results, and the identification of core underlying dimensions or attributes. This analysis provided a seven-factor solution accounting for 62% of the total variance, which was the best solution, and the results of this procedure are summarised in Table 4.

TABLE 3. Demographic Profile of the Sample

Variable	% Sample	Variable	% Sample
Usual Place of residence – International – Interstate – Intrastate	 44% 21% 35%	Age group – < 20 years – 21 - 30 – 31 - 40 – 41 - 50 – 51- 60 – 61 - 70 – > 70 years	 9% 36% 15% 12% 15% 9% 4%
Sex – Male – Female	 51% 49%		

TABLE 4. Results of the Factor Analysis of Rainforest Travel Features

Features % of Variance Explained	Factor 1 20%	Factor 2 11%	Factor 3 8%	Factor 4 7%	Factor 5 6%	Factor 6 5%	Factor 7 5%
A place that is close by	.76						
A famous place	.75						
A place tour operators go to	.70						
Has sealed road access	.61						
Experience the beauty of nature		.74					
Natural place with no built facilities		.67					
See wildlife		.63					
Environmental information		.58					
A place to rest and relax			.70				
Pleasant setting to relax in			.74				
Solitude away from others			.55				
Be close to friends and family			.49				
Go on long walks(> 1 hour)				.83			
Be physically active				.74			
Go on short walks (< 1 hour)				.73			
Have wilderness adventures					.80		
Do something new and different					.65		
Range of activities available					.58		
Go swimming					.44		
Type of facilities available						.74	
A safe place						.66	
Number of tour buses likely to be there							.83
Number of other people likely to be there							.81

Note: Features were rated on a 5-point scale from not at all important (1) to very important (5)

The resulting factor scores were then used to cluster analyse the sample using a K-Means clustering. Four-, five- and six-group solutions were analysed and the stability of the solutions was confirmed by re-running the analyses using the saved cluster centres. Discriminant analyses indicated that all three solutions were sound with 95%, 95% and 96% correctly classified in each case. The four-group solution was chosen because it provided the clearest differentiation on the factor scores used in the cluster analysis and the greatest number of statistically significant (p < 0.01) differences on rainforest activity participation variables. Table 5 provides a summary of the differences of the four segments on the rainforest travel features.

Comparing the Segments

Rainforest visitors in Cluster 1 were motivated by a need to escape and experience solitude and relaxation in a natural environment. They were primarily interested in long and short walks and didn't value places that were central to regional tourist images. Cluster 2 was more interested in experiencing the beauty of nature and accessing environmental information and sought easily accessible and famous sites. This cluster was the least concerned with the presence of others at rainforest sites and less motivated by physical activity. This was also the group most likely to take a rainforest bus tour. The third cluster was the least interested in the natural environment, solitude, or escape. These rainforest visitors were primarily motivated by opportunities to swim and to experience new and different things. The final cluster was motivated by escape, nature appreciation, and physical activity. This group gave the highest levels of importance to opportunities to experience solitude and consideration of the number of other people in their choice of a rainforest site to visit. Facilities for visitors and safety were also important travel features for this group.

The second stage in building the rainforest travel style segments was to profile and compare the four segments on the features of an ideal rainforest site (Table 6), travel behaviour (Table 7), and socio-demographic variables (Table 8). These were conducted using chi-square analyses for nominal variables, oneway ANOVAs for normally distributed interval variables and Kruskal-Wallis non-parametric tests for the other measures. As in the previous tables only statistically significant relationships are reported with the significance level set at 0.01. The results for features of ideal rainforest sites were consistent with the importance ratings given for the items related to solitude and the number of

TABLE 5. Comparing the Clusters on Rainforest Travel Features and Activity Participation

	Cluster 1	Cluster 2	Cluster 3	Cluster 4
% of sample	18%	26%	21%	35%
Travel Features				
A famous place	1.8	2.4	2.5	3.5
A place tour operators go to	1.8	2.8	2.3	2.7
Experience the beauty of nature	4.8	4.9	3.8	4.8
Natural place with no built facilities	4.2	3.8	2.8	4.3
See wildlife	4.3	4.6	3.7	4.6
Environmental information	3.9	4.5	3.2	3.9
A place to rest and relax	4.3	3.7	3.9	4.4
Pleasant setting to relax in	4.3	3.9	4.0	4.4
Solitude away from others	4.1	3.4	3.3	4.3
Be close to friends and family	2.1	1.9	2.5	3.0
Go on long walks (> 1 hour)	3.8	3.3	3.2	3.8
Be physically active	3.4	3.3	3.4	3.9
Go on short walks (< 1 hour)	4.6	4.0	3.6	4.0
Have wilderness adventures	2.2	3.7	3.3	4.0
Do something new and different	3.7	4.7	4.0	4.5
Range of activities available	2.3	3.4	3.5	3.4
Go swimming	3.1	3.2	3.8	4.1
Type of facilities available	3.9	4.3	3.7	3.5
A safe place	3.7	4.4	4.2	3.9
Number of tour buses likely to be there	2.7	2.4	2.8	3.6
Number of other people likely to be there	3.2	2.8	3.2	3.8
Activity Participation				
Take a bus tour for day	8%	20%	12%	13%
White water rafting	2%	2%	10%	10%
Viewing scenery	33%	29%	21%	19%

Only statistically significant relationships ($p < 0.01$) are reported.
Scores for the travel features are mean scores on scale from 1, not at all important, to 5, very important, and tests were Kruskal Wallis One Way Analyses of Variance.
Scores for activity participation are the percent of the cluster who did this activity at least once or more than once for viewing scenery.

other people present. Clusters 1 and 4, for example, gave the highest importance ratings for opportunities to experience solitude, and they were also the most likely to state that they preferred few people at their ideal rainforest site and the least likely to state that they didn't care about the number of people at the site.

TABLE 6. Comparing the Clusters on Features of an Ideal Rainforest Site

Variable	Cluster 1	Cluster 2	Cluster 3	Cluster 4
Facilities at an ideal rainforest site				
– Restrooms	80%	78%	74%	66%
– Barbeques	11%	15%	26%	19%
– Rainforest interpretation	66%	71%	60%	58%
Number of people at an ideal site				
– None	8%	3%	10%	7%
– Few	39%	17%	25%	37%
– Some	15%	17%	14%	16%
– Don't know	13%	21%	21%	16%
– Don't care	26%	41%	31%	23%

TABLE 7. Demographic Profiles of the Clusters

Variable	Cluster 1	Cluster 2	Cluster 3	Cluster 4
Usual Place of Residence				
– International	34%	56%	53%	58%
– Interstate	28%	24%	19%	18%
– Intrastate	38%	20%	28%	24%
Number of adults in the travel party				
– 1	14%	17%	27%	20%
– 2	66%	60%	41%	50%
– 3-5	16%	15%	25%	21%
– > 5	4%	9%	7%	9%
Travel party includes children	12%	8%	7%	9%
Mean Age	45 yrs	39 yrs	33 yrs	34 yrs

TABLE 8. Comparing the Clusters on Travel Behaviours

Variable	Cluster 1	Cluster 2	Cluster 3	Cluster 4
Main form of transport				
– Private car	48%	20%	29%	31%
– Rental car	21%	20%	20%	12%
– Bus	27%	56%	45%	47%
– Other	4%	5%	7%	10%
First visit to the region	39%	64%	53%	59%
Used travel agents for rainforest travel information	17%	33%	22%	23%
Used previous experience in the region for information	30%	14%	16%	19%
Stayed in Cairns for at least 1 night	58%	74%	74%	76%

There were also statistically significant relationships between the demographic variables and the four clusters. The first cluster contained the oldest visitors, the largest proportion of intrastate visitors, and was the most likely to have visitors travelling with children. Rainforest visitors in the second cluster were most likely to be overseas visitors, to be travelling as a couple, and were the second oldest group. The youngest group was the third cluster, and these visitors were also most likely to be travelling alone or in a small group of adults. While the majority of visitors in this group were international, more than a quarter were intrastate visitors. The final cluster had a similar demographic profile to Cluster 3 with a slightly higher number of couples.

Differences in travel behaviour were also examined and were consistent with the usual place of residence of the clusters. Cluster 1, for example, was the most likely to be travelling in a private vehicle, to be on a repeat visit to the region, and to use previous experience as a source of information about the region. This cluster was also the least likely to stay in Cairns. In addition to the variables reported in Table 8, the questionnaire asked visitors to list all the rainforest activities they participated in and where these activities were carried out. Given the extensive list of sites and locations reported and the fact that multiple answers were given, no tests for statistical significance could be conducted. Clear differences in regional travel patterns can, however, be described. Cluster 1 visited more sites per person than any other cluster, with an average of 6.2 different sites, and these were spread over a wider geographic range than any of the other clusters. Members of Cluster 1 were the least likely to visit sites in the immediate vicinity of Cairns and the areas north of Cairns, and they were six times more likely than the other groups to visit places which were more than 100 kilometres from Cairns. Clusters 2 and 4 on the other hand, were the most likely to visit sites close to Cairns and in the Port Douglas and Daintree areas to the north of Cairns. Sites reported by members of the third cluster were almost entirely restricted to the areas in the immediate vicinity of Cairns.

Summary Profiles of the Four Rainforest Visitor Groups

The first cluster was labelled *Escape to Nature,* as their key motivation for visiting rainforest sites was to view scenery, appreciate nature, and escape from other people. The main activities sought were rainforest walks. This group was the oldest and the most likely to be intrastate visitors who had been to the region before, who stayed in locations other than the main urban centre of Cairns, and who travelled in a private vehicle to a wider range of more remote rainforest locations. This group was the most critical of the quality of the facilities provided by the park agencies.

The second cluster could be called *Scenic Nature Tourers,* as this was the group most likely to take a rainforest bus tour to visit accessible and famous sites. These visitors gave low importance ratings to physical activity but sought new and different experiences, and opportunities for nature appreciation. A typical member of this group was travelling with a spouse or partner, had not been to the region before, and used tour operators for information.

The third cluster contained visitors with the lowest interest in rainforest experiences. They gave low importance ratings to all the travel style features, especially those related to nature appreciation. For this group the most important rainforest travel features were safety, novelty, and the opportunity to swim and socialise with family and friends. This was the youngest group and the most likely to be travelling alone or in a group of friends. They were given the label *Just Passing Through,* as the overall pattern of their responses suggested that they sought the rainforest primarily as a pleasant backdrop for their social experiences.

The final group was named the *Wilderness Adventurers,* as they gave the highest importance ratings to wilderness adventures, physical activities, nature appreciation, and escape from other people. These rainforest visitors were the most likely to be international tourists travelling by bus in a couple or small group, from Cairns.

Satisfaction and Service Quality

Most visitors expressed high levels of satisfaction with their rainforest visits overall, with a mean score of 8.5 (standard deviation of 1.5) on an 11 point scale from 0 meaning not at all satisfied to 10 meaning very satisfied. The same scale was used to rate their holiday in the region overall, and again the mean was high at 8.6 (standard deviation = 1.5). The majority (82%) stated that they would definitely recommend a visit to the region to family and/or friends, and a further 90% stated that would definitely return to the region in the future. The visitors were also asked to rate the quality of various features of the rainforest sites they visited on a scale from 1 meaning poor quality to 5 meaning high quality. These eight features were chosen to match factors under the control of the relevant management agencies. They were also consistent with items which have been shown to be important for perceived service quality and/or satisfaction in other comparable settings (Burns et al., 2001; Hamilton et al.,

1991; Frochot and Hughes, 2000). The eight elements and their mean quality ratings were:

- The overall rainforest environment (4.4)
- Facilities provided for visitors (4.2)
- The management of visitor impacts (3.9)
- Rainforest interpretation (3.8)
- The range of activities available for visitors (3.8)
- Cleanliness of the sites (4.3)
- Ease of access to relevant information (4.1)
- Usefulness of available information (4.0)

Significant differences were found among the four rainforest travel style groups on seven of these measures (see Table 9). Members of the *Escape to Nature* group were the least likely to state that they would definitely return and the most critical of the quality of management of visitor impacts, the quality of the rainforest interpretation provided, and the range of activities available. *Scenic Nature Tourers* were the most satisfied overall and, consistent with the type of rainforest travel style

TABLE 9. Comparing the Clusters on Satisfaction and Service Quality Ratings and Best Features

Variable	Escape to Nature	Scenic Nature Tourers	Just Passing Through	Wilderness Adventurers
Mean rating of overall holiday satisfaction	8.7	9.0	8.5	8.7
Mean rating of overall rainforest visit satisfaction	8.6	8.7	7.9	8.3
Definitely visit region again	70%	88%	81%	76%
Mean quality ratings for – usefulness of information – management of visitor impacts – rainforest interpretation – range of activities available	3.9 3.7 3.6 3.7	4.0 4.1 4.0 3.9	3.7 3.8 3.6 3.7	4.0 3.9 3.9 3.9
Key themes in best rainforest experience – Nature Appreciation – Wildlife encounters – Facilities – Scenery – Solitude – Novelty/Activity – Access – Social features	20% 21% 21% 20% 20% 34% 2% 5%	25% 9% 29% 27% 11% 29% 4% 2%	46% 4% 23% 25% 9% 21% – –	20% 12% 10% 32% 24% 31% 3% 8%

sought, these visitors were the most likely to report the facilities and scenery as key themes in their best rainforest experiences. The *Just Passing Through* visitors were the least satisfied overall and the most likely to report nature appreciation themes as contributing to their best experiences. This last finding is surprising given that this group gave the lowest importance to features related to nature appreciation.

IMPLICATIONS AND CONCLUSIONS

The first aim of the study was to explore the relationships between rainforest travel style segments and perceptions of the service quality and satisfaction with rainforest tourism experiences available in the Wet Tropics region of Australia. Overall the study found high levels of satisfaction and ratings of quality for several components of the available rainforest experiences. This provides indirect support for the scheme that is used by the management agency to organise settings for different types of activity and experience opportunity. The lowest satisfaction and quality ratings were given by the respondents in the *Just Passing Through* group. This is not surprising as this group had generally low levels of interest in visiting rainforest sites and so represent a mismatch between the product or experience offered and their overall reasons or motives for being in the area. One management option to avoid such a mismatch is to seek to provide better information before arrival in the setting so that visitors can make informed decisions about what they do and don't want to experience. This is supported by the significantly lower quality ratings given by this group for service components related to information.

The analyses of service quality and overall satisfaction ratings also indicated potential problems for the *Wilderness Adventurers* group. This group also gave lower rainforest visit satisfaction scores. A more detailed examination of their responses found, however, that they gave the highest quality ratings on all of the four components reported in Table 9. There are two possible explanations for these findings. The first is that factors other than those under the control of park management impacted on their overall satisfaction. This is consistent with the argument and research findings presented by Noe (1999). Noe (1999) proposes that satisfaction is based on two sets of factors, instrumental factors, which include the facilities and service provided by the managers of tourism or recreation sites, and expressive factors, which are those features of the experience that are focussed on the achievement of desired goals. The achievement of these goals is only partly determined by what managers do; it is also determined by factors outside management control, such as the social interactions within groups, and personal factors such as fatigue and well being. In the present case, this group was the most likely to be travelling in a tour group and the most likely to be international. Thus factors related to the tour itself are likely to have impacted on respondent satisfaction. The second explanation is that the study did not measure all the relevant features of service quality or factors likely to impact on overall satisfaction. One clear possibility in this regard is the issue of crowding. This group was the most likely to be concerned about the number of other people present at a rainforest site and the most likely to have visited popular, high-use sites within easy driving distance from Cairns. The survey did not, however, directly measure perceptions of crowding.

The second aim of the study was to compare the segments uncovered with those anticipated or assumed by the management agency. As described in Table 1, the Wet Tropics region is divided into six types of site based on the assumption that visitors mainly select rainforest sites to visit based on the number of other people likely to be there, the level of infrastructure available, the style of activity they seek, how famous the site is, and how easy it is to access the site. The rainforest travel style segmentation produced four groups that were clearly distinguished by these variables. Three groups in particular could be easily matched to the site categories. The *Nature Escapists* sought solitude and relaxation in a setting with some facilities, which matches the Core Natural 2 and Recreation 1 categories. The *Scenic Nature Tourers* were clearly seeking the style of experience provided in the two Icon categories and the Recreation 2 category that have easy access to famous sites with substantial infrastructure and interpretation. The Core Natural 1 and Recreation 1 categories offered access to the wilderness with limited numbers of people and the opportunity to engage in physical activities, which best matches the *Wilderness Adventurer* group. The fourth group, *Just Passing Through,* was not particularly matched to any site category as the rainforest itself was not the core focus of their experience. Generally this group could be suited to any of the Recreation or Icon categories, as the presence of others and the level of facilities were irrelevant, and they didn't seek wilderness experiences.

This group produced one of the few unexpected results in that these rainforest visitors gave nature experience items low importance ratings, but they were the most likely to give nature appreciation themes as part of their best rainforest experiences. In other words, they enjoyed something they weren't seeking. This is an important finding for two reasons. Firstly, it lends some support to claims that experience of a natural environment can be a force for changing perceptions, and this is an important reason for encouraging people to visit these places (Hall and McArthur, 1993; Baumel and Baumel, 1992; Mannell and Kleiber, 1997). Secondly, it reminds us that tourism and recreation experiences are dynamic, and visitors can and do change their motives and expectations. Researchers and managers need to be careful not to treat segment descriptions and classification schemes as static.

The third and final aim of the study was to consider the value of the lifestyle segmentation approach for this public sector tourism context. Overall, the lifestyle based segmentation used in this study was specific to the product domain of concern, choice of rainforest sites, and it did generate groups that were well matched to the management system in use. These four groups also differed significantly in their site choices and their evaluations of service quality and their overall satisfaction. Although there were differences between the groups in terms of socio-demographic and travel behaviour variables, these relationships were complex. Thus the results support the use of lifestyle segmentation approaches as a way of describing and understanding Wet Tropics rainforest visitors.

REFERENCES

Baumel, G., and Baumel, L.L. (1992). *Leisure and Human Behavior 2nd Edn.* Dubuque, Iowa: Wm. C. Brown.

Burns, R.C., Graefe, A.R., and Titre, J.P. (2001). *Customer Satisfaction at US Army Corps of Engineers Administered Lakes.* Portland, Oregon: US Northeastern Forest Research Station. *http://www.fs.fed.us/ne/home/publications/scanned/gtr241a.pdf* (accessed May 2001).

Clark, R.N., and Stankey, G.H. (1979). *The Recreation Opportunity Spectrum: A Framework for Planning, Management and Research.* Portland, Oregon: USDA Forest Service Research article PNW-98.

Cleaver, M., and Muller, T.E. (2002). The Socially Aware Baby Boomer: Gaining a Lifestyle-Based Understanding of the New Wave of Ecotourists. *Journal of Sustainable Tourism*, 10(3): 173-190.

Cordell, H.K., Hoover, A.P., Super, G.R., and Manning, C.H. (1999). Adding human dimensions to ecosystem-based management of natural resources. In Cordell, H.K. and Bergstrom, J.C. *Integrating Social Sciences with Ecosystem Management.* Champaign, Illinois: Sagamore, pp. 1-12.

Crompton, J.L., MacKay, K.J., and Fesenmaier, D.R. (1991). Identifying Dimensions of Service Quality in Public Recreation. *Journal of Park and Recreation Administration*, 9(3): 15-27.

Driver, B., and Brown, P.J. (1978). The Opportunity Spectrum Concept in Outdoor Recreation Supply Inventories: A Rationale. In *Proceedings of the Integrated Renewable Resources Inventories Workshop*. Washington, DC: USDA Forest Service General Technical Report RM-55, pp. 24-31.

Frochot, I., and Hughes, H. (2000). HISTOQUAL: The Development of a Historic Houses Assessment Scale. *Tourism Management*, 21: 157-167.

Galloway, G. (2002). Psychographic Segmentation of Park Visitors Markets: Evidence for the Utility of Sensation Seeking. *Tourism Management*, 23: 581-596.

Gladwell, N.J. (1990). A Psychographic and Sociodemographic Analysis of State Park Inn Users. *Journal of Travel Research*, 28(4): 15-20.

Hall, C.M., and McArthur, S. (1993). Heritage Management. In Hall, C.M. and McArthur, S. *Heritage Management in New Zealand and Australia*. Auckland: Oxford University Press, pp. 1-17.

Hamilton, J.A., Crompton, J.I., and More, T.A. (1991). Identifying Dimensions of Service Quality in a Park Context. *Journal of Environmental Management*, 32: 211-220.

Hammitt, W.E., and Cole, D.N. (1998). *Wildland Recreation: Ecology and management, 2nd Edn*. New York: John Wiley and Sons.

Juran, J.M., and Gryna, F.M. (1993). *Quality Planning and Analysis*. New York: McGraw-Hill.

Kaltenborn, B.P., and Emmelin, L. (1991). Tourism in the High North: Management Challenges and Recreation Opportunity Spectrum Planning in Svalbard, Norway. *Environmental Management*, 17(1): 41-50.

Lawson, R., Thyne, M., Young, T., and Juric, B. (1999). Developing Travel Lifestyles: A New Zealand Example. In Pizam, A. and Mansfeld, Y. *Consumer Behavior in Travel and Tourism*. New York: The Haworth Press, Inc., pp. 449-479.

Mannell, R.C., and Kleiber, D.A. (1997). *A Social Psychology of Leisure*. State College, Pennsylvania: Venture.

Moscardo, G., Pearce, P.L. and Morrison, A.M. (2001). Evaluating Different Bases for Market Segmentation: A Comparison of Geographic Origin versus Activity Participation for Generating Tourist Market Segments. *Journal of Travel and Tourism Marketing*, 10(1): 29-49.

Noe, F. (1999). *Tourist Service Satisfaction*. Champaign, Illinois: Sagamore.

Omachonu, U.K., and Ross, J.E. (1994). *Principles of Total Quality*. Delray Beach, Florida: St. Lucie Press.

Ormsby, J., Moscardo, G., Pearce, P., and Foxlee, J. (2003). *A review of research into tourist and recreational uses of protected natural areas*. Technical Report, Townsville: Great Barrier Reef Marine Park Authority.

Reisinger, Y., and Turner, L.W. (2003). *Cross-cultural Behaviour in Tourism*. Oxford: Butterworth Heinemann.

Saylor, J.H. (1992). *TQM Field Manual*. New York: McGraw-Hill.

Wet Tropics Management Authority (2000). *Wet Tropics Nature Based Tourism Strategy*. Cairns: Wet Tropics Management Authority.

Yuan, M.S., and McEwen, D. (1989). Test for Campers' Experience Preference Differences Among Three ROS Setting Classes. *Leisure Sciences*, 11: 177-186.

A Lifestyle Segmentation Analysis of the Backpacker Market in Scotland: A Case Study of the Scottish Youth Hostel Association

Maree Thyne
Sylvie Davies
Rob Nash

SUMMARY. The purpose of the research outlined in this article is to provide a travel lifestyle segmentation analysis of one particular tourist group, commonly known as 'backpackers', who reside in Scottish Youth Hostel Association hostels. This research was undertaken due to the lack of understanding and knowledge of this market in the United Kingdom, specifically their needs, wants and motivations. Five cluster groups were uncovered in total: *Typical Backpackers, Discoverers, Outdoors, Family Ties,* and *Routine Travellers.* The aim of this article is to provide a wider understanding beyond the demographics of the backpacker and thus provide useful marketing and promotional advice for suppliers to the backpacker market. It also aims to contrast the Scottish backpacker

Maree Thyne, Sylvie Davies and Rob Nash are affiliated with the Scottish Centre of Tourism (SCoT), Aberdeen Business School, The Robert Gordon University, Garthdee II, Garthdee Road, Aberdeen AB 10 7QG (E-mail: m.thyne@rgu.ac.uk) (E-mail: s.davies@rgu.ac.uk) or (E-mail: r.nash@rgu.ac.uk).

[Haworth co-indexing entry note]: "A Lifestyle Segmentation Analysis of the Backpacker Market in Scotland: A Case Study of the Scottish Youth Hostel Association." Thyne, Maree, Sylvie Davies, and Rob Nash. Co-published simultaneously in *Journal of Quality Assurance in Hospitality & Tourism* (The Haworth Hospitality Press, an imprint of The Haworth Press, Inc.) Vol. 5, No. 2/3/4, 2004, pp. 95-119; and: *Hospitality, Tourism, and Lifestyle Concepts: Implications for Quality Management and Customer Satisfaction* (ed: Maree Thyne and Eric Laws) The Haworth Hospitality Press, an imprint of The Haworth Press, Inc., 2004, pp. 95-119. Single or multiple copies of this article are available for a fee from The Haworth Document Delivery Service [1-800-HAWORTH, 9:00 a.m. - 5:00 p.m. (EST). E-mail address: docdelivery@haworthpress.com].

market with findings in Australia, to determine whether cluster groups uncovered are similar in both countries. *[Article copies available for a fee from The Haworth Document Delivery Service: 1-800-HAWORTH. E-mail address: <docdelivery@haworthpress.com> Website: <http://www.HaworthPress. com> © 2004 by The Haworth Press, Inc. All rights reserved.]*

KEYWORDS. Backpackers, SYHA, lifestyle segmentation, marketing

INTRODUCTION

To view backpackers as one homogeneous group of travellers, different from mass tourists but not from each other, can be dangerous since it will surely result in at least some of these visitors being dissatisfied or not particularly well catered to. (Loker-Murphy, 1996:25)

The overall backpacker market in Britain has been recognised as an important and growing market (Keeley, 2001); however, we know very little about the types of people that constitute this important market. Specifically, there is little understanding of their motivations, the attractions they visit and the activities undertaken (lifestyles). It is felt that current research into this market is not commensurate with the potential benefits and that it is vital that backpacker travel patterns become the subject of further research because much of the information currently available is purely anecdotal (Keeley, 2001). In 2000, Shipway stated that the backpacker market 'continues to be overlooked by both academic and market research and by the tourism industry and tourist boards in Britain' (Shipway, 2000:393). This current article argues that four years on, very little is still understood about this market in the United Kingdom and particularly Scotland.

The more a producer/supplier knows about their market, the more effective their marketing strategy will be. 'In marketing, the underlying premise is that consumers' lifestyles will strongly influence their consumption behaviour' (Craig-Lees, Joy and Browne, 1995:291). Demographic differences alone give no indication as to why people consume specific products or services; therefore, firms need to look for better ways in defining their markets (Craig-Lees et al., 1995; Lawson, Tidwell, Rainbird, Loudon and Della Bitta, 1999). 'One of the most promising approaches to selecting target markets is lifestyle and psychographic segmentation' (Lawson et al., 1999:46). It has been advocated in marketing and tourism literature that consumers do not purchase the same goods/services for the same reasons (Holt, 1997; Thyne 2001). Thyne (2001) focused on museum visitors and found that people would visit museums to fulfil quite different values-based motivations, thus determining that within the one target market, there were a number of different needs, wants and motivations. The research question for this article is whether the same theory applies to the backpacker market in Scotland?

Segmentation research has been undertaken on the backpacker market in Australasia (Loker-Murphy, 1996; Ryan and Mohsin, 2001) which showed different segments within the one target market. However, so far such research has been undertaken in only one country. Therefore, it would be useful to determine if the backpacker market in another region also consists of distinguishable segments and whether these are similar to those identified within the Australian research.

BACKGROUND

Definitions and Characteristics of Backpackers

Backpacking has emerged as a major global cultural, economic and social phenomenon, assisted by the relative ease of international travel and a growing network of budget hotels and tour operators. Increasing flexibility of work patterns and changes in life path expectations have also fuelled this growth (Chesshyre, 2003).

Research into the backpacker market has mainly been conducted in Australasia (Pearce, 1990; Loker-Murphy, 1991, 1996; Murphy, 2001; Ryan and Mohsin, 2001; Mohsin and Ryan, 2003). The work from the 1990s to the present day has had a dual purpose: (1) to refine the social/cultural interpretation of the backpacking phenomenon and (2) to provide statistics on demographics and the economic impact of the backpacker market. During this period, the shared understanding of the backpacker characteristics rested on a social definition provided by Pearce in 1990, which includes the following criteria:

- a preference for budget accommodation;
- an emphasis on meeting other travellers;
- an independently organised and flexible travel schedule;
- longer rather than very brief holidays and
- an emphasis on informal and participatory holiday activities (Pearce, 1990).

The first criterion, a preference for budget accommodation, has been seen throughout these years as the basic and determining criterion in defining backpackers. As a result, travellers staying in hostel type of accommodations have provided the sample frame for most subsequent research.

Studies following Pearce's research have not only succeeded in providing fairly consistent demographics but also in revealing additional criteria such as length of stay, travel patterns and activities and shared motivations (Loker-Murphy, 1991, 1996; Murphy 2001; Mohsin and Ryan, 2003). Loker (1991) extended Pearce's research by including demographic characteristics, which she had found through research, to be common to backpackers:

- 18-30 years of age
- A minimum length of stay of four months
- Holiday as the main purpose of the trip

It has since been recognised that these demographics are changeable. For example, a recent survey conducted in Australia suggests that backpackers may not always be differentiated by age (i.e., they are not all necessarily young); they include holidaymakers in full-time employment, some of whom are time constrained and their choice of accommodation is not limited to hostels but may include motels and B & Bs (Mohsin and Ryan, 2003). Therefore, instead of segmenting this market on their demographics, it is argued here that it is more useful to focus on lifestyle segmentation. This will be discussed in more detail under the 'lifestyles' section.

However, there does remain limited information on this market in the United Kingdom, specifically the motivations, lifestyles and expectations of backpackers. There are also a number of problems both within the United Kingdom and internationally, associated with identifying statistically just who constitutes the backpacker market, because they are no longer so easily distinguished by their economic or demographic characteristics as Keeley (2001) suggested.

BENEFITS AND VALUE OF BACKPACKER TOURISM

Governments often perceive international tourism as an engine for economic development. However, academics who study the economic impact of the backpacking market regret that, until recently, the focus has been commonly upon mass tourism and traditional tourists while ignoring the sub-sector of backpacker tourism (Loker-Murphy and Pearce, 1995; Hampton, 1998; Scheyvens, 2002). This is in spite of the fact that the World Tourism Organisation had already reported in 1995 the average annual rate of increase of youth tourism today outstrips by close to 60% the average annual rate of increase of world tourism (Loker-Murphy and Pearce, 1995).

Although the backpacker tends to spend less *per diem,* it is increasingly acknowledged that their contribution to a local economy is significant in terms of the time they spend in an area (Shipway, 2000). In an Australian context, Loker-Murphy and Pearce point to the value of this market to Australia:

> *Given that backpackers account for up to 8% of visitors to Australia, that they have an overall trip expenditure greater than the average visitor, and they are more likely to travel extensively throughout Australia, especially outside the capital cities, it is evident that backpackers are important to Australia's tourism industry. (1995:840)*

In addition to revenues from backpackers' spending outlined earlier, Elliott (2002) demonstrates that there is also a social benefit associated with backpacker travel. Backpackers are as likely to frequent urban and rural destinations. Although their value in the former is less significant alongside other tourists in higher spending categories, they are far more important as visitors to rural areas, as they seek out new destinations and have a penchant for remote and unusual places (Scheyvans, 2002). They are much more willing to endure hardships in their travels than other types of tourists and are not averse to inconvenience. According to these authors, backpackers are worth more to the local economy than they commonly receive credit for. This point is especially relevant to Scotland, where often the main benefits from tourism tend to be centred on the traditional tourist route of Edinburgh, Glasgow and Inverness, at the expense of more peripheral areas which, nevertheless, offer strong attractions based on their natural and physical environment (Nash, 2002).

In research commissioned by the English Tourism Council, Keeley (2001) estimates that the backpacker market accounts for 10% of overseas visitors to the United Kingdom and those 2.5 million travellers come to Britain for a three to four week backpacking trip. Keeley suggests that there is a potential market worldwide of 20 million young people who at any given time have the resources to visit Britain. Britain's appeal to the backpacker market includes its history, cultural diversity, visual images and the use of the English language (Keeley, 2001). However, little is known about the type of people which constitute this market, for example the types of attractions/activities they are interested in.

Shipway (2000) undertook quite comprehensive research into the backpacker market in England and Wales. Shipway identified a number of very interesting facts about the market, for example, their levels of interest and spending habits. He also looked into their attitudes, perceptions and experiences. He concluded his research with recommendations for budget accommodation providers, transport operators and host communities, emphasising the importance of the backpacker market to the United Kingdom. This current article extends Shipway's research, by picking up on his 'future research' points, specifically 'demonstrating the development of different subsets of groups' within the backpacker market (Shipway, 2000: 414). It also extends Shipway's research into a Scottish context.

Information on the general economic impact of tourists in Scotland is readily accessible from relevant government departments, yet more specific information on the backpacking phenomenon across Scotland as a whole is incomplete and sporadic. However, it is possible to derive some insight into the growth of the backpacker market from a survey on the hostel market in Scotland conducted by VisitScotland (2000) and from a profile of holiday makers staying in hostels in the Highlands and Islands between 1997 and 1999 (Highland and Island Enterprise, 2000). According to VisitScotland, the number of hostels in Scotland has doubled since 1990 to 227 in 2000, and occupancy levels in hostels at 49% are higher than in all forms of accommodation with the exception of self-catering (VisitScotland, 2000). These results may reflect a steady growth of backpacker type tourists who tend to favour this type of accommodation.

However, what is still uncertain is the type of people who constitute this market. This information would be useful to VisitScotland and individual hostels and transport companies, for example. It is the lack of research and official statistics, especially in a Scottish context, that prompted this research and it was felt that SYHA hostels would provide an appropriate field of exploratory investigation, since the SYHA marketing literature refers to its target customers as 'independent travellers' while promoting activities for 'backpackers' (www.syha.org.uk).

The Scottish Youth Hostel Association (SYHA)

Established in 1931, the SYHA is a non-profit-making organisation with charitable status. It is the leading provider of hostel type accommodation in Scotland with 4,500 beds across 73 hostels. Around 70% of SYHA visitors are from outside Scotland, contributing to tourism income and to the economic health of both city and, crucially, fragile rural communities, particularly in the North and North-West Highlands. The SYHA is a significant local employer throughout Scotland with 450 employees (SYHA Annual Report, 2002; www.syha.org.uk).

Lately, the marketing drive has been an important element in the overall development of the SYHA business strategy, and it has adopted the concept of target marketing and market segmentation which has been closely tied in with customised improvements of products and services (SYHA Annual Report, 2001 and 2002). For example, the SYHA has closed some of its hostels which were not suitable for today's standards and has undertaken major refurbishments in 27 of its hostels with the addition of en-suite facilities (www.syha.org.uk). The current emphasis is to raise the general quality of the 'core hostelling product' (SYHA Annual Report, 2002) and, at the same time, to match products and services to the tastes of visitors in differing market groups. A travel lifestyles study, as proposed in this article, can provide added insight for the development and management of the SYHA marketing mix, particularly for product development and promotional strategies.

Lifestyles

The concept of 'lifestyles' or 'style of life' originated over 50 years ago from Alfred Adler, referring to the goals that people shape for themselves and the means they employ to reach them (Lazer, 1963). 'Lifestyle relates to how people live, how they spend their money and how they allocate their time' (Craig-Lees, Joy and Browne, 1995: 291). Lifestyles have been used in marketing and consumer behaviour literature to refer to the various reasons behind different patterns of consumption. It is assumed that people who have similar lifestyles are more likely to use similar products and services (Craig-Lees et al., 1995). Clusters or segments of consumers with similar lifestyles can be identified and the appropriate marketing mixes can be developed for each group (Craig-Lees et al., 1995). It has been suggested that segmenting consumers on lifestyles is more beneficial than segmenting them on their demographics, for example, predominantly because they are related to the goals people set for themselves and they provide marketers with an understanding of the motivations forces that drive behaviour (Lawson et al., 1999).

To aid in success, marketers aim to determine the variables which distinguish people's performance in the marketplace (Kucukemiroglu, 1999). Over the past 40 years it has been recognised that these variables go beyond just demographic and socio-economic variables, and a continually larger focus has been placed on psychographic and lifestyle segmentation (Kahle and Kennedy, 1989; Gonzalez and Bello, 2002).

Marketing academics and practitioners have adopted lifestyle segmentation in a variety of areas, see for example Oates, Shufeldt and Vaught (1996); Mitchell and Haggett (1997); Kaynak and Kara (2002) and Kim, Kim and Kim (2003). Lifestyles and psychographics have also been used in a variety of contexts in tourism literature. For example, host community segmentation studies (Davis et al., 1988); hotel choice amongst themed hotels (Zins, 1998; McCleary and Choi, 1999); tourist activity choice (Madrigal and Kahle, 1994; and Gnoth, 1999) and domestic travel behaviour (Lawson, Thyne, Young, and Juric, 1999). Such studies have identified tourist 'lifestyles' through the measurement of motivations, attractions visited, activities undertaken, attitudes and demographics. This current research follows a similar methodology to Lawson et al. (1999) in its investigation into the travel lifestyles of backpackers. This point will be expanded upon in the methodology section of this article.

Lifestyle segmentation has previously been used in a backpacking context (Loker-Murphy, 1996; Ryan and Mohsin, 2001); however, this has not been specific to the United Kingdom. Loker-Murphy (1996) undertook a cluster analysis on backpackers to Australia, specifically focusing on their motivations. Four distinct groups were identified: *Social/Excitement Seekers, Escapers/Relaxers, Achievers*, and *Self-Developers*. Ryan and Mohsin (2001) undertook a cluster analysis on visitors to the Northern Territory, Australia. Again four groups were uncovered: *Mainstreamers, Passive Viewers, Explorers*, and *The Not Keen*. For both studies, nationality was the most significantly different demographic between the segments. Such an analysis has not been performed before on backpackers to the United Kingdom, therefore, it will be interesting to see if similar cluster groups are identified.

METHODOLOGY

The methodology for this current research was a two-stage process: in-depth interviews followed-up with a more extensive questionnaire. The methodology was similar to that of Lawson et al. (1999) in their travel lifestyles research. In-depth interviews were undertaken both to gather exploratory information on the backpacker market and to aid in the design of a questionnaire for wider distribution. The interviews were held with international and domestic visitors staying in SYHA hostels throughout Scotland; a mixture of urban and rural locations were used. The respondents were a mixture of age groups, nationalities and gender. In total, 22 interviews were undertaken. The themes included in the interviews are shown in Table 1.

The results from the interviews were compared to the literature to determine the items which needed to be included in the questionnaire. The questionnaire was designed to garner further information on each of the areas discussed in the interviews. Once designed, the questionnaire was pretested on 20 backpackers staying at an urban SYHA hostel. Afterwards, a few of the questions were changed mainly due to syntax suggestions.

There were seven sections in the questionnaire; see Table 2 for a summary of the content areas in the questionnaire.

Open-ended questions were also included to give respondents further opportunity to expand on their response or to suggest improvements to the current level of service.

With the support of the SYHA, 1,200 questionnaires were distributed to 12 Scottish Youth Hostels, in September and October 2002. The selection criteria for the hostels sought to achieve a balanced sample between urban and rural hostels across Scotland. Three hundred nine completed questionnaires were returned, constituting an acceptable response rate of 25.7%.

TABLE 1. Themes for the In-Depth Interviews

Interview themes
• motivation for travel
• the origin of the visitor
• length of stay
• activities undertaken and attractions visited
• patterns of expenditure
• transportation used
• sources of information gathered prior and during visit to Scotland
• booking procedures
• perceptions of the provision of facilities
• general demographics
• overall satisfaction of visit to Scotland

TABLE 2. Summary of the Questionnaire's Content

Question subject	Details about the question	Number of questions
Details of holiday in Scotland	Length of stay Regions visited Travel companions Holiday planning	Four
Reasons for travel	Motivations Expectations/Perceptions Attractions visited/intend to visit Activities undertaken/intend to undertake	Eighty-two
Transportation	Types of transport used Reasons for choosing transportation modes	Eleven
Accommodation	Types of accommodation used Reasons for choosing accommodation types Importance/Satisfaction of accommodation facilities Overall satisfaction with accommodation Suggested improvements for accommodation Reasons for staying in SYHA Booking procedure for accommodation	Thirty-four
Spending	Estimate of how much was spent on holiday Estimate of budget for holiday	Three
Information sources	Types of information sources used to plan trip	Thirteen
Demographics	Gender Age Education Work situation Household income	Seven

These were statistically analysed using SPSS (Statistical Package for Social Science) software.

First, to gain insight into the overall sample, the general demographics of the respondents were analysed. These are reported in the results section. Second, a cluster analysis was undertaken on the 32 motivation statements. However, before this was undertaken, the overall sample means, standard deviation and size of the sample for each scale item was checked. These were considered satisfactory, with no major discrepancies apparent between the standard deviations. Additionally, a reliability analysis was undertaken on the 32 items in the motivational scale, of which the overall scale Cronbach alpha was 0.9060. All alpha values were above the 0.7 threshold which Nunnally (1978) and Peterson (1994) recommend. Thus the scale was deemed reliable.

In a similar vein to the travel lifestyles research by Lawson et al. (1999), a cluster analysis was undertaken on a number of variables within the data set, to provide an in-depth portrayal of the 'style of life' of the backpacker market. Some of the variables included in the analysis were attractions visited, activities undertaken, attitudes and motivations. A hierarchical cluster analysis was first undertaken on these variables (represented on a 7-point Likert scale (1 = not at all important, 7 = extremely important), using the Wards method of agglomeration and Squared Euclidean Distances. This method was initially chosen to produce a dendrogram from which the number of clusters present could be determined. Analysis of the dendrogram indicated that a three, four or five cluster solution could be used to interpret the results. When interpreting each cluster solution, all cluster groups had recognisable cluster solutions. Therefore, it was decided to run a K-means cluster analysis on the data, requesting the results for a three, four and five cluster solution. A K-means cluster analysis will assign objects (in this case respondents) into clusters, once the number of clusters to be formed is specified. Therefore, a K-means cluster analysis can 'fine tune' the results obtained from the hierarchical analysis (Hair et al. 1998).

A reverse discriminate analysis (forecasting the cluster membership from the original variables) was then undertaken on the three, four and five cluster solutions produced by the K-Means cluster analysis. This was to determine the accuracy of the cluster group membership classifications. The discriminate analysis worked well for all three group solutions (94%, 95% and 94% of cases were correctly classified in each respective solution). Although the four cluster solution correctly classified the most cases, the authors decided after analysing the cluster profiles that if the three or four group solution was chosen over the five cluster groups, significant group profiles would be missing. The five cluster solution intuitively better represented the backpacker market and was thus chosen for further analysis.

A One-Way Analysis of Variance was undertaken and showed significant differences (p ≤ 0.001) to exist between all five groups, with regard to the 32 motivational statements. The following section outlines the profiles of each cluster group, both with respect to their motivations and also their demographics, activities undertaken and attractions visited.

RESULTS

This section will present in the first instance the results of a preliminary statistical analysis on the sample in terms of profile and tourist behaviour. In the second instance, it will describe the five clusters identified at the second stage of the analysis.

The Overall Sample

Profile

The British constitute the largest nationality (30%) of the 309 respondents in the sample, amongst whom 36% specified that they were Scottish residents (10% of the overall sample). Visitors from the rest of Europe amount to 26% of the sample with 10% from Germany. American and Canadian visitors constitute 14% of the overall numbers, behind Australian and New Zealand visitors (21% combined). A summary of the demographic profile of the sample is outlined in Table 3.

General Background Information About the Sample

It is important to note that some questions discussed in the following sections allowed respondents to make multiple responses, thus figures will not always add to 100%. The majority of respondents (84%) had planned their trip within a period of six months prior to their arrival in

TABLE 3. Summary Profile of Respondents

Components	Attributes	% of respondents
Gender	Male	46
	Female	54
Age	Under 29 years old	50
	Between 30 and 49 years old	33
	Over 50 years old	17
Highest Level of education	No secondary education	1
	Secondary education	16
	Technical/trade certificate	8
	University qualification	59
	Professional training	16
Work situation	Full-time employee	39
	Student	26
	Part-time employee	9
	Temporarily unemployed	8
	Retired	9
	Self-employed	8
	Full-time homemaker	1
Annual Household Income	£5,000 or less	15
	Between £5,001 and £10,000	15
	Between £10,001 and £20,000	23
	Between £20,001 and £30,000	21
	Between £30,001 and £40,000	17
	Over £40,000	9

Scotland while 50% did so within the previous month. Predominantly, the sample tended to travel with friends (35%) or alone (29%).

As sources of information, respondents use (in order of frequency) maps (54%), guidebooks (46%), the Internet (42%) and brochures (40%). They travel widely around Scotland both in the countryside (mainly the Highlands) and the main cities (mainly Edinburgh) where they visit the attractions that they expressed that they expected to find in Scotland, particularly natural attractions and castles. Respondents make little use of telephone accommodation reservation centres and even less of international booking networks. They tend to book directly with individual hostels either in person (44%) or by telephone (35%) and 20% have indicated that they have used the Internet for booking purposes. Respondents' main activities undertaken, in order of frequency, are 'general sightseeing' (74%), 'walking around town' (74%), 'dining-out' (53%) and 'visiting pubs' (52%). Hill walking (62%) and rambling (42%) are also expressed as being common activities respondents undertook.

Cluster Description

This section presents the findings resulting from the cluster analysis. As with the methodology adopted by Lawson et al. (1999), the cluster groups were identified and profiled by analysing a number of variables, including demographics, transportation choice, travel party, length of stay, destinations visited and perceptions. Five cluster groups were identified: *Typical Backpackers, Discoverers, Outdoors, Family Ties,* and *Routine Travellers.*

Table 4 provides demographic and other background information on the cluster groups; for the variables 'travel party' and 'forms of transport', respondents were able to list multiple responses. The information in this table will be explained in more detail within the cluster profile discussion.

Segment 1: Typical Backpackers (25%)

This group of visitors is composed mainly of European nationals, followed by British and Australians. Among the Europeans, Germans constitute the larger group with 44% (see Table 4). More than half of this segment are aged under 30 with the largest proportion being between the ages of 20 and 24. Females make up the larger proportion of this segment. The large majority of this group have university and/or professional qualifications. These *Typical Backpackers* represent the largest

TABLE 4. Summary Profiles of the Five Segments

Variable	Typical Backpackers (n = 77)%	Discoverers (n = 85)%	Outdoors (n = 68)%	Family Ties (n = 52)%	Routine Travellers (n = 26)%
Nationality					
British	22	17	58	10	42
Other Europeans	34	29	18	17	29
Australians	16	12	9	27	8
New-Zealanders	4	4	4	23	4
North Americans	8	25	6	20	9
Other nationalities	16	13	5	3	8
Gender					
male	37	41	64	35	67
female	63	59	36	65	33
Age					
under 29 years	58	76	29	43	5
old between 30 and 49	27	21	44	36	53
over 50 years old	15	3	27	21	42
Length of Stay					
less than 1 week	38	36	38	41	50
1 week to 2 weeks	35	29	42	43	36
2 weeks to 1 month	11	11	7	8	14
1 month to 2 months	1	5	7	2	0
over 2 months	15	19	6	6	0
Travel Party					
with friends	40	45	26	23	23
alone	30	22	43	19	31
family group	21	9	7	29	31
organised/club	3	13	1	4	8
Forms of Transport					
train	42	43	37	33	35
coach/bus	37	37	23	24	23
private car	30	32	44	33	46
rental car	26	26	13	48	11

percentage of members of the Youth Hostel Association, thus suggesting that they are familiar with the facilities on offer in Youth Hostels.

Members of this segment could be described as the most motivated travellers of the whole sample, since they have provided the largest number of high scoring motivations. Principally, *Typical Backpackers* have emphasised motivations that are both closely related to the 'typical', most well-known attractions of Scotland, as well as reasons that are linked to a desire for self-improvement through travel and adventure. They want to discover new things and experience adventure and travel (mean = 6.18) while having fun and excitement (mean = 5.90). They seek to enjoy the beautiful scenery and fresh air away from the hustle and bustle of daily life. They seek to see the 'real thing' and explore other cultures by meeting and interacting with people. All these reasons constitute 'push' motivations factors, yet it is a 'pull' motivation which scores the highest, namely the beautiful scenery of Scotland (mean = 6.49) followed by the availability of fresh air (mean = 5.96). It is clear that the reasons cited by these respondents are of an instrumental nature, to ultimately 'relax mentally' (mean = 6.09).

In order to achieve these aspirations, *Typical Backpackers* engage themselves in a wide range of activities which are associated both with the outdoors and the city, thus being able to test the range of typical Scottish attractions (national parks, wild life in natural habitat as well as castles, museums, cathedrals/abbeys and distilleries). These activities include: general sightseeing, hill walking, walking around town, rambling, visiting the beach, mountain climbing.

Segment 2: Discoverers (28%)

Discoverers constitute the youngest group of the overall sample with 73% of respondents under the age of 30 years. The highest percentage of students in the entire sample are found in this segment (40%). Amongst those who have completed their education, 48% hold a university degree and 16% have completed professional training. It is in this group that one finds the highest concentration of visitors from the United States: 19% compared to only 8% for the overall sample. The British constitute 17% of that particular group followed by the Germans and Australians (each 12%). See Table 4 for more detail.

Similarly to the *Typical Backpackers,* the *Discoverers* have emphasised 'adventure and travel' as important motivations (mean = 6.01) but this group also wants 'to experience new things' (mean = 5.87) and have a 'learning experience' (mean = 5.48) (see Table 4). These are the two motivations that particularly distinguish *Discoverers* from the other segments. Through these experiences they seek to have fun and excitement with friends or family. Here, too, the 'pull factor' of the 'beautiful scenery' is significant with a mean of 5.80.

This group includes the largest percentage of respondents (13%) travelling in an organised group or club compared to 4% of the overall sample. Further analysis has indicated that this percentage is constituted entirely of United Kingdom nationals.

Percentages indicate that destination preferences are evenly spread between cities and the countryside. While visiting these destinations, members of this group tend to engage mostly in activities which they hope will provide them with a learning experience or teach them something new, for example, visiting castles, cathedrals and abbeys, natural attractions (particularly national parks) and general sightseeing, including walking around towns.

This group tends to rely less on self-catering since it constitutes the largest segment eating out in restaurants and cafés and visiting pubs, possibly a reflection of their age. Also, in relation to other segments, the *Discoverers* are the most frequent shoppers (60%) visiting craft outlets and street markets.

Interestingly and perhaps because they are seeking education, as many as 14% of *Discoverers* 'did not know what to expect at all' before arriving in Scotland. This percentage is the highest across the five segments and is twice as high as the overall sample percentage.

Segment 3: The Outdoors (22%)

This group comprises mainly domestic visitors. It is in this segment that the 40 to 50 age bracket is best represented, and it also includes the highest level of university qualifications. Males make up just over two thirds of this segment (see Table 4).

For this segment the main motivations for coming to Scotland centre around experiencing and enjoying the 'beautiful' scenery of Scotland (mean = 6.40) and the fresh air (mean = 5.99) respondents also want to escape the hustle and bustle of daily life (mean = 5.68) and to get away from the city (mean = 5.15) while relaxing mentally (mean = 5.41). This is reflected in their choice of activities which include hill walking, rambling, mountain and rock climbing, cycling and offroad biking. In this segment, such outdoors activities score the highest across the whole sample.

Not surprisingly, the near majority of members of this segment (87%) chose to go to the most popular mountain areas, namely the Highlands and the Trossachs. Similarly, they sought natural attractions, particularly national parks which provide the right conditions for their outdoors pursuits. Also, visiting cities was not as popular with this group, with under half of this segment having visited, or intending to visit, Edinburgh and/or Glasgow. Given the wide range of outdoors pursuits that can attract them to rural areas, the *Outdoors* group prefer to use their private car rather than public transport, and they tend to travel alone (43%) rather than with friends.

As it would be expected, given the interest and the range of outdoor and sport activities within this segment, maps are cited as the most important source of information for this segment. The *Outdoors* do not consider the Internet as an important source of information and instead tend to rely more on their past knowledge and past experience.

Segment 4: Family Ties (17%)

Family Ties members originate mostly from outside the United Kingdom, particularly from Australia, New Zealand and North America. The age bracket is evenly distributed within the segment with a slight majority of respondents under the age of 30; females dominate this segment (see Table 4).

Members of this group are prepared to 'experience adventure and travel' (mean = 4.63) and 'to explore other cultures' (mean = 4.38), presumably in order 'to see the real thing' (mean = 4.31). However, the label given to this group derives specifically from the fact that the most differentiated variables (including motivations, activities and attractions visited) indicated by its members are centred on the family: whether it is 'to visit the place my family have been' (mean = 3.94), 'to visit family and friends' (mean = 3.48) or simply on 'family/friends' recommendations' (mean = 3.15). Their strong desire 'to visit the place my family are from' (mean = 4.15) makes them unique from the other segments. With this in mind, it is probably not surprising that most members of this segment do come from closely connected countries to Scotland.

The *Family Ties* group, possibly while visiting family or family connections, also partake in general sightseeing, walking around towns and driving. The near majority of this segment (92%) are attracted by Scottish heritage that they find in castles and museums and galleries. As travellers wishing to visit families who do not necessarily reside in tourist popular areas, the *Family Ties* are the segment which make the most use of rental cars (48% of the segment using rental cars compared to 26% for the entire sample).

Segment 5: Routine Travellers (8%)

One small segment did not indicate any single significant reason which influenced their decision to travel around Scotland (none above the rating of 2), nor emphasised any particular attitude statement throughout the questionnaire. The questionnaires completed by members of this group included the highest number of 'no responses' across the whole sample. It is therefore very difficult to provide a suitable description in terms of motivations and attitudes.

However, closer examination of the demographics of the group reveals that this segment comprises 42% of British nationals and that the majority

(86%) are over the age of 30. Furthermore, their activities differ slightly from the rest of the sample with a specific focus on hill walking, mountain and rock climbing. One therefore could assume that the respondents' motivation is mainly activity driven (hill walking and climbing); and because many are U.K. nationals, they have possibly performed this activity routinely for years and they are familiar with the Scottish outdoor environment. Moreover, as already stated, this segment includes the largest number of non-responses within the questionnaire. One possible explanation could be that their wish to pursue their chosen activity governs any other consideration in terms of motivations and behaviour, which suggests that they may not have seen, in some of the questions, much relevance to themselves. One such activity could be the pursuit of 'Munro bagging'[1] for example, a popular hobby amongst British residents which consists of climbing all mountain tops above 3000 feet (914 m). The determination involved in pursuing such a goal determines their mode of transport and choice of accommodation in so far as it must serve their purpose effectively. It is important to note that the possible explanation behind this cluster group can only be an assumption; however, one way of checking this assumption would be to undertake further qualitative research.

DISCUSSION AND CONCLUSIONS

This research has highlighted a number of interesting points about the backpacker market in Scotland. Not only is it noteworthy that there are a number of varying activities undertaken, attractions visited and important motivations within this one target market, but there are also demographic and attitudinal characteristics in this sample that differ from the traditional view of what constitutes a backpacker.

The analysis of the results of this research has highlighted behaviour trends that can be compared with backpacker tourists identified in the literature reviewed earlier. The respondents to the SYHA questionnaire closely match the following characteristics listed by Pearce 1990:

- low spending patterns.
- unstructured travelling patterns by booking in person at hostel reception (44%) or by telephoning specific hostels (35%). If they use a centralised booking system, respondents tend to favour the Internet (20%) rather than a telephone reservations centre (13%).
- few specialist activities (with the exception of hill walking).

However, the respondents in the current research differ in the following areas:

- relatively short length of stay (probably because Scotland may be part of a wider trip across Europe or even the U.K.).
- relatively short planning period (again possibly for the same reason).
- they travel with a group of friends, instead of alone.

The results of this current research support the findings of Mohsin and Ryan (2003), in that:

- the sample is not all young (for example, 32% are over 40 years).
- the sample includes holiday makers in full-time employment.
- their choice of accommodation is not limited to hostels.

Respondents were also segmented on their travel lifestyles, that is, a cluster analysis was performed on travel motivations, activities participated in and attractions visited, and these were tied to other aspects of the travel such as travel companions, transport, information search and the respondent's demographics to determine cluster profiles.

Five cluster groups were identified, the profiles of each were analysed, which showed each group to be clearly distinct from the other. The cluster groups display the various attitudes, interests and motivations apparent in the backpacker market, for example, 'outdoor experiences' through to 'spending time with family' and 'discovering ancestral routes'. With this in mind, SYHA may look at addressing their promotional mix to include information on ancestral routes, for example. The SYHA is beginning to realise the change in its market, as stated earlier in the article, and they are redesigning their accommodation accordingly. However they also need to look at how they market activities and attractions to attract visitors. On their Website *http://www.syha.org.uk*, there is a link pointing visitors towards information sites (such as transport options, other International Youth Hostel Federation sites, the Association of Scottish Visitor Attractions and other associations such as Scottish Mountaineering Club, VisitScotland, Wilkingwild.com). This is a very informative site, but in view of the results of this research, it is suggested that the Website would also benefit from including sites related to Genealogy, such as 'Tracing your Scottish Ancestry': *http://www.geo. ed.ac. uk/home/scotland/genealogy.html* and *http://www.ancestralscotland.com/*.

An additional aim of this research was to compare the backpacker segments identified in this research with those found in previous studies. Table 5 shows a comparison of the cluster groups.

TABLE 5. A Comparison of Backpacker Cluster Groups

Study	Cluster 1	Cluster 2	Cluster 3	Cluster 4	Cluster 5	Cluster 6	Cluster 7	Cluster 8
Loker-Murphy (1996)	Social/ Excitement Seekers (21%)	Escapers/ Relaxers (20%)	Achievers (24%)	Self-Developers (35%)				
Ryan and Mohsin (2001)			Explorers (8%)		Mainstreamers (74%)	Passive viewers (12%)	The Not Keen (6%)	
Current research:		Outdoors (22%)	Discoverers (28%)		Typical Backpackers (25%)		Routine Travellers (8%)	Family Ties (17%)

Although not identical, four of the groups found in this research are similar to previously identified segments (*Outdoors, Discoverers, Typical Backpackers, Routine Travellers*). Although the *Outdoors* segment want to 'escape the hustle and bustle of daily life', as Loker-Murphy's *Escapers/Relaxers* do, the *Outdoors* choices of activities are quite physical and, not surprisingly, take place outdoors. This segment may be a reflection of VisitScotland's increasing focus on marketing Scotland as an outdoors destination (For example, the U.K. Market Walking and Cycling campaign: *http://www.scotexchange.net/PromoteYourBusiness/promote_campaigns_walking.asp.* However, promoters do need to consider the perceptions of poor weather in Scotland, as this may affect this market. This was reflected by comments in the in-depth interviews undertaken. A number of people noted that it had rained a lot during their travels in Scotland and a few times they were 'stuck inside the hostel'. With this in mind, hostel owners may want to consider alternative activities which they could promote to their customers. This is an opportunity for a network to be established between the SYHA, Visit Scotland and the Association of Scottish Visitor Attractions. The lack of co-operation between sectors in the tourism industry in Scotland has been acknowledged (Hassan, 2000; Nash; 2002) and this is one opportunity to address such a shortfall.

Discoverers, like *Achievers* (Loker-Murphy, 1996) and *Explorers* (Ryan and Mohsin, 2001) express a strong interest in 'experiencing new things' and 'having a learning experience', thus stressing an education element which tours, for example, could capitalise on. Again this is an opportunity to create networks between accommodation outlets, tour operators and attractions, for example.

Typical Backpackers are similar to Ryan and Mohsin's *Mainstreamers*. They are the youngest group in the sample and have a relatively high interest in most activities/attractions, as do the *Mainstreamers*. This segment is probably the closest to the stereotypical backpacker that many people perceive.

Routine Travellers, although not identical to *The Not Keen* (Ryan and Mohsin, 2001) are similar in that they do not rate any motivations as especially important, nor do they highlight any specific attractions/activities as particularly featuring in their travel experience. As stated in the results section, one possible explanation for this may be because they are routine travellers who are only residing in the SYHA for 'somewhere to stay' and they are quite different from the typical resident of the SYHA. Possible explanations for this segment may be that they may be staying in a hostel with their family for the sole purpose of taking a family holiday. Or they may be just using the accommodation while they are involved in a specific activity, for example hill walking. Additional qualitative research should be undertaken to gain a better understanding of this cluster.

The one cluster in this research that has not appeared in previous studies is *Family Ties*. The distinguishing motivations of this group are 'to visit places that their family are from', 'to visit places their family have been' and 'to visit friends and family'. This segment is unique in that it has not been identified in previous studies. This is possibly due to sample differences. It is likely that New Zealanders, Australians and North Americans (who make up the largest proportion of this segment) will visit Scotland because of genealogy interests, as many of their ancestors would have originated from Scotland. This is almost like the traditional 'pilgrimage'.

Although there may be a number of people visiting Australia and New Zealand to visit friends/family, they may be more likely to stay with them than pay for accommodation. It is obviously not as likely that younger people will travel from the United Kingdom to Australia and New Zealand to 'discover their ancestors', thus it is not surprising that this segment shows up in the U.K. research and not in the previous backpacking segmentation studies undertaken in Australia.

This segment would be of particular interest to VisitScotland, especially considering they are currently trying to extend the genealogy market for Scotland (*http://www.ancestralscotland.com/*). *Family Ties* confirms the existence of such a market and again provides an opportunity for a network to exist between accommodation, activities/attractions and VisitScotland. For example, it would be interesting to follow-up this research with interviews of accommodation providers to discover how much they know about the genealogy market and how much they can tell customers about it, if asked.

Loker-Murphy (1996) and Ryan and Mohsin (2001) both found nationality to be the demographic variable that differentiated their segments the most. This research also shows a difference in nationality; for example, *Routine Travellers* and *Outdoors* are made up mainly of British nationals, whereas *Family Ties* is made up predominantly of New Zealanders, Australians and North Americans. There are also differences between the age groups, with *Discoverers* being the significantly younger segment and *Routine Travellers* consisting of 42% over 50 years. Thus supporting Loker-Murphy (1996), that the backpacker market can no longer be defined by age.

The methodology utilised in this research is recommended for future research; by undertaking travel lifestyle segmentation, marketing managers receive information on why someone chooses to visit Scotland as a backpacker, not just who has visited. As stressed at the beginning of this article, the more a producer/supplier knows about their market, the more effective their market strategy.

To conclude, this article has shown that travel lifestyle segmentation can be applied to the Scottish backpacker market, as it has been in the past to the Australian market. Interestingly, similar cluster groups were identified, suggesting that there are communalities within the backpacker market worldwide; however, to determine whether this is true on an international context, further comparisons need to be drawn between destinations, for example, Thailand, China, Europe, Central and South America. Additionally, research in the United Kingdom needs to expand into the Independent Hostel market, to identify any major market differences between themselves and the SYHAs. To date, research suggests that backpackers can no longer be considered as young, spendthrift travellers, who will stay in one place for a number of months and who usually travel alone. It is now clear that this market is shifting to include more diverse demographics, activities and attractions, and marketers need to change with the market, so they do not lag behind and thus miss out on the economic and social benefits of the backpackers.

NOTE

1. The Munros are the highest of Scotland's mountains, 284 mountaintops above 3000 feet, named after the man who first catalogued them, Sir Hugh Munro.

REFERENCES

Ancestral Scotland. (2003) [Online] Available World Wide Web: *http://www.ancestralscotland.com/,* (Accessed 7 August 2003).

Chesshyre, T. (2003). 'A mass exodus, despite trouble overseas'. *The Times,* January 4th 2003. London.

Craig-Lees, M., Joy, S., and Browne, B. (1995). *'Consumer Behaviour'.* Singapore: John Wiley and Sons.

Davis, Allen, D. J. and Consenza, R. (1988). 'Segmenting Local Residents by their Attitudes, Interests and Opinions toward Tourism'. *Journal of Travel Research, 27*(2), 2-8.

Elliot, M. (2002). 'Must the backpackers stay home?' *The Times.* December 16th 2002. New York.

Gnoth, J. (1999). 'Tourism expectation formation: The case of camper-van tourists in New Zealand'. In Pizam, A., and Mansfield, Y. *Consumer Behaviour in Travel and Tourism.* New York: The Haworth Hospitality Press.

Gonzalez, A. M. and Bello, L. (2002). 'The construct "lifestyle" in market segmentation'. *European Journal of Marketing, 36*(1/2), 51-85.

Hair, J. F., Anderson, R. E., Tatham, R. L., and Black, W. C. (1998) *Multivariate Data Analysis.* 5th Edition. New Jersey: Prentice-Hall International, Inc.

Hampton, M. P. (1998). 'Backpacker Tourism and Economic Development'. *Annals of Tourism Research, 25*(3), 639-660.

Hassan, S. (2000). 'Determinants of market competitiveness in an environmentally sustainable tourism industry'. *Journal of Travel Research, 38*(3), 239-245.

Highlands and Islands Enterprise (2000). *'Profiles of Holidaymakers staying in Hostels in the Highlands and Islands'* [Online], Available World Wide Web: *http://www.scotexchange.net/KnowYourMarket/kym-accom.htm* (Accessed 6 August 2003).

Holt, D. (1997). 'Poststructuralist Lifestyle Analysis: Conceptualizing the Social Patterning of Consumption in Post modernity'. *Journal of Contemporary Research, 23,* 326-350.

Kahle, L. R. and Kennedy, P. (1989). 'Using the list of values (LOV) to understand consumers'. *Journal of Consumer Marketing, 6*(3), 5-12.

Kaynak, E. and Kara, A. (2002). 'Consumer perceptions of foreign products-country images and ethnocentrism'. *European Journal of Marketing, 36*(7), 928-949.

Keeley, P. (2001). 'The Backpacker Market in Britain'. *Insights,* B53-B66.

Kesic, T. and Piri-Rajh, S. (2003). 'Market segmentation on the basis of food related lifestyles of Croatian families'. *British Food Journal, 105*(3), 162-174.

Kim, S., Kim, H., and Kim, W. G. (2003). 'Impacts of senior citizens' lifestyle on their choices of elderly housing'. *Journal of Consumer Marketing, 20*(3), 210-226.

Kucukemiroglu, O. (1999). 'Market segmentation by using consumer lifestyle dimensions and ethnocentrism'. *European Journal of Marketing, 33*(5/6), 470-487.

Lawson, R., Thyne, M., Young, T., and Juric, B. (1999). 'Developing Travel Lifestyles: A New Zealand Example'. *Consumer Behaviour in Travel and Tourism,* pp. 449-511. New York: The Haworth Hospitality Press.

Lawson, R., Tidwell, P., Rainbird, P., Loudon, D., and Della Bitta, A. (1999). *Consumer Behaviour in Australia and New Zealand.* Sydney: McGraw-Hill Inc.

Lazer, W. (1963). 'Lifestyle Concepts and Marketing.' *Toward Scientific Marketing*. S. Greyser (Ed.) Chicago: American Marketing Association.

Loker, L. (1991). 'More answers to further questions'. *The Backpacker Phenomenon II*. Townsville Australia: Department of Tourism James Cook University.

Loker-Murphy, L. (1996). 'Backpackers in Australia: A Motivation Based Segment Study'. *Journal of Travel and Tourism Marketing*, *54*(4), 23-45.

Loker-Murphy L. and Pearce, P. L. (1995). 'Young budget travellers: Backpackers in Australia'. *Annals of Tourism Research*, *22*(4), 819-843.

Madrigal, R. and Kahle, L. R. (1994). 'Predicting Vacation Activity Preferences on the Basis of Value-System Segmentation'. *Journal of Travel Research*, *32*(3), 22-28.

McCleary, K. W. and Choi, B. M. (1999). 'Personal Values as a Base for Segmenting International Markets'. *Tourism Analysis*, *4*, 1-17.

Mitchell, V. W. and Haggett, S. (1997). 'Sun-sign astrology in market segmentation: An empirical investigation'. *Journal of Consumer Marketing*, *14*(2), 113-131.

Moshin, A. and Ryan, C. (2003). 'Backpackers in the Northern Territory of Australia–Motives, Behaviours and Satisfactions'. *International Journal of Tourism Research*, *5*, 113-131.

Murphy, L. (2001). 'Exploring social interactions of backpackers'. *Annals of Tourism Research*, *28*(1), 50-67.

Nash, R. (2002). *Tourism in peripheral areas: The use of causal networks and lesson drawing as analytical methods*. A thesis submitted in partial fulfilment for the Degree of Doctor of Philosophy, The Robert Gordon University, Aberdeen.

Nunnally, J. (1978). *Psychometric Theory*. 2nd Edition. New York: McGraw-Hill.

Oates, B., Shufedt, L., and Vaught, B. (1996). 'A psychographic study of the elderly and retail store attributes'. *Journal of Consumer Marketing*, *13*(6), 14-27.

Pearce, P. L. (1990). *The Backpacker Phenomenon: Preliminary Answers to Basic Questions*. James Cook University of North Queensland.

Peterson, R. A. (1994). 'A Meta-Analysis of Cronbach's Coefficient Alpha'. *Journal of Consumer Research*, *21*(3), 381-391.

Ryan, C. and Moshin, A. (2001). 'Backpackers: Attitudes to the Outback'. *Journal of Travel and Tourism Marketing*, *10*(1), 69-91.

Scheyvens, R. (2002). 'Backpacker Tourism and Third World Development'. *Annals of Tourism Research*, *29*(1), 144-164.

Scottish Youth Hostel Association (2001). *Annual Report and Financial Statements 2001*.

Scottish Youth Hostel Association (2002). *Annual Report and Financial Statements 2002*.

Shipway, R. (2000). 'The international backpacker market in Britain: A market waiting to happen'. In Long, P., Evans, N., Sharpley, R., and Swarbrooke, J. *Motivations, Behaviour and Tourist Types, Reflections on International Tourism*. Sunderland: Centre of Travel and Tourism.

SYHA website [Online] *http://www.syha.org.uk* (Accessed 6 August 2003).

Thyne, M. (2001). 'The importance of values research for non-profit organisations: The motivation-based values of museum visitors'. *International Journal of Non-profit and Voluntary Sector Marketing*, *6*(2), 116-130.

Tracing your Scottish Ancestry (2003). [Online], Available World Wide Web *http://www.geo.ed.ac.uk/home/scotland/genealogy.html* (Accessed 7 August 2003).

U.K. Market Walking and Cycling campaign (2003). [Online], Available World Wide Web *http://www.scotexchange.net/PromoteYourBusiness/promote_campaigns_walking.asp* (Accessed 7 August 2003).

Visit Scotland. (2000). *The Growth, Development and Future Prospects for the Hostels Market in Scotland*. [Online], Available World Wide Web: *http://www.scotexchange. net/KnowYourMarket/kym-accom.htm* (Accessed 6 August 2003).

Zins, A. (1998). 'Leisure traveller choice models of hotels using psychographics'. *Journal of Travel Research*, *36*(Spring), 3-15.

Lifestyle Segmentation in Tourism and Leisure: Imposing Order or Finding It?

Noel Scott

Nick Parfitt

SUMMARY. This article examines three different approaches to lifestyle segmentation in improving the quality of tourism and leisure marketing decisions in three separate cases. Tourism and leisure products are prototypical lifestyle purchase yet in many tourism research studies visitors are described by demographics or tourism behaviour only. These cases illustrate different approaches to lifestyle segmentation. Firstly, there are segmentation schemes based on external logic that can be broadly applied across a range of markets, including tourism and leisure. Alternatively, there are schemes that are based on a 'conversation' with the data and which rely on an internal logic within that data that may not transfer to other market contexts. Between these two lie

Noel Scott is a doctoral candidate at the School of Tourism and Leisure Management, University of Queensland, 11 Salisbury Road Ipswich, 4305, Queensland, Australia (E-mail: noel.scott@uq.edu.au).

Nick Parfitt is Managing Director of Researchworks, P.O. Box 1081, Milton Central, Queensland, 4064 Australia (E-mail: parfittnick@optusnet.com.au).

[Haworth co-indexing entry note]: "Lifestyle Segmentation in Tourism and Leisure: Imposing Order or Finding It?" Scott, Noel and Nick Parfitt. Co-published simultaneously in *Journal of Quality Assurance in Hospitality & Tourism* (The Haworth Hospitality Press, an imprint of The Haworth Press, Inc.) Vol. 5, No. 2/3/4, 2004, pp. 121-139; and: *Hospitality, Tourism, and Lifestyle Concepts: Implications for Quality Management and Customer Satisfaction* (ed: Maree Thyne and Eric Laws) The Haworth Hospitality Press, an imprint of The Haworth Press, Inc., 2004, pp. 121-139. Single or multiple copies of this article are available for a fee from The Haworth Document Delivery Service [1-800-HAWORTH, 9:00 a.m. - 5:00 p.m. (EST). E-mail address: docdelivery@haworthpress.com].

schemes that apply external paradigms to specific datasets. The cases selected illustrate points along this spectrum.

The first case study examines the use by government tourism organizations of lifestyle segmentation 'bought in' from an external source. Here lifestyle segmentation data is collected from a representative sample of the Australian population as part of a commercial "single source" data set. The second case is based on a regional tourism study, which has utilized prior theory to develop its own lifestyle segmentation and at the same time related this to boarder characteristics of tourists in Tropical North Queensland. The third case examines the development of tailored lifestyle segmentation among 'event' spectators based on purely internal criteria unrelated to the broader population. These cases provide insight into the appropriate development and application of lifestyle segmentation and the use of the data by tourism and leisure managers. Managers may think about the type of lifestyle segmentation approach required based on how the segmentation scheme results need to be related to the wider market or population. *[Article copies available for a fee from The Haworth Document Delivery Service: 1-800-HAWORTH. E-mail address: <docdelivery@haworthpress.com> Website: <http://www.HaworthPress.com>*

KEYWORDS. Lifestyle segmentation, tourism, leisure, case study

INTRODUCTION

Segmentation is a central topic of many business related disciplines including tourism, leisure and recreation (Chen 2003) and marketing (Kotler 2000). Segmentation is relevant to both managers and academics. Segmentation allows a focus on particular customer types leading to efficiencies in targeting (Papadopoulos 1989; Perdue 1996). It allows a better understanding of market structure and customers and hence assists in the development or modification of products that better match market needs (Bojanic & Warnick 1995). Use of segmentation allows a portfolio approach to destination management (A'guas, Costa & Rita 2000) and the adoption of yield management practices (Upchurcha, Ellis & Seo 2002) by allowing destination visitors or product purchasers to be differentially targeted. The concept of segmentation underpins theories of tourism such as the destination life cycle model (Butler 1980, 2001) and Plog's theory of destination development (Plog 1974).

In this article, a number of issues related to use of one type of segmentation–lifestyle segmentation–are discussed theoretically and then in practice through three case studies. The issues discussed are directed at the practicalities of use of lifestyle segmentation in solving real world marketing problems in terms of designing the appropriate research. One focus of the article is the tension between the general application of findings of research versus the specificity and insight into a particular situation. This identifies a dimension that should be considered by managers involved in the design of segmentation research studies. A second focus is the selection and sourcing of data suitable for lifestyle segmentation and how to make this more efficient and affordable. Here the issue relates to methodology and practicalities and efficiencies of data collection. However, before discussing these three cases, the theory of lifestyle segmentation is discussed.

CHARACTERISTICS OF DIFFERENT SEGMENTATION APPROACHES

Segmentation approaches have been classified in terms of the bases (or type of variables) used and whether such bases are specified prior to analysis (*a priori*) or during analysis of the data (*post hoc*) (Chen 2003). In turn, the bases used for segmentation have been described in terms of their level (generally applicable or product specific) and type (observable or unobservable) (Wedel & Kamakura 1999: 7). General applicable lifestyle segmentation may use schemes that have been applied across a population for many purposes. An example is the VALS™ scheme (Mitchell 1983). Such a scheme is developed without consideration for a particular type of product or service to which it would be applied. It is considered to be generally applicable. Alternatively, a product specific lifestyle segmentation scheme is developed to inform decisions about a specific consumer product or service. Here the applicability of the scheme to the whole population is of no consequence and the focus is on explaining some aspect of the usage of a particular product.

Segmentation bases can also be examined in terms of their observability. Age and gender are examples of observable segmentation bases while psychographics and motivation are examples of unobservable bases (Ralston & Stewart 1990). The degree of observability of a segmentation base is an important consideration in implementation of findings of research. Thus if a particular segment is found to be a useful target market, then the next step in a marketing program may be development of an advertising campaign. However, if there is no knowledge of the media viewing habits of this segment then an advertising campaign cannot be implemented. Single source data avoids this problem by collecting lifestyle, purchase and media usage data at the same time. Alternatively, a particular research study may collect a variety of information not directly useful for lifestyle segmentation for the same market targeting purpose.

Van Raaij uses a similar classification for the type of segmentation bases but recognises three levels of analysis for bases: general, domain specific and brand specific (Van Raaij 1994). The distinction between general, domain specific and brand specific segmentation bases is an important one. In contemporary attitude theory (Fishbein & Ajzen 1975), the context of a particular decision is important for prediction of behaviour. In other words the person-situation-product match is important in examination of purchasing decisions in relation to some consumer goal.

A domain is defined as an area of behaviour that is aimed at a particular goal. A number of authors have noted aspects of tourism to be domain specific including innovative decision making (Szmigin & Carrigan 2001) and vacation behavior (Oppedijk van Veen & Verhallen 1986). The importance of domain specific segmentation has been noted by Van Raaij (1994) who indicates that the strength of relationship between general values and domain specific values and between domain specific values and between specific product evaluations is strong but the relationship between general values and specific product evaluations is weak.

As a result, one issue that requires consideration in the development of segmentation studies is the trade-off between the general application of segmentation results and the need for domain specific insight. This is especially true of segmentation schemes that rely on numerical post hoc grouping procedures such as cluster analysis. Classifications developed through grouping procedures seldom are generalized beyond their original database. Rather than developing classification systems for marketing phenomena in general, the use of these procedures has been developed to provide specific insight into problems that are highly situation specific. Segmentation schemes based on numerical grouping procedures may be called pre-classification techniques since their purpose is to describe the natural groupings that occur in large masses of data. From these natural groupings (or clusters) the researcher can sometimes develop a conceptual framework for classification that relates to wider theory (Hunt 1991:183).

Lifestyle: A Basis for Segmentation

One approach to developing more general, theoretically based approaches to segmentation has been termed lifestyle segmentation. Segmentation bases that are applicable outside a specific consumption domain have a number of uses for marketers. As they may allow constellations of different product purchases to be grouped, they provide insight into consumer behaviour that may allow sponsorship or cross-selling opportunities and a better ability to target a particular customer segment (Chaney 1996:32).

Lifestyle as a concept has a rich history as a means of trying to understand the basis for patterns of consumption. Drawing on the work of Veblen, Simmel, Weber and other authors, lifestyle researcher demonstrated that consumption patterns provided insight into social classification (Holt 1997). The rapid changes in society and culture over the past 50 years have led to an increasing personalization of consumer behaviour patterns (Gonzalez and Bello 2002). However, this fragmentation of markets has not reduced the need of marketers for clues into consumer behaviour.

This desire for knowledge about why customers purchase products is evident in the leisure and tourism domain. The commercialisation and commodification of leisure and pleasure travel has been noted by many authors (Chaney 1996:22). Indeed, leisure and tourism products such as package holidays, sports events and cultural exhibitions are quintessential lifestyle purchases reflecting changes in society and culture as much as being determined by these changes.

Lifestyle as a general basis for segmentation has been much discussed and debated in the literature both in terms of its definition and its usefulness. Some authors suggest lifestyle is related to similarity in behavioural patterns (Van Raaij 1994:55). Similarly, Anderson and Golden have reviewed definitions of lifestyle (Anderson & Golden 1984) and defined it as 'characteristic patterns of overt behaviour'. However, Frank, Massy and Wind (1972:58) define lifestyle as '*refecting* the overall manner in which people live and spend time and money.' Thus we may distinguish between the concept of lifestyle, as common behavioural patterns, and the operationalization of the concept as, those things that reflect these common behaviour patterns. Lifestyle may be operationalized in two major methods: by the examination of the products the person consumes or by the examination of the person's activities, interests, opinions, and values (Frank, Massy & Wind 1972:58). In practice, the second method (termed the AIO method) is usually adopted. The concept of a lifestyle may be applied either at the individual, group or overall societal level (Anbascher 1967). It may be applied to a particular domain specific problem or additionally to a product specific situation. However, in these later applications, the issue is to ensure that the results may be usefully applied in marketing programs.

Lifestyle has been usefully applied in a number of studies. Gonzalez and Bello have reviewed use of lifestyle segmentation in tourism and applied an AIO base for the study of Spanish tourism (Gonzalez & Bello 2002). Shih used the VALS™ segmentation scheme for tourism marketing strategy purposes (Shih 1986). Todd and Lawson used an AIO method for understanding the characteristics of visitors and non-visitors to museums (Todd & Lawson 2001). Zins (1998) has discussed the overlap of lifestyle and travel style. Lawson et al. discuss lifestyles in relation to travellers to New Zealand (Lawson et al. 1999). Several studies have examined segmentation issues and use of lifestyle segmentation in sports marketing (Green & Chalip 1998; Pitts 1999; Tuppen 2000).

Based on this discussion of lifestyle and approaches to segmentation, this article will now examine three different approaches to lifestyle segmentation used in prior research by the authors. These cases have been chosen to illustrate the trade-off between generalizability and specificity of segmentation schemes and means to make specific segmentation results able to be implemented using techniques such as analysis of single source data and collection of both product specific and domain specific data at the same time.

Three Case Studies of Lifestyle Segmentation

The first case examined in this article uses an approach to lifestyle segmentation based on a general segmentation scheme. In particular, the case examines the use of a proprietary values typology called the Roy Morgan Values Segments™ by Australian and International tourism managers in a number of situations.[1] Roy Morgan Research Pty Ltd collects a wide range of information about the general population via a syndicated research product, Roy Morgan Single Source. Roy Morgan Single Source allows profiling of markets based on general lifestyle segments, specific travel behaviours and intentions, media usage and other characteristics in a cost effective manner.

In the second case, brand specific, domain specific and general theoretically based segmentation approaches have been used to examine and contrast the users of tourism products (hotels in Port Douglas) with visitors in general to Port Douglas and Tropical North Queensland. While the segmentation process is specific to data collected from hotel guests and visitors to the region as part of the project, the basis for segmentation has been derived from a long established lifestyle model.

The third case is based on development of a lifestyle segmentation scheme derived from collection of attitudes, interests and opinions of users of a specific product (rugby union spectators at Ballymore in Brisbane, Australia). Here the issue is to focus on one market domain with less opportunity for generalizability, since the marketing task is very much focused on developing loyalty among specific markets.

Case 1: Use of an Externally Derived Lifestyle Typology

The first case study examines use of lifestyle and values segmentation for tourism planning and marketing purposes based on an externally derived segmentation model. Such segmentation models have a number of uses for tourism planners and managers including market targeting and new product development. Firstly, Roy Morgan Single Source data allows lifestyle segmentation based on tourism activities such as usage of national parks, visiting movies and outdoor sports (Reed, Hepper & Tilley 1999).

Secondly, it allows proprietary lifestyle segmentation descriptions to be applied to segments selected on the basis of recent travel behaviour. This has been used in a number of tourism plans as a means of describing current visitors (City of Ballarat 2002; Tourism Victoria 2002). Another use of Roy Morgan Single Source data is by tourism media planners as a method of estimating the relative concentration of product users in media audiences in order to evaluate media vehicle efficiency (Assael & Poltrack 1991; Assael & Poltrack 2002). Not all media vehicles are of equal importance. Planners are interested in efficient, or selective, media–those with relatively high concentrations of product users. To do this they use single source data that collects data on product usage and media usage simultaneously.

In Australia one important source of single source data for tourism studies is the Roy Morgan Research Holiday Tracking Survey (HTS). The HTS is part of the Roy Morgan Single Source omnibus survey. This omnibus survey includes questions that track preferences, intentions and actual travel behaviour. Questions are directed to a base survey sample of over 50,000 people aged 14 years and over. Data is collected on advertising awareness of holiday destinations in Australia; where people would prefer to go for short and long trips; intention of taking such trips as well as media usage and many other respondent characteristics. A proprietary segmentation scheme is used to classify each respondent into one of ten Roy Morgan Values Segments™3.[1] These segments are based on four human social dimensions (Individualism, Life Satisfaction, Conservatism and Innovation) and two dimensions that ground the Values Segments™ in marketplace reality (Quality Expectations and Price Expectations).[1]

A number of Australian tourism studies using Roy Morgan HTS single source data are provided in Table 1. Lifestyle segmentation based on the HTS is used to supplement and create depth for the description of the characteristics of types of tourists such as wine tourists (Tourism Queensland 2002). Life cycle segments are used for describing prospective customers (City of Ballarat 2002) and for advertising effectiveness studies (South Australian Tourist Commission 2003).

This case illustrates the use of general lifestyle segmentation scheme in examining tourism. By using a database such as the Roy Morgan HTS database, a tourism manager has access to single source data. This

TABLE 1. Examples of Use of Roy Morgan Single Source Data in Australia

Report	Usage	Source:
Tasmanian Attractions Study	Develop an activities 'index' based on attractions and compare to all travellers	(Reed, Hepper & Tilley 1999)
Tourism Victoria Strategic Plan 2002-2006	Tourism Victoria segments the domestic market in a number of ways using a number of segmentation techniques including the Roy Morgan Value Segments, MOSAIC and Lifecycle	(Tourism Victoria 2002)
Wine Tourism	Describe lifestyle segments of Australian Wine tourism visitors	(Tourism Queensland 2002)
Ballarat Tourism Strategic Plan	Describe lifestyle segments	(City of Ballarat 2002)
ACT Tourism Strategic Plan 2001-2005	Describe lifestyle segments of Australian Wine tourism visitors.	(Canberra Tourism and Events Corporation 2001)
South Australia Tourism Plan 2003-2008	Used for advertising effectiveness studies	(South Australian Tourist Commission, 2003 #3200)

Source: Prepared for this research

allows identification and profiling of tourism activities and destinations based on a variety of traveller characteristics. Use of lifestyle segments supplements the preference, intention and behavioural data available from the HTS. Thus it provides a cost-effective method of segmentation for a range of different tourism activities.

Case 2: Hotels in Tropical North Queensland

The second study discussed here discusses research previously examined from other perspectives in prior articles (Laws, Scott & Parfitt 1999; Laws, Scott & Parfitt 2002). The objective of the research was to examine the relationship between the marketing images and competitive positioning of hotels and those of the overall destination of Tropical North Queensland (TNQ) and constituent sub-regions (including Port Douglas) in the context of visitor segmentation. In order to do this, the visitors to individual hotels and the overall destination and sub-regions were compared both in terms of demographics and also in terms of a lifestyle segmentation scheme developed for the study. A dedicated segmentation scheme was used in order to allow the specific characteristics of the travelers to the region and hotel to be examined in fine detail.

The research program was multi-staged involving three separate components. This methodology was designed to be able to compare key issues across the various geographic levels by developing similar question and analysis formats. The research process, therefore, moved from detailed qualitative interviews to wider structured questionnaire research, and from a focus on the particular Port Douglas resort hotels to a wider regional study.

The first stage of the program incorporated 70 qualitative interviews with guests at the two hotels. Australian-resident guests were approached randomly via the resorts' front office database, a letter from the General Manager and a follow-up telephone call from the researcher. The interviews took the form of 30-minute 'in depth' interviews and 90-minute focus groups, and were used to examine in detail issues of decision making, reasons for choosing the destination and accommodation, overall attitudes towards vacations and motivation, and imagery.

The semi-structured nature of qualitative interviewing allowed the use of indirect (projective) questioning, including mapping, creative pictorial techniques and repertory grid techniques to examine motivations and expectations (Kelly 1955; Young 1995). The information generated by this stage of the research was the basis for formulating a structured questionnaire for subsequent research. It also prompted the research partners to start to identify motivational groups, and devise appropriate advertising strategies as discussed below.

The findings of the 'in depth' interviews and focus groups were then quantified among a sample of 220 guests. Guests completing this questionnaire were again selected randomly from resort records. Here differences between visitation to the region and hotel usage were examined in detail and a number of reasons for visiting both determined. The third component of the research consisted of face-to-face interviews with 600 Australian visitors to Tropical North Queensland. This questionnaire included items common to those asked in the resort survey in order to enable comparisons of data to be made. Interviewing for this stage was conducted equally between the three main TNQ holiday centres.

As mentioned in Case 1, tourism authorities may use an origin-lifecycle segmentation approach derived from single source data at the level of the destination. However, in this case, due to the involvement of individual hotel operators and sub-regions there was a need to develop both domain-specific and brand-specific segmentation. For this reason a lifestyle segmentation was undertaken to complement the destination segmentation approach.

Qualitative research was used to establish why resort guests had decided to visit Tropical North Queensland on vacation and the decision making process for so doing. Guests differed in their specific motivations for their vacation, and, based on these specific motivations, a four-segment typology was constructed. These were measured quantitatively using self-completion questionnaires among resort guests, and face-to-face surveys among TNQ visitors. From the analysis of these surveys, four major segments were identified based on specific motivations described in Table 2, but it should be noted that membership of one group does not necessarily preclude leanings towards another.

The four motivational segments were refined through a number of stages in the research process. Firstly, at the 'qualitative' stage guests and visitors were asked directly their reasons for taking a vacation and the factors on which they distinguished between competitive destinations and different vacation styles. These verbatim comments were then used as the basis for nineteen statements that the sample of resort guests (217 interviews) and the broader sample of visitors to the region (600 interviews divided equally between Cairns, the Northern Beaches and Port Douglas) were asked to rate on a five-point scale (from 'Very Important' to 'Not at all Important'). Cluster analysis using a four-cluster k-means method was then used to establish the four major segments. The characteristics of each group are best represented through their mo-

TABLE 2. Lifestyle Segmentation Groups

Segment	Description	Marketing implications
Activity-focused	This group goes on vacation and to particular destinations with clear objectives of undertaking particular activities or visiting specific locations, for example, observing coral on the Reef or viewing flora and fauna in the rainforests. The appeal of a holiday for them is marked by achievement and growth. This group tends to be well-informed and strong vacation planners.	Focus on detailed information in support of their particular interest.
Image focused	This group are motivated by general regional attributes since their primary motivation is to go somewhere different from home. They look for a different climate, different environments and life-styles. They are likely to consider a wide range of vacations since their criteria for choice is fairly broad.	They rarely have specific reasons for choice and are the group most amenable to overall regional imagery and marketing.
Other people focused	This group chooses their vacation based on what they have been told by other people. A primary motivation for them is then to relay back to the reference group their own experiences. In a sense this group might be referred to as 'snobs' although they occur across the range of socio-economic and income groups.	Marketing needs to generate the sense of a destination as 'the place to be.' They are particularly excited, for example, by the visits of President Clinton and various movie stars to Port Douglas.

tivational ratings. In Table 3, mean scores are shown where +2.5 is equivalent to a rating of 'Very Important' and −2.5 is equivalent to a rating of 'Not at all Important').

This technique was considered appropriate to achieve understanding of the decision making process for the vacation since it identified the overall competitive context of TNQ and Port Douglas, the motivations which visitors seek to fulfill, the way in which different destination and holiday experiences are distinguished and clustered by visitors, establish a market structure, as illustrated in Table 4.

This research allowed the various organizational levels involved in destination marketing (the region, the sub-region and the hotels) to assess the viability of cooperative promotion, and the extent to which they might share image elements and target markets. For example, the re-

TABLE 3. Comparison of Groups by Individual Factor

Motivation factor:	Self-directed	Image-directed	Activity-directed	Other-directed
To relax	2.13	1.76	1.41	1.55
To spend time with my partner	1.47	0.89	0.0	0.90
To visit new places	1.38	1.76	1.71	1.60
To celebrate a special event or anniversary	−0.55	−1.25	−1.10	−0.60
To exercise my choice to do nothing	1.18	0.77	−0.19	1.05
To take the chance to think things over	0.30	−0.18	−0.23	0.45
To be pampered and waited on	0.07	−0.66	−1.09	−0.10
To indulge my senses	0.91	0.40	0.63	1.10
To feel fitter and healthier	0.77	0.52	0.51	1.35
To live life at a different pace	1.44	1.66	1.32	1.80
To feel warmer	1.25	1.63	0.69	2.20
To be active	0.53	0.53	1.90	0.78
To get close to nature	0.65	0.86	1.58	1.45
To travel as far north as possible	−0.19	−0.18	0.38	0.55
To be challenged	−0.46	−0.66	0.85	−0.03
To find out new things	0.41	0.64	2.10	1.02
To see somewhere that people have told me about	0.58	0.88	0.88	2.25
To visit a unique attraction	1.10	1.37	2.24	2.00
To have experiences I can tell others	0.83	1.13	1.41	2.05

TABLE 4. Alternative Destinations Considered

Segment	Alternative destinations considered	Activity preferences
Activity-focused	TNQ; Northern Territories; Fiji; Pacific islands	Bushwalking, rainforest walks, Skyrail, Diving, visiting Cape Tribulation, Cooktown
Image focused	Barrier reef islands; Bali; Fiji; New Caledonia; Hawaii; Lord Howe; Norfolk Island	Visiting Cape Tribulation
Other people focused	Barrier reef islands; Noosa	Reef cruising, visiting Daintree, Mossman, Craft shops, Cairns
Self-focused	Warm area resorts; overseas islands; Resorts in S.E. Asia; Cruises; Europe	Relaxation and indulgence

search indicates that, among visitors staying in four- or five-star resort accommodation, the image of the region as a whole is less strong than the image presented by the hotel. The overall image map for Tropical North Queensland is shown in Figure 1. The particular lifestyle segmentation scheme developed to describe customers to the hotels and destination was central to this study as it clearly demonstrated both the overlap and differences in consumption clusters.

Case 3: Rugby Union

The third case examines rugby union spectators in Queensland. In an increasingly competitive sporting and events market, Queensland Rugby Union (QRU) conducts research to measure spectator satisfaction and develop loyalty among both spectators and sponsors. Analysis of QRU research results using lifestyle segmentation rather than simply by standard demographics (age, occupation) or by behavioural details (ticket type, frequency of support) provided a further level of understanding to be derived from the data. The lifecycle segments described were derived as follows. Firstly, 'qualitative' information on questionnaires from a number of rugby seasons (unprompted written-in com-

FIGURE 1. Elements in Lifestyle Groupings: Tropical North Queensland

ments on reasons for supporting rugby and for attending matches) were reanalysed and provided a series of 13 segmentation statements. The statements were in a questionnaire covering activities undertaken during a game and satisfaction with aspects of the visit. This questionnaire was used in a survey of respondents conducted by telephone after contact details were obtained from a random sample of spectators entering the Ballymore football ground prior to the match. A final sample of 300 people was achieved with a participation rate of 44%.

Results were analysed using SPSS's k-means clustering method. Possible cluster solutions (6-8) were run to determine the optimum solution. Cluster group membership was then parsed back into the datasets to check validity, i.e., that the segments derived made sense in describing individual responses. The seven-segment solution was chosen on balance because it produced the clearest distinguishable and insightful spectator segments. The segments that emerged were named based on differences in aggregate characteristics and are shown in Figure 2. The largest single segments are the 'traditionalists', the 'entertainment seekers' and the 'socialisers'.

FIGURE 2. Rugby Union Lifestyle Segments (Note that percentages have been changed due to commercial sensitivity)

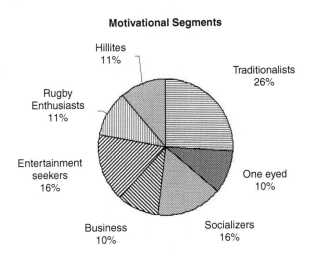

Motivational Segments

Hillites 11%

Rugby Enthusiasts 11%

Entertainment seekers 16%

Traditionalists 26%

One eyed 10%

Business 10%

Socializers 16%

These segments vary in loyalty to Rugby Union. For example, the *traditionalists* have the strongest bond with rugby; they tend to have grown up with it and some have played it. Rugby forms an important part of their social and recreational life and they are staunch supporters of the enduring 'values' of the game and have some resistance to the increasing commercialisation of the sport. The *rugby enthusiasts* are similar to the *traditionalists* in that they support what they perceive as the values of the game (intelligent, tactical, gentlemanly, international in comparison to Australia's two other major football codes). This segment includes a high proportion of families who want their children to grow up with these values. Unlike the *traditionalists*, the *rugby enthusiasts* do not have a long-term association with the game and they have a less developed network within the game. Over time they are likely to develop these networks and to move into the *traditionalist* segment. The *socialisers* segment place as great an emphasis on the social aspects of a rugby match as upon the game itself. The *Hillites* take their name from the XXXX Hill. The *Hillites* are similar to the *socialisers* segment in that they enjoy the social aspects of rugby as much as the game itself but they differ markedly from the *socialisers* segment in that they place little premium on comfort. The *entertainment seekers* are drawn to any event, sporting or otherwise, which promises excitement, fun, entertainment and the opportunity to 'be seen'. They may know relatively little about rugby. The *one eyed* spectators love the Reds and Queensland teams as much as they love rugby. They are motivated primarily by the desire to see their team win and they will transfer their support between Queensland and Australian teams across a variety of sports. Finally, the *business* segment comprises business people who support rugby because it makes good business sense. Most corporate spectators fit into other segments–they belong to the *traditionalist* or *socialisers* segments and they have based a decision to support rugby on more personal criteria. The *business* segment have not–they may enjoy the game to a greater or lesser extent but they see it as the opportunity to develop contacts and business opportunities as well as projecting the right values for their own business activity.

The Rugby Union lifestyle segments developed are primarily useful for decision making within a very specific domain. In this case the emphasis was on a very detailed understanding of the market in terms of differences in loyalty (see Figure 3).

FIGURE 3. Rugby Union Segments–A Loyalty Continuum

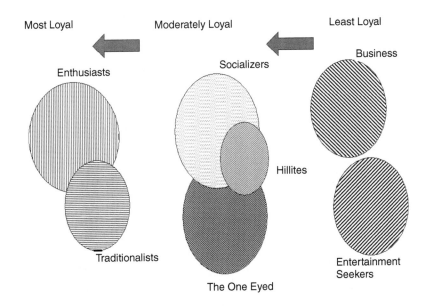

CONCLUSIONS

These three cases have illustrated approaches to lifestyle segmentation based on varying requirements of generalizability and specificity for the research results. The first illustrated use of single source data in conjunction with a standard method of developing lifestyle segments that is well used among Australian tourism destination management organizations. The second developed a lifestyle segmentation approach that linked to customer data at a number of geographic levels. Finally, the last examined a case study that was specific to a particular context.

These cases illustrate the importance of deciding whether to impose order on a particular problem or find it. Is the problem one where the market for a particular product is established in the market and the manager requires information about usage of related products? Use of single source data may reveal patterns of consumption based on imposing a proprietary lifestyle segmentation approach. These patterns of consumption relate to both usage of products and different media viewing habits. Here the approach is to move from the user of a specific product to describing the general pattern of other purchases. The additional information will often provide a better perspective on who buys a product and why.

Alternatively, lifestyle segmentation may be self-contained and focused on understanding how different market segments use a particular product. Here the focus may be on increasing total revenue through increasing repeat purchase or add-on purchases. Understanding the various market segments and their characteristics may allow targeting of the more profitable one or suggest ways of moving existing buyers to higher value segments. However in this approach, the focus is on the meaning of the product alone for particular segments rather than in relation to other products.

Lastly, it may be necessary to understand both the specific segments that purchase of a product as well as the relationship of the product to other similar products. The approach taken in examining hotels in Port Douglas when required to understand both hotel usage and the relationship of this to usage of the destination was to develop a number of segments based on both destination and hotel characteristics. In all three examples using lifestyle segmentation provided useful information on the specific consumption contexts and general consumption patterns.

Understanding the lifestyle of customers is a valuable tool in marketing in order to understand how the product 'fits a customer's life'. Recreational travel and leisure activities have always been lifestyle choices and are increasingly lifestyle purchases. Viewing these products within the framework of lifestyle segmentation is both logical and, as previously discussed insightful.

NOTE

1. Developed in conjunction with Colin Benjamin of The Horizons Network.

REFERENCES

A'guas, P., Costa, J. & Rita, P. 2000, 'A tourist market portfolio for Portugal', *International Journal of Contemporary Hospitality Management*, vol. 12, no. 7, pp. 394-401.

Anbascher, H. 1967, 'Life style: A historical and systematic review', *Journal of Individual Psychology*, vol. 23, pp. 191-212.

Anderson, W. T. & Golden, L. L. 1984, 'Lifestyle and psychographics: A critical review and recommendation', in *Advances in Consumer Research*, ed. T. Kinnear, Association for Consumer Research, Provo, UT, vol. XI, pp. 405-11.

Assael, H. & Poltrack, D. F. 1991, 'Using Single Source Data to Select TV Programs Based on Purchasing Behavior.' *Journal of Advertising Research*, vol. 33, no. 1, pp. 9-17.

_____2002, 'Consumer Surveys vs. Electronic Measures for Single-Source Data', *Journal of Advertising Research*, vol. 42, no. 5, pp. 19-25.

Bojanic, D. & Warnick, R. 1995, 'Segmenting the market for winter vacations', *Journal of Travel and Tourism Marketing*, vol. 4, no. 4, pp. 85-90.

Butler, R. W. 1980, 'The concept of a tourist area cycle of evolution: Implications for management of resources', *Canadian Geographer*, vol. 24, no. 1, pp. 7-14.

_____2001, 'The resort cycle two decades on', in *Tourism in the 21st Century: Reflections on Experience*, eds B. Faulkner, E. Laws & G. Moscardo, Continuum, London, pp. 284-99.

Canberra Tourism and Events Corporation 2001, *ACT Tourism masterplan 2001-2005*, Canberra Tourism and Events Corporation, Canberra.

Chaney, D. 1996, *Lifestyles*, Routledge, London.

Chen, J. S. 2003, 'Market segmentation by tourists' sentiments', *Annals of Tourism Research*, vol. 30, no. 1, pp. 178-93.

City of Ballarat 2002, *Ballarat Tourism: 3 Year Strategic Plan*, City of Ballarat, Ballarat.

Fishbein, M. & Ajzen, I. 1975, *Belief, Attitude, Intention and Behaviour: An Introduction to Theory and Research*, Addison-Wesley, Reading, MA.

Frank, R. E., Massy, W. F. & Wind, Y. J. 1972, *Market Segmentation*, Prentice Hall, Englewood Cliffs, NJ.

Gonzalez, A. M. & Bello, L. 2002, 'The construct 'lifestyle' in market segmentation: The behaviour of tourist consumers', *European Journal of Marketing*, vol. 36, no. 1/2, pp. 51-85.

Green, B. C. & Chalip, L. 1998, 'Sports tourism as the celebration of subculture', *Annals of Tourism Research*, vol. 25, no. 2, pp. 275-91.

Holt, D. B. 1997, 'Poststructuralist lifestyle analysis: Conceptualizing the social patterning of consumption in postmodernity.' *Journal of Consumer Research*, vol. 23, no. 4, pp. 326-50.

Hunt, S. D. 1991, *Modern Marketing Theory*, South Western, Cincinnati.

Kelly, G. 1955, *The psychology of personal constructs*, Norton, New York.

Kotler, P. 2000, *Marketing Management*, Millennium edn, Prentice-Hall, Upper Saddle River, NJ.

Laws, E., Scott, N. & Parfitt, N. 1999, 'Co-Operative Destination and Hotel Brand Image Management in Port Douglas Tropical North Queensland', article presented to Asia Pacific Tourism Association Fifth Annual Conference, Hong Kong.

_____2002, 'Synergies in destination image management: A case study and conceptualisation', *International Journal of Tourism Research*, vol. 4, no. 1, pp. 39-55.

Lawson, R., Thyne, M., Young, T. & Juric, B. 1999, 'Developing Travel Lifestyles: A New Zealand Example', in *Consumer Behaviour in Travel and Tourism*, ed. A. Pizam, The Haworth Hospitality Press, New York.

Mitchell, A. 1983, *Nine American Life-Styles*, Warner, New York.

Oppedijk van Veen, W. M. & Verhallen, T. W. M. 1986, 'Vacation Market segmentation: A domain-specific value approach', *Annals of Tourism Research*, vol. 13, no. 1, pp. 37-58.

Papadopoulos, S. 1989, 'Strategy development and implementation of tourism marketing plans: Part 2', *European Journal of Marketing*, vol. 23, no. 3, pp. 37-47.

Perdue, R. 1996, 'Target market selection and marketing strategy: The Colorado downhill skiing industry', *Journal of Travel Research*, vol. 34, no. 4, pp. 39-46.

Pitts, B. 1999, 'Sports tourism and niche markets: Identification and analysis of the growing lesbian and gay sports tourism industry', *Journal of Vacation Marketing*, vol. 5, no. 1, pp. 31-50.

Plog, S. C. 1974, 'Why destination areas rise and fall in popularity', *Cornell Hotel and Restaurant Administration Quarterly*, vol. 14, no. 4, pp. 55-68.

Ralston, L. & Stewart, W. P. 1990, 'Methodological perspectives on festival research studies', *Annals of Tourism Research*, vol. 17, no. 2, pp. 289-92.

Reed, D., Hepper, J. & Tilley, P. 1999, *The Tasmanian Attractions Study: An independent study of current Tasmanian tourist attractions and a vision for growth into the 21st century*, http://www.tourism.tas.gov.au/corp/tasind/attractions99/attract99.html, viewed 7/5/2003.

Shih, D. 1986, 'VALS as a tool of tourism market research: The Pennsylvania experience', *Journal of Travel Research*, vol. 24, no. 4, pp. 2-10.

Szmigin, I. & Carrigan, M. 2001, 'Leisure and tourism services and the older innovator', *Service Industries Journal*, vol. 21, no. 3, pp. 113-29.

Todd, S. & Lawson, R. 2001, 'Lifestyle segmentation and museum/gallery visiting behaviour', *International Journal of Nonprofit and Voluntary Sector Marketing*, vol. 6, no. 3, pp. 269-77.

Tourism Queensland 2002, *Wine Tourism*, http://www.tq.com.au/research/pdf/free/spec_interest/tq_wine.pdf, viewed 1/5/2003.

Tourism South Australia 2003, *South Australia Tourism Plan 2003-2008*, Tourism South Australia, Adelaide.

Tourism Victoria 2002, *Victoria's Tourism Industry Strategic Plan 2002-2006*, Tourism Victoria, Melbourne.

Tuppen, J. 2000, 'The restructuring of winter sports resorts in the French Alps: Problems, processes and policies', *International Journal of Tourism Research*, vol. 2, pp. 327-44.

Upchurcha, R. S., Ellis, T. & Seo, J. 2002, 'Revenue management underpinnings: An exploratory review', *Hospitality Management*, vol. 21, pp. 67-83.

Van Raaij, W. F. 1994, 'Domain-specific Market Segmentation', *European Journal of Marketing*, vol. 28, no. 10, pp. 49-68.

Wedel, M. & Kamakura, W. A. 1999, *Market Segmentation: Conceptual and Methodological Foundations*, Kulwer Academic Publishers, London.

Young, M. B. 1995, 'Evaluative Constructions of domestic tourist places', *Australian Geographical Studies*, vol. 33, no. 2, pp. 272-86.

Zins, A. H. 1998, 'Leisure traveller choice models of theme hotels using psychographics', *Journal of Travel Research,* vol. 36, no. 4, pp. 3-15.

Improved Understanding of Tourists' Needs: Cross-Classification for Validation of Data-Driven Segments

Sara Dolničar

SUMMARY. Data-driven segmentation has become standard practice in strategic marketing. Typically, however, respondents are grouped only once, implicitly assuming deterministic nature of the segmentation methods applied. Once the segments are derived, background variables are used to test the significance of the difference between clusters indicating external validity of the market segments. High external validity implies a high level of trustworthiness of the solution and thus managerially useful market segments to choose from. However, single runs of explorative analysis remain only a weak basis for good long-term managerial decisions. In this study a different approach is suggested to im-

Sara Dolničar is affiliated with the School of Management, Marketing & Employment Relations, University of Wollongong, Northfields Avenue, Wollongong, NSW 2522, Australia (E-mail: sara_Dolničar@uow.edu.au).

The author would like to thank Jess Pointing, Martin Fluker and The Surf Travel Company for providing the interesting empirical data set that allows illustrating the validation concept proposed.

[Haworth co-indexing entry note]: "Improved Understanding of Tourists' Needs: Cross-Classification for Validation of Data-Driven Segments." Dolničar, Sara. Co-published simultaneously in *Journal of Quality Assurance in Hospitality & Tourism* (The Haworth Hospitality Press, an imprint of The Haworth Press, Inc.) Vol. 5, No. 2/3/4, 2004, pp. 141-156; and: *Hospitality, Tourism, and Lifestyle Concepts: Implications for Quality Management and Customer Satisfaction* (ed: Maree Thyne and Eric Laws) The Haworth Hospitality Press, an imprint of The Haworth Press, Inc., 2004, pp. 141-156. Single or multiple copies of this article are available for a fee from The Haworth Document Delivery Service [1-800-HAWORTH, 9:00 a.m. - 5:00 p.m. (EST). E-mail address: docdelivery@haworthpress.com].

Digital Object Identifier: 10.1300/J162v05n02_08

141

prove the quality of the market structure insight for decision-making: two data-driven segmentation solutions are constructed independently. Association between them is used as an additional internal validity indicator.

Benefit and behavioural segmentation bases are used to illustrate the concept: surfers provided information regarding the importance of aspects of proposed surf destinations and destinations they had previously visited. Segments resulting from both bases are profiled: they notably differ in background information. Significant association between these solutions supports the validity and managerial usefulness for target segment choice for the following targeted marketing action.

Using this procedure results in the identification of stable consumer groups, which in turn leads to an improved understanding of customer segments; and thus enables the industry to improve the quality by customizing the product. *[Article copies available for a fee from The Haworth Document Delivery Service: 1-800-HAWORTH. E-mail address: <docdelivery@haworth press.com> Website: <http://www.HaworthPress. com> © 2004 by The Haworth Press, Inc. All rights reserved.]*

KEYWORDS. Segmentation, validation, post-hoc (a posteriori, data-driven) segmentation

INTRODUCTION

It has become a standard procedure to account for consumer heterogeneity in the marketplace by grouping individuals based on the similarity of their answers given in a survey. Responsible for this might be:

- *Socio-demographic criteria.* For instance, Dodd and Bigotte (1997) group winery visitors according to demographics.
- *Behavioural information.* An example is provided by Hsu and Lee (2002) who construct segments based on motor coach selection criteria.
- *Benefit variables.* This concept was first introduced by Haley in 1968 and has rapidly risen in popularity; a recent example is provided by Silverberg, Backman and Backman (1996) who investigate benefit segments among nature-based tourists.

The procedure of investigating existing or constructing artificial but managerially useful groups of similar customers is referred to as *a posteri-*

ori (Mazanec, 2000), *post-hoc* (Wedel & Kamakura, 1998), or data-driven market (Dolničar, 2002a) segmentation. Homogeneous market segments derived in such way can be subsequently targeted in a more efficient manner (Frank, Massy & Wind, 1972; Wedel & Kamakura, 1998): sub-group's demands can be met better.

Typically, market segments are derived by clustering (determining sub-groups by computing the similarities of consumers) the data only once. Detailed reviews of emerged standards in data-driven market segmentation were investigated by Baumann (2000) and Dolničar (2002). In general, very little effort is made to validate the managerial usefulness of segments. Accepted ways of validating results include the use of repetitive algorithms, manual repetition, or testing of additionally available information. The latter approach can often be found in segmentation studies published in academic journals. In the present article, an additional approach for validation of data-driven segmentation results is illustrated which makes use of multiple segmentation bases existing in one data set. After independent data-driven grouping, the association of the solutions is used as an indicator of validity.

The procedure proposed has been used prior to this study for the purpose of identifying integrated vacation styles (Dolničar & Mazanec, 2000; Dolničar & Leisch, 2003). Here this approach is presented as a useful additional tool for evaluating the internal validity of data-driven market segments. By evaluating the validity of segmentation results, the customer segments chosen as targets are tested more thoroughly; as such they form a stronger basis for understanding the needs of defined customer groups. Better understanding of the customers enables the hospitality and tourism industry to better customize its products and consequently better match the customers' needs and desires. This is expected to lead to higher quality products optimally harmonized with demand for the particular target segments chosen, higher consumer satisfaction and increased loyalty.

METHODOLOGY

The proposed validation procedure is illustrated using an empirical example. The data set includes 430 respondents (active surfers) to an online-survey. Two pieces of information were used for independent construction of segments: (1) the importance attached to different destination factors (benefits tourists seek when choosing a particular destination), and (2) determination of prior visits to 30 international surf destinations. The latter consists of Yes or No statements. The importance block includes 17 items indicating importance of factors for destination choice. In addition, the survey includes other questions relating to surf behaviour, personal characteristics and general travel behaviour, the answers to which can be used for profiling and determining significant differences between segments.

For the construction of the surfer segments self-organising neural network procedures were applied: self-organising feature maps (SOFMs, Kohonen, 1984) and topology representing networks (TRNs, Martinetz & Schulten, 1994). The term *neural network* refers to techniques from the area of artificial intelligence that can be used for the purpose of data analysis. Self-organising neural network procedures–meaning that they "learn" without being given feedback about the correct answer–were first introduced into the area of market segmentation by Mazanec (1992), their main advantage being additional topological market structure information resulting from only one step of partitioning analysis. The benefit segments based on importance statements were built using the less rigid TRN approach, whereas the behavioural segments were forced into a SOFM grid, in order to reveal possible topological neighbourhood patterns using a framework that allows simple definition of similarity of segments. For both networks random starting points were chosen and training was allowed for 90 epochs with a decreasing learning rate. The software used is freely available from the Vienna University of Economics and Business Administration (*http://charly.wu-wien.ac.at/software/*).

Behavioural Segmentation

Six segments were chosen, because this solution rendered sufficiently large and yet well-profiled segments.[1] The resulting solution is described in detail with regard to the implications for surf tourism marketing in Dolničar and Fluker (forthcoming) and is outlined in Figure 1. Each bar chart represents one segment. The bars indicate the proportion of segment members stating that they had visited each destination, and the line represents the sample average. The resulting segments are surprisingly distinct. Behavioural segment 1 (Indonesia segment) has a very strong focus on Indonesia as a surf destination and includes roughly 10% of the respondents,[2] B2-members (America segment, 24%) are above average in surfing American destinations. Segment B3 (Western Australia and Indonesia segment, 8%) is characterized by a combination of Western Australian and Indonesian destinations, B4

FIGURE 1. Behavioural Segments (Source: Dolničar & Fluker, forthcoming)

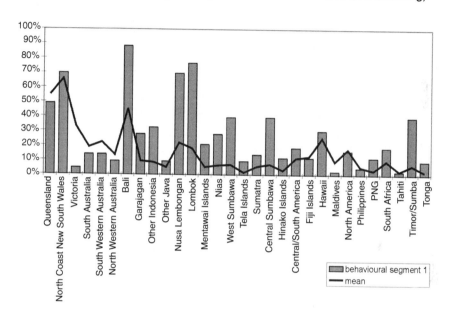

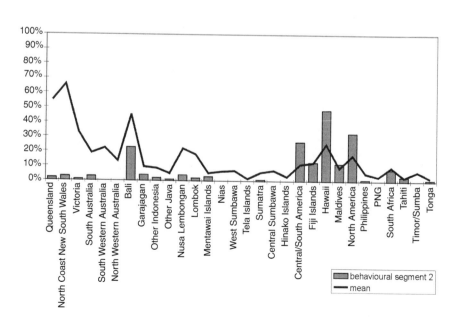

FIGURE 1 (continued)

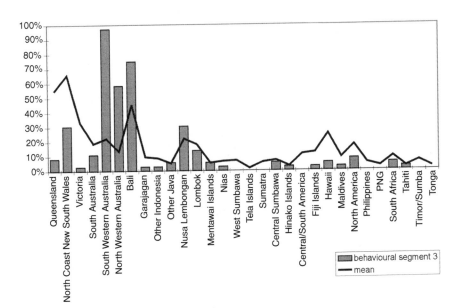

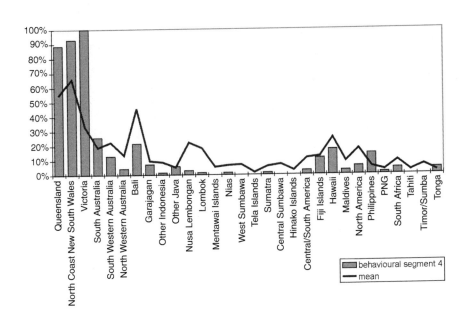

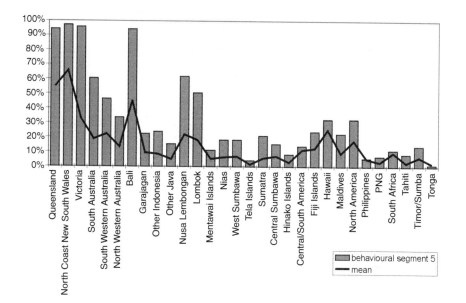

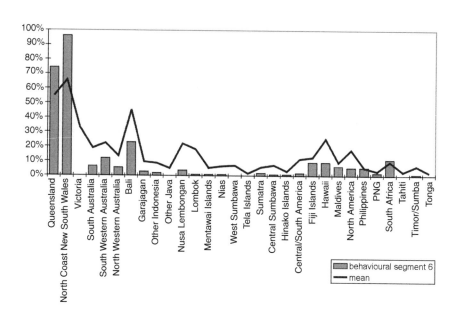

(Australia segment, 16%) represents a group of surfers that almost exclusively surfs at the coasts of Australia (the only other destinations mentioned, on average, more often was the Philippines). Surfers assigned to B5 (all destinations, 17%) declare that they have surfed anywhere in the world more often than the average. Here, answer tendencies might distort results; the segment should be interpreted with care. Finally, B6-surfers (North Eastern Australia, 25%) have so far surfed in Queensland and at the north coast of New South Wales; they represent a second group of Australia-surfers.

In addition to the segmentation base, descriptive information was available in the data set. Such information is used to further describe the segments and to investigate whether the grouping chosen actually represents distinct groups.

A number of significant differences between the segments are revealed: The average age varies (ANOVA p-value = 0.000) from 27 to 33 years, with surfers focusing on American sites representing the oldest group. The years of surfing experience (Chi square p-value = 0.000, this p-value is Bonferroni-corrected to adjust for the fact that multiple tests are computed on the basis of the same data set) distinguish the behavioural segments: again, the America-surfers apparently have most experience, whereas the surfers visiting Indonesia and Western Australia as well as the NSW/Queensland group are least experienced. With regard to the length of stay (0.000), Indonesia-surfers stay longest, with 23% stating that they stay for 5-8 weeks. The America-surfers (B2), the Indonesia and Western Australia segment (B3) as well as the Eastern Australia group (B6) have the shortest lengths of stay with about two thirds staying less than two weeks.

Further significant distinguishing criteria of defining segments include the preferred wave type (0.004), the regularity of undertaking surf trips (0.001), the interest in destination novelty (0.048), education level (0.010) and income (0.006) although no significant differences in daily budget are detected.

Benefit Segmentation

A five-cluster solution was chosen because contingency tables between solutions with different numbers of clusters reveal that there is a high congruence of surfer types with both the four- and the six-segment solution indicating local stability of types over solutions with a different number of segments. Figure 2 outlines the segments derived (they were discussed in detail with regard to tourism marketing implications in

FIGURE 2. Benefit Surfer Segments (Source: Dolničar & Fluker, 2003)

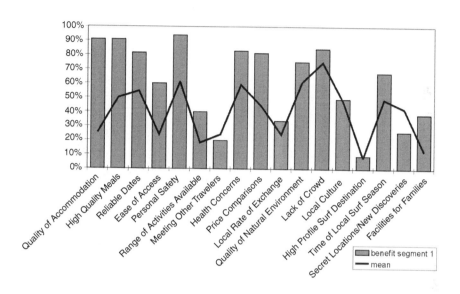

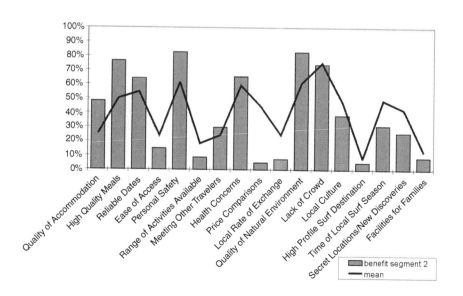

FIGURE 2 (continued)

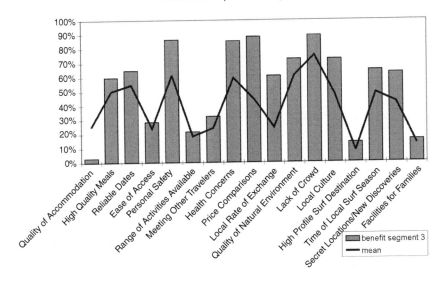

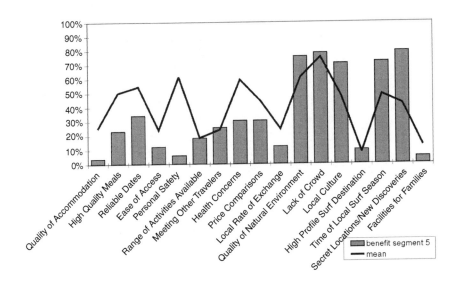

Dolničar & Fluker, 2003). Segment 5 (P5, "radical adventurers," 19%) represents the most distinct group of surfers: the time of the local surfing season as well as secret locations are important to the majority of this segment, local culture, the lack of crowd and quality of natural environment also play a central role. P4 (23%, not given in Figure 2) does not identify anything to be important at all.[3] Segment P2 ("luxury surfers," 19%) is interesting from the viewpoint that neither price nor exchange rate are of particular interest. It is more important to this group that accommodation is good, food is excellent and safety is assured. Segments P1 and P3 are very similar to each other. The surfing-related items are important to these segments, personal safety and health play an important role, high-quality meals and reliable dates are appreciated. The main differentiating factors are the availability of facilities for families and the quality of accommodation in P1 ("price-conscious safety seekers," 15%) and the search for new locations and discoveries as well as the lack of crowd in P3 ("price-conscious adventurers," 24%).

The analysis of descriptive variables indicates significant discrimination between these segments. Radical adventurers (P5) are the youngest group; the price-conscious safety seekers (P1) represent the oldest group (ANOVA p-value = 0.000). This is well mirrored in the years of surfing experience (Bonferroni-corrected Chi square p-value = 0.009), where 37% of the latter claim that they have been surfing for more than 20 years. Regarding surfing ability (0.001), very few members of each segment dare to call themselves "highly advanced," but half of both the price-conscious safety seekers (P2) and the price-conscious adventurers (P3) regard themselves as "advanced." Also of interest: the highest number of "beginner" classifications appears in group P3. Further significant differences include the preferred wave size (0.010), the preferred wave type (0.009), movement during the stay (0.004), education (0.000) and income level (0.000).

Association Between Solutions

The contingency table of memberships for both segmentation solutions is presented in Table 1. This is the core component of the proposed validation procedure. The assumption underlying this internal validity investigation is that segments of consumers that truly exist in the market can be repeatedly revealed from different perspectives, looking at different tourist characteristics.

TABLE 1. Interdependence of Benefit and Behavioural Segments

		P1 price-conscious safety seeker	P2 luxury surfer	P3 price-conscious adventurers	P4	P5 radical adventurer
B1 Indonesia	Observed	4	2	10	13	14
	Expected	6,5	8,1	10,2	10,0	8,2
	% of behavioural	9,3	4,7	23,3	30,2	32,6
	% of benefit	6,2	2,5	9,8	13,0	17,1
B2 America	Observed	22	18	27	24	10
	Expected	15,3	19,0	24,0	23,5	19,3
	% of behavioural	21,8	17,8	26,7	23,8	9,9
	% of benefit	33,8	22,2	26,5	24,0	12,2
B3 Western Australia and Indonesia	Observed	5	3	8	9	11
	Expected	5,4	6,8	8,5	8,4	6,9
	% of behavioural	13,9	8,3	22,2	25,0	30,6
	% of benefit	7,7	3,7	7,8	9,0	13,4
B4 Eastern Australia	Observed	8	16	17	10	19
	Expected	10,6	13,2	16,6	16,3	13,3
	% of behavioural	11,4	22,9	24,3	14,3	27,1
	% of benefit	12,3	19,8	16,7	10,0	23,2
B5 All destinations	Observed	10	14	18	16	13
	Expected	10,7	13,4	16,8	16,5	13,5
	% of behavioural	14,1	19,7	25,4	22,5	18,3
	% of benefit	15,4	17,3	17,6	16,0	15,9
B6 North Eastern Australia	Observed	16	28	22	28	15
	Expected	16,5	20,5	25,9	25,3	20,8
	% of behavioural	14,7	25,7	20,2	25,7	13,8
	% of benefit	24,6	34,6	21,6	28,0	18,3

The association is tested using the Pearson Chi square test that renders a p-value of 0.022, thus indicating significant interdependence between the two solutions at the 95% level (Cramer's V is significant with a p-value of 0.022 as well and amounts to 0.142). The values for the segments conspicuous of being (at least partially) answer tendencies are given in grey. The cells in which the observed counts strongly exceed the expected number of respondents appear in boldface; cells in which the observed counts are lower than the expected value are marked in italic. For each cell the observed counts, the expected cell frequency and the percentages with regard to both segmentations are provided. Managerially, the boldface cells are of interest as they point to the market segments that are identified both from the benefit as well as from the behavioural perspective. Surfers are consequently significantly more often than one would expect located in both the behavioural and benefit segment represented by the boldface cross-tabulation cell.

Including one third of the members of the price-conscious safety seekers (P1) this group is highly over-represented in the behavioural segment that surfs in American waters. The luxury surfers (P2) prefer Australia: 23% are assigned to B4 (Eastern Australia) and 26% to B6 (North Eastern Australia), but are under-represented in the Indonesia-segment. A slight deviation from the expected values occurs for the price-conscious adventurers (P3): they are under-represented among the surfers that include Queensland and New South Wales in their portfolio of surfing destinations (B6). Finally, the radical adventurers show the most profiled distribution: These surfers are more often than expected found in behavioural segments B1, B3 and B4 where the two first segments represent the Indonesia-region on the topological map and B4 the East of Australia. On the other hand, the less radical adventurers can be found among the members of B2, the America-centred segment, and B6, the group focusing on Queensland and New South Wales when going for a surf vacation. Those segments thus represent good opportunities for managers of surfing destinations because they are independently revealed both from the behavioural and the benefit side. The internal validity of such segments is higher than it is the case for the remaining surfer groups. This gives management more confidence that the chosen target segment is not a random result or a methodological artefact.

CONCLUSIONS, LIMITATIONS AND FUTURE WORK

Two data-based market segmentations of surf tourists were cross- tabulated for the purpose of internal validation of derived market segments. One was constructed on the basis of benefits sought and the other on the basis of surfing destinations visited in the past. Both segmentation solutions render distinct segments significantly differing in various background variables. Significant association is detected between the two groupings that indicate systematic association between the benefit segments and the behavioural segments. This ads validity to the solution (besides the external substantiation obtained by testing of significant differences in descriptive information) and supports the assumption that segments that are homogeneous with regard to the importance respondents attach to different destination factors when choosing among them does interact with their actual choice of destinations.

The proposed procedure assists hospitality and tourism managers to avoid selecting market segments that are not backed by both behavioural and benefit characteristics. Australia as a surfing destination, for instance, is lucky to find that the market segment named "luxury surfers" likes to surf at Eastern and North Eastern Australian destinations. This segment is not very price-sensitive but the quality of accommodation and food is important for these tourists, and safety must be assured. Realising these facts enables the destination management to provide the expected kind of service and product thus increasing the quality of the service.

This study is only the first step toward investigating the usefulness of cross-classification for the validation of data-driven segment solutions. The limitation lies in the requirement to have at least two question blocks of different nature in the guest survey to enable independent segment construction. In case of this particular illustration based on the surfer data set, the limitations are that only one single data set was studied that was not optimal due to the data collection method. The sample size was too small for a managerially relevant segmentation study given the large number of variables. The representativeness could not be assumed given the online survey technique used. Future work must include multiple replications of this approach with numerous data sets of varying nature and dimensionality. Analysis with artificial data could give guideline values for the various cluster combinations studied.

NOTES

1. The author is aware of the fact that every grouping of 430 respondents in a thirty dimensional space is a very rough partitioning and that the sample size does represent a major limitation. However, the aim of this article is to illustrate a simple internal validity measure, not to gain insight into surf tourist. In case the latter were the aim, a larger and representative sample size would be needed.

2. These percentages are only rough because the sample was not drawn following a representative sampling procedure. Strictly speaking the percentages are proportions of the sample only, not the population.

3. This is a typical phenomenon that occurs in data-driven market segmentation: one or two segments function as collecting points for answer patterns that are either above or below average with regard to all variables. Such segments profiles are ambiguous, because they could either represent a real answer pattern that can be interpreted (in this case, for instance, that none of the tourists see any benefit in any of those aspects) or an answer pattern that should not be interpreted, because it might result from respondent fatigue or lack of motivation to complete the questionnaire properly.

REFERENCES

Baumann, R. (2000). *Marktsegmentierung in den Sozial- und Wirtschaftswissenschaften: eine Metaanalyse der Zielsetzungen und Zugänge.* Vienna: Vienna University of Economics and Management Science.

Dodd, T., & Bigotte, V. (1997). Perceptual Differences among Visitor Groups to Wineries. *Journal of Travel Research,* 35(3), 46-51.

Dolničar, S. (2002a). Review of Data-Driven Market Segmentation in Tourism. *Journal of Travel & Tourism Marketing,.* 12(1), 1-22.

Dolničar, S. (2002b). A Review of Unquestioned Standards in using Cluster Analysis for Data-driven Market Segmentation. *CD Proceedings of the Australian and New Zealand Marketing Academy Conference (ANZMAC).*

Dolničar, S., & Fluker, M. (2003). Who's Riding the Wave? An Investigation into Demographic and Psychographic Characteristics of Surf Tourists. *CD proceedings of the 13th International Research Conference of the Council for Australian University Tourism and Hospitality Education (CAUTHE).*

Dolničar, S., & Fluker, M. (forthcoming). Behavioural Market Segments Among Surf Tourists–Investigating Past Destination Choice. *Journal of Sports Tourism.*

Dolničar, S., & Leisch, F. (2003). Winter Tourist Segments in Austria–Identifying Stable Vacation Styles for Target Marketing Action. *Journal of Travel Research,* 41(3), 281-193.

Dolničar, S., & Mazanec, J. (2000). Holiday Styles and Tourist Types: Emerging New Concepts and Methodology, in: Gartner, W.C., and Lime, D.W. (eds.), *Trends in Outdoor Recreation, Leisure and Tourism.* New York: CAB International, pp. 245-255.

Frank, R.E., Massy, W., & Wind, Y. (1972). *Market Segmentation.* Engelwood Cliff: Prentice-Hall.

Haley, R.J. (1968). Benefit Segmentation: A Decision-Oriented Research Tool. *Journal of Marketing,* 32, 30-35.

Hsu, C.H.C. & Lee, E.-J. (2002). Segmentation of Senior Motorcoach Travelers. *Journal of Travel Research,* 40(4), 364-374.

Kohonen, T. (1984). *Self-Organisation and Associative Memory.* New York: Springer-Verlag.

Martinetz, Th., & Schulten, K. (1994). Topology Representing Networks. *Neural Networks,* 7(5), 507-522.

Mazanec, J.A. (1992). Classifying Tourists into Market Segments: A Neural Network Approach. *Journal of Travel & Tourism Marketing,* 1(1), 39-59.

Myers, J.H., & Tauber, E. (1977). *Market structure analysis*. Chicago: American Marketing Association.

Silverberg, K.E., Backman, S.J., & Backman, K.F. (1996). A Preliminary Investigation into the Psychographics of Nature-Based Travelers to the Southeastern United States. *Journal of Travel Research*, 35(2), 19-28.

Wedel, M. & Kamakura, W. (1998). *Market Segmentation–Conceptual and Methodological Foundations*. Boston: Kluwer Academic Publishers.

Lifestyle Market Segmentation, Small Business Entrepreneurs, and the New Zealand Wine Tourism Industry

Ken Simpson
Phil Bretherton
Gina de Vere

SUMMARY. Wine tourism is an important niche activity for which participant needs and motivations have been somewhat under-researched. This paper describes a case study investigation to evaluate the nature of buyer/seller relationships that evolve in a wine tourism setting. Visitors to three small New Zealand wineries were interviewed to gather data relating to their lifestyle behaviors and their attitudes towards the wine tourism experience, and factor analysis used to categorize these visitors in terms of the List of Values typology of lifestyle characteristics. Results indicate that the 'achiever' and 'funlover' segments are well

Ken Simpson is affiliated with the School of Management and Entrepreneurship, UNITEC Institute of Technology, Auckland, New Zealand.

Phil Bretherton is affiliated with the School of Marketing and Tourism, Central Queensland University, Rockhampton, Queensland, Australia.

Gina de Vere is affiliated with Masters Consulting, Warkworth, North Auckland, New Zealand.

Address correspondence to: Ken Simpson (E-mail: ksimpson@unitec.ac.nz).

[Haworth co-indexing entry note]: "Lifestyle Market Segmentation, Small Business Entrepreneurs, and the New Zealand Wine Tourism Industry." Simpson, Ken, Phil Bretherton, and Gina de Vere. Co-published simultaneously in *Journal of Quality Assurance in Hospitality & Tourism* (The Haworth Hospitality Press, an imprint of The Haworth Press, Inc.) Vol. 5, No. 2/3/4, 2004, pp. 157-188; and: *Hospitality, Tourism, and Lifestyle Concepts: Implications for Quality Management and Customer Satisfaction* (ed: Maree Thyne and Eric Laws) The Haworth Hospitality Press, an imprint of The Haworth Press, Inc., 2004, pp. 157-188. Single or multiple copies of this article are available for a fee from The Haworth Document Delivery Service [1-800-HAWORTH, 9:00 a.m. - 5:00 p.m. (EST). E-mail address: docdelivery@haworthpress.com].

157

represented amongst winery visitors, but that there is an appreciably lower incidence of 'belonger' personalities. Implications of these findings for the wine tourism industry are considered. *[Article copies available for a fee from The Haworth Document Delivery Service: 1-800-HAWORTH. E-mail address: <docdelivery@haworthpress.com> Website: <http://www. HaworthPress.com> © 2004 by The Haworth Press, Inc. All rights reserved.]*

KEYWORDS. Wine tourism, List of Values, lifestyle segmentation, buyer/ seller relationships

INTRODUCTION

The provision of superior service quality is a foundation element of success in all tourism industry sectors, though it is often argued to be a particularly vital consideration for smaller, special interest categories of visitor activity. One such 'niche' activity is wine tourism, here defined as "visitation to vineyards, wineries, wine festivals, and wine shows, for which grape-wine tasting and/or experiencing the attributes of a grape-wine region are the prime motivating factors for visitors" (Hall & Macionis, 1998:197).

The scale of participation in this particular niche has grown rapidly in recent years and, based on a lengthy period of sustained growth in the parent wine industry, wine tourism has become a significant sector of the inbound visitor industry for many New World countries (Hall & Mitchell, 2000). For example, Hall and Macionis (1998) report an annual visitation of around 5.3 million people to wineries in Australia, and expect that wine tourism receipts may reach $A1,100 million by 2025; similarly, it has been estimated that New Zealand wineries welcome around 250,000 international and 500,000 locally resident visitors each year (Hall et al., 1997). Clearly, the wine tourism industry is one that offers significant potential.

For the small wine producer, there are significant advantages in choosing to participate in the tourism industry. There is the obvious attraction of direct product sales, at the winery and following positive visitor reaction to tastings; there is income to be derived from food, wine-related products, and sundry merchandising; and additional downstream sales can be realized by treating the winery visitor as a potential long-term, repeat-purchasing customer (King & Morris, 1998). However, access to these income streams implies a commitment to the customer experience, as opposed to a solitary concentration on the sale of wine, and suggests the need for winery proprietors to add a concern for service quality to their existing focus on product quality (Ali-Knight & Charters, 2001).

In this respect, much of the wine tourism literature to date has concentrated on the behavior patterns of winery visitors, and has consequently attempted to categorize or classify these visitors in terms of motivation. For example, Hall and Macionis (1998) have suggested a tripartite typology of winery visitors, incorporating the 'wine lovers' (those for whom a winery visit is a central, and possibly sole, motivation for their tourist activity); the 'wine interested' (those for whom wine is a pastime rather than a passion, and whose tourist activity may be motivated by a number of additional factors); and the 'curious tourists' (those who are largely unaware of wines and wine drinking, and view the winery visit as a novelty experience). Similarly, Hall and Winchester (1999) hypothesize the existence of four clusters of wine visitor, labelled in self-explanatory fashion as connoisseurs, aspirational wine drinkers, beverage wine drinkers, and new wine drinkers.

If visitor segments such as these do in fact exist, it is reasonable to suggest that their needs and motivations may significantly differ from each other. The wine tourism experience desired by a 'connoisseur,' in search of a particular bottle of wine or a special taste experience, will be quite distinct from that desired by a 'new wine drinker' out for a Sunday drive on a pleasant summer's day. Yet each of these visitors may visit the same winery on the same day, their distinctive set of values, attitudes, and behaviours combining to pose quite different challenges to the winery's service design. From this point of view, the wine tourism operator may well be required to develop and demonstrate a multi-faceted mastery of the service delivery process.

For many small wine entrepreneurs who claim an association with the visitor industry, there has historically been some difficulty in reconciling the 'product' driven demands of quality wine production with the 'service' perspective required by wine tourism operations (Morris & King, 1998; Macionis & Cambourne, 1998; Hall & Macionis, 1998). When small wineries attempt to cater for the on-site visitor, a palpable strength in product knowledge is frequently counter-balanced by a demonstrable lack of familiarity with the tourism industry and a parallel lack of ability in terms of product and services marketing (Hall & Mitchell, 2000; Ali-Knight & Charters, 2001). As Hall et al. (2000) comment, small wineries seem unable to recognize the possibility that their core product may actually be a visitor experience, not just a bottle of wine–as such, many wine tourism operations are much better at wine than they are at tourism.

This paper suggests that the growing popularity of wine tourism has placed a series of demands upon winery proprietors that they have historically been ill-equipped to contend with. The visitor industry has, for many small wineries, moved from supporting role to core business activity, and the provision of superior service quality to multiple market segments has become a vital element in delivery of that core competence. Yet, these businesses are patronized by a range of market segments whose needs and motivations have not been adequately analyzed (Dodd & Bigotte, 1997; Ravenscroft & van Westering, 2001; Ali-Knight & Charters, 2001). Thus, the primary goal of this paper is to investigate wine tourism from a service quality perspective, contrasting the business practices of small wine tourism operators with the motivations, needs and behavior patterns of their visitors. In this manner, we attempt to better understand the complex relationships between buyers and sellers in a niche tourism industry which continues to grow in importance for those geographical regions that depend on wine production for their economic prosperity.

LITERATURE REVIEW

The Wine Tourism Industry

Wine tourism has quickly become an important industrial activity for many countries, especially in the New World where it has been often seen as an attractive strategy to combat economic deprivation in depressed rural areas (O'Neill & Charters, 2000; Hall & Mitchell, 2000; Ali-Knight & Charters, 2001). In addition, it is said to offer a long-term source of high profit wine sales, an excellent opportunity to gather consumer feedback on product and service quality, an augmented reputation for the host region and its individual winemakers, and a valuable addition to the existing range of visitor attractions (Dodd, 1995; Beverland et al., 1998; Charters & O'Neill, 2000). At an individual producer level, however, it is necessary to note that wine production and wine tourism are not necessarily parallel activities of equal importance.

In most New World countries, the production and distribution of wine is controlled by a handful of larger producers, for whom wine tourism is but a minor concern, commonly regarded as a useful public relations exercise at best (Beverland et al., 1998). In contrast, the host of smaller wineries that typically complement the market leaders–Treloar (2002)

reports that 1,400 Australian wineries account for just 11% of total production–are often reliant on wine tourism activities as an integral component of their sales strategies, most commonly participating through the
on-site sale of wine to visitors 'at the cellar door.' Dodd (1995) reports
that almost half of the wineries in New York State offer the cellar door
option, with approximately 60% of all product sales taking place on site,
whilst a new wine industry in Canada's Okanagan Valley relies heavily
on direct sales to promote its product (Verburg, 1999). In both Australia
(Hall & Macionis, 1998) and New Zealand (Hall et al., 2000), around
80% of wineries offer a cellar door sales facility.

Individual wineries can also choose to work within marketing con-
sortia created to support a designated 'wine trail' touring route. For this
type of tourism, well-established in the USA and Australia (Hall &
Macionis, 1998), throughout much of Europe (Hall et al., 1997), and
even in Israel (Hall & Mitchell, 2000), it is often difficult to determine
whether it is the region's wineries, or simply the generic appeal of the
region itself, that provides the key impetus to visit. In this respect, the
participation of local government in the development of wine trails has
frequently led to the establishment of a local wine tourism organization
and the subsequent preparation of a formal wine tourism strategy for the
area (Macionis & Cambourne, 1998). Though uncommon in New Zealand, this type of arrangement flourishes in Australia (Hall et al., 1997),
where one important result has been the development of public/private
partnerships to create and maintain a regional wine centre and visitor information office (O'Neill & Charters, 2000)–in these circumstances,
the smaller winery can gain significant benefits from the creation of a
regional branding for the local wine tourism product.

This latter point serves to remind us that there is a monetary cost involved when wineries decide to enter the cellar door market. Yes, their
product will be sold at full retail price, but sales volume is likely to be
low and associated staff costs high, for there is a need to invest in
knowledgeable and friendly people to conduct the tastings and secure
the sales (Dodd, 1995). Previous research (King & Morris, 1998) suggests that the investment may well be worthwhile–it is said that 75% of
winery visitors will buy at the cellar door and that 33% of those will repeat purchase in the next twelve months–but that the thin demarcation
line between success and failure may well owe its origins to the service
quality performance of the winery's proprietor and staff.

Service Quality and Wine Tourism

As would be the case in virtually all other service industry environments, our discussion of wine tourism service quality begins with an acknowledgement of the SERVQUAL instrument that has been developed, modified and refined through a series of articles by Parasuraman, Zeithaml and Berry (1985, 1988, 1991, 1993). Though subject to robust discussion and debate since its introduction (Babakus & Boller, 1992; Cronin & Taylor, 1992, 1994: Teas, 1993; Buttle, 1996; Robinson, 1999), SERVQUAL appears to have offered a common foundation for research into service quality issues specific to the tourism and hospitality industries (Fick & Ritchie, 1991; Saleh & Ryan, 1991; Johns, 1993; Ryan & Cliff, 1997; Mei, Dean & White, 1999).

In an attempt to adapt SERVQUAL to the specific requirements of wine tourism, O'Neill and Charters (2000) incorporated the central principles of Martilla and James' (1977) importance-performance analysis (IPA) into the SERVQUAL framework, using the resulting WINOT instrument to measure wine tourism service quality in Western Australia–the model was again used, in a modified form, by O'Neill, Palmer and Charters (2002). Meanwhile, in New Zealand, the Wine Institute had already commissioned a survey investigating the involvement of wineries in tourism (Hall & Johnson, 1998), and the results of that survey are reported in Hall et al. (2000). In addition, Mitchell (2002) describes a New Zealand Winery Visitors Survey conducted over the 1999-2000 season, with questionnaires administered by 33 wineries in nine separate regions–this latter research was particularly important for its inclusion of lifestyle items in the instrument, alongside the more conventional measures of visitor behavior and demographics.

Despite the examples cited above, Augustyn (1998) is probably correct when she argues that most tourism businesses, though fully aware of the need for quality in the design and delivery of the visitor experience, are noticeably lacking when it comes to the implementation of a quality measurement system. According to Augustyn, this weakness is most clearly evident amongst those small tourism businesses that are dependent on service quality for their competitive advantage and survival. From this point of view, and especially given the growing stature of the wine tourism sector, there is a clear need to build on the service quality investigations of researchers such as Hall and Johnson (1998), O'Neill and Charters (2000), and Mitchell (2002)–the 'methods' section of this paper outlines the ways in which these authors' ideas were incorporated into the current work.

Market Segmentation and the Winery Visitor

In order for smaller wineries to take full advantage of the opportunities offered by wine tourism, it is essential for them to understand the forces that drive winery visitors' behavior. Table 1 summarizes the main findings of previous investigations into this topic.

Though any attempt to interpret this table is clearly subjective, it is interesting to note the bias towards a winery visit as part of a rural tourism experience, and what might be seen as three associated motivations–the product motivation shown by a desire to taste and purchase wines; the experiential motivation shown by a desire to partner the wine product with a programme of attractions, activities, food and entertainment; and the educational motivation shown by a desire to learn more about the product, take a winery tour, and meet the winemaker.

There has also been a significant volume of work done in attempting to isolate and describe the typical purchase behaviours of a wine tourist market segment. For example, from a specifically demographic view-

TABLE 1. Wine Tourists' Motivations–A Research Summary

Motivation to Participate	Beverland et al., 1998	Hall and Macionis, 1998	Macionis and Cambourne, 1998	Mitchell, Hall and McIntosh, 2000	Ali-Knight and Charters, 2001
Winery as rural tourism attraction	x	x	x	x	x
Taste wine	x	x		x	x
Buy wine	x	x		x	x
Eat at winery	x	x	x	x	x
Learn about wine/ winemaking		x	x	x	x
Take a winery tour		x	x	x	x
Meet the winemaker		x	x	x	
A day out in the countryside			x	x	
Enjoy other attractions/ activities	x	x	x		
Attend festivals and events		x	x	x	x
Enjoy other entertainments		x	x		
Socialize with friends and family		x	x	x	

point, Charters and O'Neill (2000) report that females tend to be more positively disposed to their cellar door experience than males, and are consequently heavier spenders; King and Morris (1998) suggest that purchase value increases in tandem with age, education and income levels; and Dodd and Bigotte (1997) recognize the positive buying behaviors of a 'seniors' group who are less demanding, better pleased, and bigger spenders, though often seeking to purchase from the range of lower quality wines on offer.

Perhaps most importantly, Greenwell et al. (2002) use the context of a major sporting event to point out the vital importance of a product/service blend that functions as the key determinant of spectator ticket sales. For these authors, that blend includes such elements as the physical setting for the game, the attitudes and behaviours of host personnel, and the bundle of service elements offered to augment the core product. So it may well be for wineries and the wine tourist–just as we don't sell a baseball game as stand-alone proposition, but instead sell a baseball-centred entertainment package, so it seems reasonable to posit that a winery is not judged solely on the quality of its wines, but will rather be evaluated in terms of the total visitor experience.

The discussion above suggests that past research has tended to classify the component parts of wine tourism demand through the application of traditional segmentation criteria, such as demographics, behavior patterns, and benefits sought–as such, the fourth significant segmentation tool, that of psychographic or lifestyles segmentation, has been noticeably absent from past research efforts.

Kotler (1994) presents psychographics as a psychological, as opposed to a physical or behavioral, construct, an approach to understanding the complex range of influential characteristics that are thought to contribute towards the buying behavior of individuals. Traditionally, psychographic characteristics have included social class, personality, and lifestyle, the latter concept held to embody "an understanding of individuals' needs, benefits sought, and motivations" (Middleton, 1997:80). Therein lies the applicability of lifestyle segmentation to the wine tourism industry.

Wine Tourism, Service Quality and Lifestyle Segmentation

Proponents of lifestyle segmentation argue that, though traditional demographic criteria can indeed help to build valuable customer profiles, leisure service providers can reap greater benefits from an analysis of customers' values, beliefs, attitudes, interests and opinions (Pearce et al., 1998). Thus, large scale lifestyle surveys have become well established in the mainstream tourist industry–Australia's Roy Morgan Holiday Tracking Survey (Macionis & Cambourne, 1998) and the New Zealand Consumer Lifestyle Analysis (Todd et al., 1998) are good examples.

The earliest implementation of lifestyle segmentation in the tourism industry is represented by the work of Plog (1974), who used psychographic criteria to develop a typology of tourists based on their attitude to risk behaviors in their choice of tourist experience–thus, Plog's 'allocentric' travellers were portrayed as constantly in pursuit of new and exciting experiences, whilst their 'psychocentric' counterparts sought the reassurance of well-established destinations and reputable tour companies. An individual's positioning on Plog's continuum can be easily related to the typologies of traveller presented by Cohen (1972) and Smith (1977), both of whom described a range of attitudes amongst travellers that varied from "drifters" and "explorers," driven by a need to forever achieve new and exciting experiences, to the "organized mass" or "charter" tourist who was content to follow a tourism trail that had been earlier established by multiple others.

From this perspective, some form of lifestyle classification may offer a useful basis by which to categorize winery visitors, for previous motivational research has suggested the existence of a wine tourist typology that parallels the more generic ideas of Cohen and Smith. For example, based on psychographic criteria, the wine connoisseur and beverage drinker (Hall and Winchester, 1999) can be seen in a similar light to Cohen's (1972) explorers and organized mass tourists, or Smith's (1977) elite and incipient mass categories. As with these authors' research, in both mainstream and niche tourism activities, an ability to categorize winery visitors according to their psychographic profile would make a useful contribution towards understanding their motivations and subsequent behaviours. If motivation and behaviour can be better understood, then the critical elements of required service delivery can also be more clearly comprehended, and appropriate adjustments made to the winery's service design and delivery.

There are multiple contenders for the title of most-used lifestyle category assessment instrument, primary amongst which appear to be Rokeach's Value Survey (Rokeach, 1973) and the VALS instrument developed by the Stanford Research Institute (Mitchell, 1983). However, these and other instruments or processes have attracted frequent criticism that this type of research is cumbersome and impracticable, and is often weighed down by excessively long questionnaires (Plog,

1994; Ryan, 1995). Indeed, much of the psychographic research used in tourism settings can be 'question heavy'–Davis et al. (1988) used 31 items to segment a local resident community; Silverberg et al. (1994) asked nature travellers to evaluate 46 items; and Hudson and Shephard (1998) included 97 variables in their ski field work. There is a real danger of respondent fatigue in each of these instances, and a consequent need for a simpler method of measuring individual values.

In response to that need, the List of Values (LOV) instrument (Kahle, 1983) seeks to measure the extent to which just nine identifiable values exert an influence over an individual's behaviour patterns. A substantial literature of debate since Kahle's original proposals (Novak & MacEvoy, 1990; Muller, 1991; Madrigal & Kahle, 1994; Madrigal, 1995), has resulted in a number of refinements to the original model, culminating in the identification of three 'value system categories' of consumer. These categories, along with the specific values believed to most strongly influence each category's behaviour patterns, are shown in Table 2 below.

When combined with the type of conventional demographic and behavioural data collection suggested earlier in this section, the LOV format offers a simple and effective form of psychographic research design that has been tested and proven in multiple settings–in essence, it offers significant benefits over its competitors in terms of administration sim-

TABLE 2. The List of Values Approach to Consumer Personality Measurement

Funlovers:
- Fun and enjoyment in life
- Excitement in things to do
- Warm relationships with others
Achievers:
- Sense of accomplishment
- Feeling of self-fulfilment
- Self-respect and self-esteem
Belongers:
- Sense of belonging
- Being well respected by others
- Safety and security

Sources: Kahle, 1983; Kahle, Beatty and Homer, 1986; Kennedy, Best and Kahle, 1988; Kamakura and Novak, 1992

plicity, and has no apparent disadvantages when compared to competitor options. It was for these reasons that the LOV approach was selected as a central element in the design of the current research.

CASE STUDY SETTING

Like many of its New World counterparts, the New Zealand wine industry is dominated by a handful of relatively large scale producers. More than half of all total output is produced by one clear market leader, there are two significant market challengers and a handful of moderately sized market followers, and the bulk of industry product is sourced from three primary grape-growing and wine-producing regions. However, as a valuable adjunct to the efforts of these core producer characteristics, a number of localized sites are becoming recognized as important niche locations.

The Rodney District region, and in particular the area surrounding the small village of Matakana, has been one of the more recent entrants into wine production, aided to no small extent by its favourable location, approximately 75 minutes northwards by road from Auckland (New Zealand's largest urban population centre). Matakana's reputation as a pleasant summer day trip destination for Aucklanders is founded on its attractive rural surroundings, its carefully tended farmland, gently rolling hills, and white sandy beaches–the consequent image of laid back rural relaxation provides a useful backdrop for a cottage industry based on food and beverage production/consumption, and was at least partly responsible for the development of the area's first wineries in the early 1990s.

A decade later, Matakana supports nine privately owned wineries, all of them being boutique producers with a maximum output of no more than 3,500 cases each year. To assist in the building of a locally owned wine tourism industry, the majority of these wineries have joined together to create both a 'Matakana Wine Trail' brand (Wineries of Matakana Internet website) and a tourism industry partnership that promotes the region as 'Matakana Coast Wine Country'–the objectives of this latter exercise are best summarized by a mission statement that seeks to "brand the Matakana Coast as being recognized for wine, food, country lifestyle, coast artisans and adventure" (Matakana Coast Internet website).

Though it should be clearly understood that Matakana wines are of excellent quality, and can more than hold their own against most local or imported products, their marketability is certainly enhanced by the milieu in which they are produced. When a significant volume of day-trip tourism meets with quality food and wines, the resulting outcome is often the realization of a 'total wine experience' and the emergence of a niche market segment that is primarily motivated by the component characteristics of that experience. Thus, the paragraphs that follow describe an investigation of the extent to which locally designed and delivered wine tourism initiatives have been successful in meeting the needs of that particular market segment.

OBJECTIVES

The research described in this paper began with two prior assumptions–first, that the historical evolution of Matakana winemaking would combine with the personal values of winery owners to assign a distinctive local flavour to the wine tourism product; and, second, that visitors to the region would share an identifiable portfolio of common lifestyle characteristics. These foundations suggested specific objectives for the current research, expressed below as a series of key questions.

1. What are the demographic characteristics of visitors to the Matakana cellar door?
2. What are the motivations for a visit to the region in general, and the winery in particular?
3. What are the primary behavioural patterns displayed by cellar door visitors?
4. What are the usual wine buying and consuming patterns of cellar door visitors?
5. What are the primary leisure pursuits of cellar door visitors?
6. Which of the LOV values are held to be most important by cellar door visitors?
7. What were cellar door visitors' evaluations of key service quality elements?
8. How did these evaluations equate to an intention to return and an intention to recommend?
9. What was the nature of relationship between visitors' lifestyle characteristics, demographic characteristics, and quality perceptions of the service encounter?

METHODOLOGY

The research questions presented above were addressed through the self-completion of a written survey instrument by visitors to three separate Matakana wineries over two weekends in June and July, 2003. The instru-

ment comprised a battery of questions sourced from a review of the literature, and selected on the basis of their previous application to the type of
objective established for the current research–its content is summarized in
Table 3 below.

In particular, the items included under 'motivations,' 'visitor behaviour patterns,' 'usual wine behaviours' and 'primary leisure pursuits'
were designed as wine tourism measures that would replicate the Wine
Institute of New Zealand's previous investigations (Hall & Johnson,
1998; Mitchell, 2002), and were consequently framed as open ended
questions designed to elicit unprompted responses. The structure and
wording of questions designed to measure the LOV variables was taken
verbatim from the recommendations of Kahle and Kennedy (1989),
whilst the items that sought to measure visitors' service quality evaluations were based on O'Neill and Charters' (2000) WINOT instrument,
adjusted for local conditions. In striving to replicate these authors'
methods, a five-point Likert scale was used for contributing quality
items, though a ten point scale was used for the summary evaluations–
the latter has been claimed as a superior predictor of future consumer

TABLE 3. Matakana Wineries' Survey Instrument

Category	Content	Number of Items
Demographics	Gender, residence, family life cycle, age, education, occupation, income	7
Motivations	Reasons for visiting the region, reasons for visiting the winery	2
Visitor Behaviour Patterns	First time or repeat visitor, number of wineries to be visited, party size, spending on wines, spending on other products	5
Usual Wine Behaviours	Claimed wine expertise, number of wine purchase occasions annually, purchase outlets used, size of wine cellar	4
Primary Leisure Pursuits	Favourite leisure activities, publications read, preferred TV channels	3
LOV Assessment	Scale rating of each LOV item; identification of two most influential values	10
Visitor Evaluations	Site ambience and atmosphere Staff knowledge, friendliness Wine and food quality and value	3 4 5
Summary Evaluations	Overall quality rating, intention to return, intention to recommend	3
Total Number of Items		**46**

behaviour intentions (Tull & Hawkins, 1987), a valuable attribute in the context of the current research objectives. In this manner, the three key concepts–wine tourism, service quality, and lifestyle segmentation–were measured through the application of methodology that had, as far as possible, been already tried and tested in similar circumstances.

Each of the three selected wineries has chosen to include an on-site café in its efforts to meet visitor needs, and the instrument was offered to every café visitor over the three days on which data collection took place. Visitors were invited to complete the instrument at the lunch table, immediately before departure, and the refusal rate was estimated to be less than 5%. A total of 243 surveys were therefore returned for analysis, though partial completion was a notable feature of the response pattern. Part of this phenomenon may have resulted from an acknowledged complexity in the instrument itself, though part was clearly due to the completion of a survey within an extremely convivial and social environment–more than one respondent noted that it would be a "good idea to ask people to complete this *before* the wine tasting!"

Though the data collected are argued to be representative of the overall pattern of visitation over the two weekends, it is important to note that the time period in question is undoubtedly classifiable as 'mid-winter'–as a result, there may well be a significant potential for respondent bias that limits the generalisability of results to a summer visitor market. In view of this bias potential, and the somewhat erratic completion statistics referred to above, each of the following result categories is accompanied by an indication of the number of respondents who contributed to the data presented.

Data were initially analyzed through calculation of basic descriptive statistics for each of the 46 variables, before two separate principal components analyses (PCA) were conducted across responses to the nine LOV items and the twelve quality evaluation items. PCA was used with the LOV items to verify the existence of three distinctive value based lifestyles as posited by Kennedy et al. (1988), and was used with the quality evaluation items in order to replicate the methods used by O'Neill et al. (2002) in their West Australian wine tourism research. In keeping with the suggestions of Mitchell (1994), a varimax rotation was used in the interests of isolating a smaller set of predictor variables for use in subsequent correlational analysis. Factors with an eigenvalue greater than 1.00 were retained, and were then incorporated, alongside a range of single variables taken from the survey instrument, into the comparative matrix shown in Table 4.

RESULTS

The visitors who completed the survey display a demographic pattern that is clearly distinguishable from that of the general population of New Zealand. As Table 5 shows, respondents are predominantly female of an older generation, are well educated, share their residence with a partner and (often) their children, and enjoy a household income that comfortably exceeds the New Zealand average of $56,212 (Statistics New Zealand Internet website).

The majority of visitors are essentially local people, with 11% of respondents originating from the immediate vicinity of the winery, 21% from the surrounding Rodney district, and 55% from Auckland city and suburbs–the bias towards central and north Auckland is indicative of a higher socio-economic status for those districts and of their comparative ease of access to Matakana.

For many, a permanent residence or holiday home in Rodney district was an obvious reason for them being in the area at the time, with 'a day out in the countryside' and 'visiting friends and relatives' the other key contributors. In contrast, winery visit motivations were mostly attributable to either a previous experience of visiting that winery or to the recommendation of a friend. Details of visit motivation, and subsequent behaviours, are contained in Table 6.

Respondents had travelled in a wide variety of party sizes, but more than three-quarters were with a party of four or fewer–for more than 80% of their number, the survey site winery was to be the only one visited in the course of the day. They typically spent between $26 and $75 during their visit (mean spending was $67), though 10% of visitors spent nothing at all–this could perhaps be attributable to those who had their costs paid by a travelling companion, and who had responded literally to the question "how much did *you* spend?"

TABLE 4. Comparative Rating Model

Demographic Variables	Intervening LOV Factors	Intervening Quality Factors	Dependent Variables
Gender Residence Age Group Education Occupation Income	F1 Achievers F2 Funlovers	F1 Cafe Factor F2 Winery Factor	Overall spending Intention to return Intention to recommend Overall rating

TABLE 5. Demographic Data

Variable	Options	Count	Proportion
Gender (n = 233)	Male	98	0.42
	Female	135	0.58
Age Group (n = 233)	0-19	2	0.01
	20-29	29	0.12
	30-39	62	0.27
	40-49	48	0.21
	50-59	58	0.25
	60+	34	0.14
Education (n = 231)	Bachelor degree	62	0.27
	Postgraduate	56	0.24
	Some university	43	0.19
	Trade qualifications	35	0.15
	Secondary school	35	0.15
Family Status (n = 234)	Partner, no children at home	121	0.52
	Partner and children	63	0.27
	Single, no children at home	44	0.19
	Single with children	6	0.02
Employment (n = 233)	Administrative/services	82	0.35
	Self employed	69	0.30
	Home maker/retired/student	45	0.19
	Trade/technical	27	0.12
	Central/local government	10	0.04
Income (n = 207)	$60,000+	140	0.67
	$40,000-59,999	37	0.18
	$20,000-39,999	20	0.10
	$0-19,999	10	0.05
Residence (n = 233)	Central Auckland	57	0.25
	Rodney district	48	0.21
	East, West, South Auckland	40	0.17
	North Auckland	31	0.13
	Immediate vicinity	25	0.11
	Other NZ	18	0.08
	International	13	0.05

Given subsequent claims of wine knowledge level and purchase behaviours, a significantly higher average spend was recorded for the café as opposed to the wine shop (café average $45, wine shop average $31). From these statistics, it seems possible that many visitors will have called at the winery primarily for lunch rather than for wine tasting, and taken away one or perhaps two bottles of wine at the conclusion of their visit. This analysis is supported by the data presented in Table 7.

Table 7 suggests that many respondents are enthusiastic and frequent wine purchasers, though their wine is bought for drinking rather than cellaring–nearly 80% of respondents buy wine at least monthly, yet half of their number have less than 12 bottles in stock at home. The 'buy to drink now' interpretation is supported by examination of the sources from which respondents acquire their stocks, with 80% of buyers acknowledging the supermarket as a significant option–frequent cellar

TABLE 6. Visitor Behaviour Patterns

Variable	Options	Count	Proportion
Why visit Rodney? (n = 243)	Resident here	77	0.32
	Day out in country	73	0.30
	Visiting friends and relatives	37	0.15
	En route to elsewhere	19	0.08
	Wine tasting and/or purchase	13	0.05
	Other	24	0.10
Why visit this winery? (n = 243)	Past experience with the winery	94	0.39
	Recommendation of a friend	71	0.29
	Recommendation–other media	23	0.09
	Followed road signage	17	0.07
	Other	38	0.16
Size of travelling party (n = 232)	One	6	0.02
	Two	90	0.39
	Three	37	0.16
	Four	47	0.20
	Five/Six	34	0.15
	Seven or more	18	0.08
Number of wineries to be visited (n = 195)	One	161	0.81
	Two	15	0.08
	Three	13	0.07
	Four or more	6	0.04
Total winery spend (n = 213)	Nil	21	0.10
	$1-25	16	0.07
	$26-75	109	0.52
	$76-125	43	0.20
	$126-175	16	0.07
	$176 or more	8	0.04
	Average spend	$67	
Wine spend (n = 182)	Nil	55	0.30
	$1-25	29	0.16
	$26-75	88	0.49
	$76-125	6	0.03
	$126-175	2	0.01
	$176 or more	2	0.01
	Average spend	$31	
Café spend (n = 193)	Nil	48	0.25
	$ 1-25	18	0.09
	$ 26-75	93	0.48
	$ 76-125	26	0.13
	$ 126-175	3	0.02
	$ 176 or more	5	0.03
	Average spend	$45	

TABLE 7. Wine Consumption Behaviours and Other Leisure Pursuits

Variable	Options	Count	Proportion
Number of wine purchase occasions (n = 242)	Once a month or more 7-12 times annually 2-6 times annually Once a year	192 22 21 7	0.79 0.09 0.09 0.03
Bottles of wine in cellar (n = 213)	Less than 12 12-36 37-96 97 and more	107 42 30 34	0.50 0.20 0.14 0.16
Source of purchases (n = 242)	Supermarkets Cellar door Liquor stores Specialty wine shops Wine clubs	194 140 128 116 48	0.80 0.58 0.53 0.48 0.20
Number of cellar door visits annually (n = 236)	One Two/Three Four-Six Seven or more	40 83 45 68	0.17 0.35 0.19 0.29
Claimed level of wine knowledge (n = 240)	Intermediate Basic Expert None	105 101 21 13	0.44 0.42 0.08 0.06
Leisure interests (n = 230)	Wining, dining, entertaining Participation sport Walking, tramping, hiking Fishing, sailing, marine leisure Reading, indoor games Travel	96 70 63 63 61 42	0.42 0.30 0.27 0.27 0.26 0.18
Preferred print media topics (n = 242)	Wining, dining, entertaining Home and garden Quality women's magazines Populist women's magazines Business and trade journals TV and entertainment News magazines (NZ published)	66 57 24 22 22 21 21	0.27 0.23 0.10 0.09 0.09 0.09 0.09
Preferred television (n = 184)	TV One Prime TV TV3 TV Two Other/none	82 36 31 25 10	0.44 0.20 0.17 0.14 0.05

door visits, liquor merchants, and specialty wine retailers are also important sources.

Respondents are cautious in their self-evaluations of wine expertise, with just 6% claiming to be advanced or expert. A further 86% claim some knowledge, at a basic or intermediate level, and there is evidence of a well-established wining and dining culture outside of the basic wine purchase patterns. Eating, drinking and entertaining are the key elements in terms of both leisure time activities and preferred print media, and the related topic of 'home and garden' also features strongly in the preferred media category—other leisure activities cover a broad range of popular New Zealand pastimes, including sport participation (golf is a major activity), walking and hiking, and a whole range of water-based activities. Finally, a clear preference for TV One is indicative of a segment who would prefer BBC-TV in Britain or PBS in the USA—in the absence of any publicly funded and commercial-free channel in New Zealand, TV One is recognized as the preferred 'information and education' (as opposed to 'entertainment') option.

Scores for each of the LOV items reveal some suggestion of an 'end-loading' effect in that respondents appear to have accorded high value to each of the items—when all scores can be incorporated within a bracket between 3.84 and 4.51 on a 1-5 scale, it seems likely that any information of value to be obtained from such a distribution will be limited at best. However, a different pattern emerges when respondent's 'two most influential' values are taken into account. Table 8 clearly shows that the 'belonger' value system is poorly represented amongst respondent attitudes, and that the dominant values are those related to the 'funlover' and 'achiever' segments.

The 'end-loading' phenomenon was equally noticeable amongst ratings of service quality elements. Here, all twelve mean ratings fell within a range between 3.89 and 4.47, with the highest scores being awarded to winery cleanliness, staff friendliness and welcoming environment; at the lower end of the scale, wine value and quality, range of

TABLE 8. The LOV Variables

Variable	Value System Category	Influential (Count)	Influential (Proportion)	Mean Rating
Warm relationships with others (n = 201)	Funlovers	79	0.39	4.48
Sense of accomplishment (n = 193)	Achievers	69	0.36	4.44
Fun and enjoyment in life (n = 197)	Funlovers	60	0.30	4.51
Feeling of self-fulfilment (n = 194)	Achievers	41	0.21	4.37
Self-respect and self-esteem (n = 196)	Achievers	40	0.20	4.45
Excitement in things to do (n = 194)	Funlovers	20	0.10	4.14
A sense of belonging (n = 193)	Belongers	16	0.08	3.84
Safety and security (n = 193)	Belongers	13	0.07	4.17
Being well respected by others (n = 195)	Belongers	12	0.06	4.03

wines available, and wine presentation standards were rated appreciably lower. The overall quality ratings of the winery experience were uniformly high, at a mean of 8.31 on a ten-point scale, and this was supported by a mean 'intention to return' of 8.35 and a mean 'intention to recommend' of 8.60. Table 9 summarizes these findings.

Both PCA procedures yielded a two-factor solution, explaining 54-55% of total variation (see Table 10). Though this result is appreciably below the 70% of total variation identified as acceptable by Aaker et al. (2001), it is in line with the 51% of total variation explained by O'Neill et al.'s (2002) study.

Examination of responses to the LOV questions revealed that five elements loaded onto a factor that appeared best described by the 'achiever' terminology proposed by the original authors, whilst three elements were clearly associated with a factor that was subsequently labelled 'funlover.' The LOV element 'warm relationships with others' did not load significantly on either factor. Therefore, though caution needs to be exercised in view of the low proportion of total variation explained, these results were believed to tentatively suggest that two out of the three LOV lifestyles were considerably better represented amongst winery visitors than the remaining 'belonger' category. Given the assigned importance of lifestyle segmentation within the context of this research, this tentative finding is further evaluated in the discussion section.

Similarly, in terms of quality evaluations, five elements loaded onto a factor that appeared to include aspects of food, cleanliness, and friendly

TABLE 9. The Quality Evaluations

Variable	Likert Rating
Winery cleanliness (n = 190)	4.47
Staff friendliness, helpfulness (n = 201)	4.43
Welcoming environment at winery (n = 209)	4.36
Food quality (n = 187)	4.26
Winery layout and décor (n = 218)	4.26
Staff wine knowledge (n = 111)	4.16
The wine tasting process (n = 104)	4.14
Food value (n = 183)	4.05
Wine value (n = 141)	3.96
Wine quality (n = 140)	3.95
Range of available wines (n = 127)	3.93
Wine presentation standards (n = 193)	3.89
Overall quality rating (n = 201)	8.31
Intention to return (n = 201)	8.35
Intention to recommend (n = 201)	8.60

TABLE 10. Factor Analysis Results

The LOV Factors			The Quality Factors		
Variable	F1 Achiever	F2 Funlover	Variable	F1 The Café Factor	F2 The Winery Factor
Sense of accomplishment	.798		Food quality	.794	
Sense of belonging	.684		Food value	.727	
Feeling of self-fulfilment	.670		Welcoming environment	.725	
Being well respected by others	.606		Winery cleanliness	.713	
Self-respect and self-esteem	.602		Friendly helpful staff	.695	
Fun & enjoyment in life		.884	Range of wines		.824
Excitement in things to do		.751	Wine tasting process		.738
Safety & Security		.562	Staff wine knowledge		.704
			Wine value		.683
			Wine quality		.680
Eigenvalue	2.672	2.188	Eigenvalue	3.419	3.231
Variance explained	29.69%	24.30%	Variance explained	28.49%	26.93%
KMO Test (Sampling Adequacy)	.818		KMO Test (Sampling Adequacy)	.854	

welcome, and was therefore named the 'café factor'; and five elements were similarly related to wine tasting processes, staff wine knowledge, wine range, quality and value–this second factor was therefore labelled the 'winery factor.' Variables related to the visual appeal of the winery, and the manner in which wine was presented for sale, did not load significantly on either factor. The important implication here is the potential existence of café visitation as a core visitor motivation, in contrast to the *a priori* assumption of wine products as the central drawcard.

DISCUSSION

The objectives of the research described in this paper were earlier expressed as a portfolio of key questions, and it is appropriate to frame the discussion that follows in the light of the issues raised by those questions.

Visitor Demographics

Much of the previous wine tourism research has identified the winery visitor as an older, wealthier and better educated individual, and the results obtained from this project were mostly supportive of that view. Though the gender mix was skewed towards female visitation, other findings were much as expected–nearly three quarters of visitors were aged between 30 and 60 years, more than half held a university degree, and two-thirds of all responses indicate a household income of more than $ 60,000 per annum. Findings therefore tend to confirm the perception of wine tourism as a relatively 'high-end' pursuit, and there are associated implications here for participants in terms of the need to maintain quality and value in their product and service offering.

A series of correlation coefficients had earlier been calculated to establish the nature and extent of relationships between the demographic variables, intervening LOV and quality factors, and dependent variables shown in Table 4. Though few noteworthy results emerged from this exercise, there was a negative relationship between gender and both the 'achievers' factor (–0.20) and the 'winery' factor (–0.20). Though the strength of this relationship can be appropriately described as no more than 'low-to-definite' (Malhotra et al., 1996), there is at least some suggestion that the 'achiever' group was slightly more likely to be female and to view their experience as primarily a winery visit. It may therefore prove profitable for proprietors to vary the style of their tasting processes to accommodate these characteristics, perhaps by ensuring that the product range is expanded to incorporate partner merchandising of wine accessories, coffee-table books, and condiments such as olive oil and spices.

One interesting result was the identification of a substantial local market, in the form of the one-third of all respondents who lived either in the immediate vicinity or in other parts of Rodney district–interesting, as these people are (strictly speaking) disqualified as wine tourists because of their local resident status and are therefore representative of a quite separate visitor segment with presumably separate needs and motivations. Though the authors know of no literature that seeks to differentiate local market segments from their more distantly resident counterparts, and though no significant attitudinal differences were uncovered by the current research, it seems reasonable to suggest that further research into the behaviours of locally resident visitors may prove valuable for participating wineries.

Visitor Motivations and Behaviours

If we discount Rodney district residents, the primary purpose of travel was "a day out in the countryside," with just 5% of respondents claiming a winery visit as the prime reason for their presence. This categorization of winery visitation, as an incidental rather than a primary motivation, is supportive of much of the foundation literature–it seems that people visit a winery because they are already in Rodney (rather than visit Rodney because of its wineries), and this primacy of region over attraction is something that wine tourism operators should be well aware of.

As a parallel observation, it was especially interesting to note the claimed spending practices of visitors, with significantly greater amounts of money being spent in the café or restaurant than in the wine tasting area. We therefore believe it essential for each participating winery to develop a clear idea of how their business is perceived by visitors–future advertising strategies might then be more profitably directed towards promotion of the destination, rather than promotion of the winery, on the expectation that once in the area the visitors will naturally gravitate towards a winery with a café attached, or a café with some grapevines out back, dependent on their perceptions.

The other significant factor for operators is the high proportion (two-thirds) of visitors who had visited the winery as either a repeat customer or as a result of a friend's recommendation. These figures are encouraging, and suggest the existence of a sound core product that is for the most part successful in attracting and retaining customers. Identification of a sound repeat purchase pattern is both an encouraging strength and an enticing opportunity, and wineries would do well to develop and maintain an accurate database of repeat clientele who would be favored with preferential treatment in terms of product availability and pricing.

Wine Purchase, Consumption and Other Leisure Activities

Winery visitors buy a lot of wine–from the cellar door, from supermarkets, from liquor merchants and from wine stores–and it appears that 'frequently, in small quantities' is the typical pattern. In a circumstance where nearly 80% of respondents buy wine at least once monthly, but 50% have less than one dozen bottles currently in their home cellar, the winery's premium product (that which is recommended for medium-to-long term cellaring) may not necessarily be appreciated by cellar door visitors. In order to reach the 92% of visitors who do not regard themselves as experts, there may be greater value in promoting the ready drinkability of basic labels, wine for drinking rather than cellaring, and this is a conceptualization of wine (as a fun beverage) that is strongly supported in later stages of this discussion.

Evaluation of respondent answers to the 'leisure pursuits' questions serves to augment our increasingly well-defined view of target market characteristics. More than 40% of respondents cited wining, dining and entertainment as a preferred activity, and more than half subscribe to either home entertaining or home and garden type magazines. The market segment descriptor is completed through the presence of 'healthy outdoor pursuits' as a common leisure activity, with strong support for participant sport, walking and tramping, and marine related activities like fishing and boating. It was this 'fun-loving, outdoors' classification that emerged within one of the two main value systems identified by LOV analysis.

Evaluations and Future Purchase Intentions

Two clearly discrete factors emerged from the battery of quality evaluation items. Here, it is firstly important to note the high standard of achievement across all criteria, with eight out of twelve mean values exceeding four on a five-point scale. Highest ratings were awarded to what might be termed 'ambience' variables—winery cleanliness, staff friendliness and helpfulness, and welcoming environment; whilst it was intriguing to note that it was the theoretical core product—wine value, wine quality, range of wines available, and presentation standards—that brought up the rear.

This distribution of opinion would suggest that those who perceived the site as a café with vineyard attached were more likely to be satisfied with their experience than those who thought they were visiting a vineyard with an associated eatery. Indeed, the correlation coefficients referred to earlier provides some support for this prediction, as there was a low-to-definite correlation between the café factor and 'intention to recommend' (0.28), and the cafe factor and 'intention to return' (0.28). More significantly, there was a moderate-to-substantial (Malhotra et al., 1996) correlation between the café factor and the 'overall quality rating' variable (0.48). In the context of a generally inconclusive series of correlations, these three relationships stood out as the most significant—the visitors who were motivated by the café environment were more likely to award high summary evaluations than those who were motivated by the core wine product. From the point of view of the participating winery, this discrepancy can either be seen as a threat to be combated or an opportunity to be exploited–in either case, it reinforces our previous comment that winery proprietors need to ensure they are fully aware of why their customers choose visit, and what it is that drives them to do so. Only then can the winery take appropriate steps to meet the customer needs that these comments imply.

Demographics, Lifestyles, and Perceptions of Service Quality

So, is there any meaningful relationship between visitor demographics and lifestyles on the one hand, and perceptions of service quality on the other? Does categorizing visitors according to their underlying lifestyle characteristics provide wineries with any assistance in designing their product offering and service delivery methods? Our answer to these questions appears to be a cautious "maybe," based firstly on the existence of a visitor demographic pattern that was identifiably similar to that observed by researchers such as Dodd (1995), Morris and King (1998), and O'Neill and Charters (2000). In each of these studies, the visitors surveyed were extremely enthusiastic about their vineyard experience, and it seems that there may be a well-established affinity between the wealthy middle aged demographic and the type of recreational experience offered by wine tourism.

Given this consistency of demographic description, principal components analysis of the LOV items adds a further dimension to the gradual picture that is being built up of the winery visitor. According to Kamakura and Novak (1992), the 'achiever' lifestyle is associated with a need to display competence, success and socially desirable behaviours– these are the labelled clothing buyers and conspicuous consumers of fashionable brands, people whose behaviour patterns are driven by a need to demonstrate their significant portfolio of achievement to the world. The current research confirms Kamakura and Novak's (1992) findings, in that 'achievers' are attracted by healthy living pursuits, sophisticated entertaining, quality magazines and informative television.

The 'funlover' lifestyle is portrayed as one which values social interaction, hedonistic enjoyment, often with a hint of risk implied. Its adherents are often younger, somewhat obsessed with self as opposed to the welfare of others, and (as a result?) has appreciable lower income levels than the 'achiever' group. Their focus is on short-term entertainment, experienced out of the home, and their leisure pursuits will often be characterized by energetic participation as opposed to passive immersion. Finally, their choice of reading material is likely to tend towards daily newspapers, rather than monthly magazines, and their television of choice will lean heavily towards comedy, game shows and light entertainment (Kamakura & Novak, 1992).

Coupled with a well defined demographic and a duality of lifestyles, the picture is completed by the existence of two distinct patterns of motivation amongst visitors. Though the characteristics of any one lifestyle could not be conclusively related to any specific quality assessment pattern, it is anecdotally attractive to visualize the wine-motivated visitors as confident, intelligent, articulate, and experienced 'achievers' who appreciate their winery visit as an entertainment as opposed to a retail purchase. If this is the case, it would seem sensible for wineries to ensure that their staff experience and qualifications are maintained at a high level, that ongoing attention is given to the maintenance of a friendly and welcoming environment, and that the introduction of customer retention schemes (such as formal wine tastings and loyalty programmes) are carefully considered.

On the other hand, it is equally attractive to conceptualize the café-motivated visitors as a younger and rather less affluent segment, though equally intelligent and articulate. Here the café-winery visit is more likely to be seen as a fun time to be shared with friends, a time in which the consumption of food is a necessary complement to conversation and informal entertainment, and a time in which the provision of wine plays a secondary role only. These visitors may be more attracted by a modern and trendy décor, a young and enthusiastic waiting staff, and the provision of lively entertainment to accompany the meal. It should be abundantly clear that any individual winery needs to know its customer lifestyles well, for 'getting it wrong,' in terms of service design, could create some serious difficulties.

Though suggestions like these, clearly focussing on the second rather than the first word in 'wine tourism,' may seem rather depressing to the traditional winemaker, they are supported by the comparatively weaker quality ratings awarded for the 'wine' variables. Though respondents remained generally favorable to the wine products on offer, it is fair to say that wine presentation, taste, and perceived value were by no means a highlight of their visit–in this context, the very satisfactory dependent variable ratings, for overall quality, intention to return, and intention to recommend, suggest that the wine elements are of lesser significance in determining overall satisfaction levels than are the supporting elements of ambience, food, and customer service.

Thus, we were able to observe a well-defined demographic that was guided by two primary value categories, that had fully expected to enjoy its winery experience, and that had essentially been satisfied with what it received. Though there were few significant within-group differences, there is some suggestion that female visitors may be significantly more numerous, slightly more achievement oriented, and (through their generally lower reported incomes) more likely to rate the experience highly. For the participating winery, there may therefore be some potential for marketing the wine tourism experience to female business people, and it may be profitable to consider the extent to which the cellar door site is designed with this type of visitor in mind.

Perhaps the single most important contribution to be highlighted here is the suggestion that lifestyle categorization does in fact have some influence over whether an individual is likely to be enthusiastic about wine tourism participation; and the consequent implication that a service provider's knowledge of the customer can be greatly expanded through recognition of the lifestyle category he or she is dealing with. A significant segment of the population, the careful and conservative 'belonger' category, is notably under-represented amongst winery visitors, and the products and services that have been traditionally associated with this segment are therefore unlikely to prove successful for wine tourism participants. In contrast, the needs and motivations of both the 'achiever' and the 'funlover' lifestyles have been well documented–thus, the fundamental marketing equation of 'find out what the customer wants and give it to them' is halfway complete.

CONCLUSIONS

The research described in this paper has sought to investigate the relationships between wine tourism, lifestyle market segmentation, and service quality evaluations. Acknowledging some important study limitations, introduced through the conduct of research in just one region and in an off-season climate, the authors offer the following tentative conclusions:

- Winery visitors are well-educated professional people with a well-developed set of expectations in terms of the quality of the wine tourism experience.
- Winery visitors can be categorized, through the application of lifestyle segmentation, as representative of the 'achiever' and 'funlover' LOV segments.

- Winery visitors can be categorized, through the application of motivational segmentation, as seekers after a wine experience, or seekers after a café-based package of benefits.
- The overall entertainment experience is at least as important to visitors as the tasting and purchase of wine, and visitors spend more money on non-wine products than they do on wine purchases.
- Winery proprietors need to be aware of the underlying lifestyle elements that determine the behavior of their own wine tourism customers.

It would be interesting to replicate this research through the design of a larger scale exercise, in other regions of New Zealand and in other countries, in order to eliminate the spatial and temporal limitations referred to earlier and to search for complementary and contradictory aspects of the findings reported here–though many of our findings are supportive of previous work done in New Zealand and in other New World countries, the small scale of this and previous surveys makes it impossible to offer definitive conclusions. However, as our knowledge of the wine tourism phenomenon builds, we suggest that the focus of attention for smaller wineries may well shift from a 'wine' orientation to a 'tourism' orientation–at that point, the existence of a reliable and informative guide to winery visitor behaviours will have become an industrial necessity rather than just a sociological curiosity.

REFERENCES

Aaker, D.A., Kumar, V. and Day, G.S. (2001). *Marketing Research* (7th edition). New York: John Wiley & Sons.

Ali-Knight, J. and Charters, S. (2001). The winery as educator: Do wineries provide what the tourist needs? *Australian and New Zealand Wine Industry Journal*, 16(6), 79-86.

Augustyn, M.M. (1998). The road to quality enhancement in tourism. *International Journal of Contemporary Hospitality Management*, 10(4), 145-158.

Babakus, E. and Boller, G.W. (1992). An empirical assessment of the SERVQUAL scale. *Journal of Business Research*, 24(3), 253-268.

Beverland, M., James, K., James, M., Porter, C. and Stace, G. (1998). Wine-tourists–a missed opportunity or a misplaced priority? In Kandampully, J. (ed.). Proceedings, New Zealand Tourism and Hospitality Research Conference, Advances in Research (Part 1), Akaroa 1-4 December.

Buttle, F. (1996). SERVQUAL: Review, critique, research agenda. *European Journal of Marketing*, 30(1), 8-32.

Charters, S. and O'Neill, M. (2000). Delighting the customer–how good is the cellar door experience? *Australian and New Zealand Wine Industry Journal*, 15(4), 11-16.

Cohen, E. (1972). Towards a sociology of international tourism. *Social Research*, 39(1), 169-184.

Cronin, J.J. and Taylor, S.A. (1992). Measuring service quality: A re-examination and extension. *Journal of Marketing*, 56(3), 55-68.

Cronin, J.J. and Taylor, S.A. (1994). SERVPERF versus SERVQUAL: Reconciling performance-based and perceptions-minus-expectations measurement of service quality. *Journal of Marketing*, 58, 125-131.

Davis, D., Allen, J. and Cosenza, R.M. (1988). Segmenting local residents by their attitudes, interests and opinions towards tourism. *Journal of Travel Research*, 27(2), 2-8.

Dodd, T. (1995). Opportunities and pitfalls of tourism in a developing wine industry. *International Journal of Wine Marketing*, 7(1), 5-16.

Dodd, T. and Bigotte, V. (1997). Perceptual differences among visitor groups to wineries. *Journal of Travel Research*, 35(3), 46-51.

Fick, G.R. and Ritchie, J.R.B. (1991). Measuring service quality in the travel and tourism industry. *Journal of Travel Research*, 30(2), 2-9.

Greenwell, T.C., Fink, J.S. and Pastore, D.L. (2002). Perceptions of the service experience: Using demographic and psychographic variables to identify customer segments. *Sport Marketing Quarterly*, 11(4), 233-241.

Hall, C.M., Cambourne, B., Macionis, N. and Johnson, G. (1997). Wine tourism and network development in Australia and New Zealand: Review, establishment and prospects. *International Journal of Wine Marketing*, 9(2-3), 5-31.

Hall, C.M. and Johnson, G. (1998). Wine and tourism: An imbalanced partnership? In Dowling, R. and Carlsen, J. (eds). Proceedings: Wine tourism–perfect partners. 1st Australian wine tourism conference. Margaret River, Western Australia, May.

Hall, C.M., Longo, A.M., Mitchell, R. and Johnson, G. (2000). Wine tourism in New Zealand. In Hall, C.M., Sharples, L., Cambourne, B. and Macionis, N. (eds.). *Wine tourism around the world: Development, management, and markets*. Oxford: Butterworth-Heinemann.

Hall, C.M. and Macionis, N. (1998). Wine tourism in Australia and New Zealand. In Butler, R.W., Hall, C.M. and Jenkins, J.M. (eds.) *Tourism and Recreation in Rural Areas*. Chichester: John Wiley and Sons.

Hall, C.M. and Mitchell, R. (2000). Wine tourism in the Mediterranean: A tool for restructuring and development. *Thunderbird International Business Review*, 42(4), 445-465.

Hall, J. and Winchester, M. (1999). An empirical confirmation of segments in the Australian wine market. *International Journal of Wine Marketing*, 11(1), 19-35.

Hudson, S. and Shephard, G.W.H. (1998). Measuring service quality at tourist destinations: An application of importance-performance analysis to an alpine ski resort. *Journal of Travel and Tourism Marketing*, 7(3), 61-77.

Johns, N. (1993). Quality management in the hospitality industry, part 3: Recent developments. *International Journal of Contemporary Hospitality Management*, 5(1), 10-15.

Kahle, L.R. (1983). *Social Values and Social Change: Adaptation to Life in America.* New York: Praeger.

Kahle, L.R., Beatty, S.E. and Homer, P. (1986). Alternative measurement approaches to consumer values: The List of Values (LOV) and Values and Life Style (VALS). *Journal of Consumer Research*, 13, 405-409.

Kahle, L.R, and Kennedy, P. (1989). Using the List of Values (LOV) to understand consumers. *Journal of Consumer Marketing*, 6(3), 5-12.

Kamakura, W.A. and Novak, T.P. (1992). Value-system segmentation: Exploring the meaning of LOV. *Journal of Consumer Research*, 19, 119-132.

Kennedy, P.F., Best, R.J. and Kahle, L.R. (1988). An alternative method for measuring value-based segmentation and advertisement positioning. *Current Issues and Research in Marketing*, 11, 139-155.

King, C. and Morris, R. (1998). Wine tourism: Costs and returns. In Dowling, R. and Carlsen, J. (eds). Proceedings: Wine tourism–perfect partners. 1st Australian wine tourism conference. Margaret River, Western Australia, May.

Kotler, P. (1994). *Marketing Management: Analysis, Planning, Implementation and Control* (8th edition). Englewood Cliffs: Prentice Hall.

Macionis, N. and Cambourne, B. (1998). Wine tourism: Just what is it all about? *The Australian and New Zealand Wine Industry Journal*, 13(1), 41-47.

Madrigal, R. (1995). Personal values, traveller personality type, and leisure travel style. *Journal of Leisure Research*, 27(2), 125-142.

Madrigal, R. and Kahle, L.R. (1994). Predicting vacation activity preferences on the basis of value-system segmentation. *Journal of Travel Research*, 32(3), 22-28.

Malhotra, N., Hall, J., Shaw, M., and Crisp, M. (1996). *Marketing Research: An Applied Orientation.* Sydney: Prentice Hall.

Martilla, J. and James, J. (1977) Importance-performance analysis. *Journal of Marketing*, 41, 77-79.

Matakana Coast Internet Website. *http://www.matakanacoast.com*, accessed 4 June 2003.

Mei, A.W.O., Dean, A.M. and White, C.J. (1999). Analyzing service quality in the hospitality industry. *Managing Service Quality*, 9(2), 136-143.

Middleton, V.T.C. (1997). *Marketing in Travel and Tourism* (2nd edition). Oxford: Butterworth Heinemann.

Mitchell, A. (1983). *The Nine American Life Styles.* New York: Warner.

Mitchell, R. (2002). The generation game: Generation X and baby boomer wine tourism. In Croy, W.G. (ed.). Proceedings, New Zealand Tourism and Hospitality Research Conference, Rotorua, 3-5 December.

Mitchell, R., Hall, C.M. and McIntosh, A. (2000). Wine tourism and consumer behaviour. In Hall, C.M., Sharples, L., Cambourne, B. and Macionis, N. (eds.). *Wine Tourism Around the World: Development, Management, and Markets.* Oxford: Butterworth-Heinemann.

Mitchell, V-W. (1994). How to identify psychographic segments: Part 1. *Marketing Intelligence and Planning*, 12(7), 4-10.

Morris, R. and King, C. (1998). Delighting the wine tourist. In Dowling, R. and Carlsen, J. (eds). Proceedings: Wine tourism–perfect partners. 1st Australian wine tourism conference. Margaret River, Western Australia, May.

Muller, T. E. (1991). Using personal values to define segments in an international tourism market. *International Marketing Review*, 8(1), 57-70.

Novak, T.P. and MacEvoy, B. (1990). On comparing alternative segmentation schemes: The List of Values (LOV) and Values and Life Styles (VALS). *Journal of Consumer Research*, 17, 105-109.

O'Neill, M. and Charters, S. (2000). Service quality at the cellar door: Implications for Western Australia's developing wine tourism industry. *Managing Service Quality*, 10(2), 112-122.

O'Neill, M., Palmer, A. and Charters, S. (2002). Wine production as a service experience–the effects of service quality on wine sales. *Journal of Services Marketing*, 16(4), 342-362.

Parasuraman, A., Zeithaml, V. and Berry, L. (1985). A conceptual model of service quality and its implications for future research. *Journal of Marketing*, 49(4), 41-50.

Parasuraman, A., Zeithaml, V.A. and Berry, L.L. (1988). SERVQUAL: A multiple-item scale for measuring customer perceptions of service quality. *Journal of Retailing*, 64(1), 12-40.

Parasuraman, A., Berry, L.L., and Zeithaml, V.A. (1991). Refinement and reassessment of the SERVQUAL scale. *Journal of Retailing*, 67(4), 420-450.

Parasuraman, A., Berry, L.L., and Zeithaml, V.A. (1993). More on improving service quality measurement. *Journal of Retailing*, 69(1), 140-147.

Pearce, P.L., Morrison, A.M. and Rutledge, J.L. (1998). *Tourism: Bridges across continents*. Sydney: McGraw-Hill.

Plog, S. (1974). Why destinations rise and fall in popularity. *The Cornell Hotel and Restaurant Administration Quarterly,* 14(4), 55-58.

Plog, S.C. (1994). Developing and using psychographics in tourism research. In Ritchie, J.R.B. and Goeldner, C.R. (eds.) *Travel, tourism and hospitality research: A handbook for managers and researchers* (2nd edition). New York: Wiley.

Ravenscroft, N. and van Westering, J. (2001). Wine tourism, culture and the everyday: A theoretical note. *Tourism and Hospitality Research*, 3(2), 149-162.

Robinson, S. (1999). Measuring service quality: Current thinking and future requirements. *Marketing Intelligence and Planning*, 17(1), 21-32.

Rokeach, M. (1973). *The Nature of Human Values*. New York: Free Press.

Ryan, C. (1995). *Researching Tourist Satisfaction: Issues, Concepts, Problems*. London: Routledge.

Ryan, C. and Cliff, A. (1997). Do travel agencies measure up to customer expectations? An empirical investigation of travel agencies' service quality as measured by SERVQUAL. *Journal of Travel and Tourism Marketing*, 6(2), 1-28.

Saleh, F. and Ryan, C. (1991). Analyzing service quality in the hospitality industry using the SERVQUAL model. *Service Industries Journal*, 11(3), 324-343.

Silverberg, K.E., Backman, S.J. and Backman, K.F. (1996). A preliminary investigation into the psychographics of nature-based travellers to the South-Eastern United States. *Journal of Travel Research*, 35(2), 19-28.

Smith, V. (ed.) (1977). *Hosts and Guests*. Philadelphia: University of Pennsylvania Press.

Statistics New Zealand Internet Website. *http://www.stats.govt.nz*, accessed 26 July, 2003.

Teas, R.K. (1993). Expectations, performance evaluation, and consumers' perceptions of quality. *Journal of Marketing*, 57(4), 18-34.

Todd, S., Lawson, R. and Faris, F. (1998). A lifestyle analysis of New Zealand consumers. *Asia Pacific Journal of Marketing and Logistics*, 10(3), 30-47.

Treloar, P. (2002). An investigation into the significance of relationship marketing on the young winery tourist. In Croy, W.G. (ed.). Proceedings, New Zealand Tourism and Hospitality Research Conference, Rotorua, 3-5 December.

Tull, D.S. and Hawkins, D.I. (1987). *Marketing Research* (4th edition). New York: Macmillan.

Verburg, P. (1999). Bring a corkscrew. *Canadian Business*, 72(16), 54-57.

Wineries of Matakana Internet Website. *http://www.matakanawine.com*, accessed 4 June 2003.

Delivering the Right Tourist Service
to the Right People–
A Comparison
of Segmentation Approaches

Sara Dolničar
Friedrich Leisch

SUMMARY. Market segmentation has developed to become a generally accepted and widely applied concept in strategic marketing. However, the gap between academic research aiming at increased sophistication of the methodology and managerial use has steadily increased. This paper takes the perspective of a destination manager and compares two segmentation approaches. One typically used in destination management (*a priori* geographical segmentation) and another one that is common in academic literature (*a posteriori* behavioural segmentation). The comparison emphasizes managerial usefulness (implying maximization of match between the tourists' vacation needs and the des-

Sara Dolničar is affiliated with the School of Management, Marketing, & Employment Relations, University of Wollongong, Wollongong, NWS 2522, Australia (E-mail: saraDolničar@uow.edu.au).

Friedrich Leisch is affiliated with the Department of Statistics and Probability Theory, Vienna University of Technology, Wiedner Hauptstrasse 8-10, 1040 Vienna, Austria (E-mail: friedrich.leisch@ci.tuwein.ac.at).

[Haworth co-indexing entry note]: "Delivering the Right Tourist Service to the Right People–A Comparison of Segmentation Approaches." Dolničar, Sara and Friedrich Leisch. Co-published simultaneously in *Journal of Quality Assurance in Hospitality & Tourism* (The Haworth Hospitality Press, an imprint of The Haworth Press, Inc.) Vol. 5, No. 2/3/4, 2004, pp. 189-207; and: *Hospitality, Tourism, and Lifestyle Concepts: Implications for Quality Management and Customer Satisfaction* (ed: Maree Tyne and Eric Laws) The Haworth Hospitality Press, an imprint of The Haworth Press, Inc., 2004, pp. 189-207. Single or multiple copies of this article are available for a fee from The Haworth Document Delivery Service [1-800-HAWORTH, 9:00 a.m. - 5:00 p.m. (EST). E-mail address: docdelivery@haworthpress.com].

tinations' offer) and is illustrated with an empirical guest survey data set for Austria. *[Article copies available for a fee from The Haworth Document Delivery Service: 1-800-HAWORTH. E-mail address: <docdelivery@haworthpress.com> Website: <http://www.HaworthPress.com> © 2004 by The Haworth Press, Inc. All rights reserved.]*

KEYWORDS. Market structure analysis, a priori market segmentation, a posteriori market segmentation, comparative analysis

INTRODUCTION

Due to the very nature of the tourism industry, the concept of market segmentation has been implemented since the early days of tourism promotions. Despite being a global industry, and developing to become more and more global each year, the budget for tourism promotion has to be spent in a concentrated manner to maximize the impact. It is therefore impossible to target all kinds of tourists from all countries in the world. Smaller groups that have something in common (market segments) have to be defined and addressed. Typically, national tourism organisations are responsible for the task of market segment selection (Heath and Wall, 1992; Morrison et al., 1995; Moutinho, Rita & Curry, 1996) and, typically, geographical segments are defined and worked with (Dolničar & Grabler, 2003; Mazanec, 1986a and b). In academic publications, however, more complex segmentation approaches based on multiple pieces of information about the tourist are propagated.

The aim of this article is to take the perspective of a destination manager in Austria and compare the managerial usefulness of a typical geographical segmentation with the usefulness of a segmentation that is based on vacation behaviour. For the purpose of comparison, both procedures are described, computed and interpreted. Managerial conclusions based on the results are drawn, and dangers and advantages of each of the two approaches are outlined. The significance of the comparison of procedures lies in the fact, that any organisation in the tourism industry has to choose which segment will be targeted. It is not possible to choose multiple segmentation solutions resulting from various approaches and simultaneously use them as strategic basis. The need to choose one segmentation solution makes the question of the most useful solution highly relevant. This article illustrates the two fundamental options thus providing guidance for management to follow the presented procedure in making this crucial strategic marketing decision.

MARKET SEGMENTATION IN TOURISM

The fundamental assumption underlying the concept of market segmentation is essentially a quality-driven concept: matching the touristic offer available at a particular destination with a market segment that is interested in precisely the characteristics this particular destination offers. This maximizes visitor satisfaction, which consequently will (1) increase attractiveness/utility of the product to the consumers in the segment, (2) increase sales, (3) strengthen the competitive position because the destination develops a strong specialized image position within the chosen target segment that can not be copied easily by competing destinations. The entire service quality from the information phase before the vacation to the minimization of an expectation–satisfaction gap is thus increased by consequent implementation of suitable market segmentation strategies. The concept of matching market demand and organisation/destination strengths is the fundamental idea of marketing (McDonald, 1984).

There are two different ways of determining segments: If destination management knows exactly which tourist characteristics are relevant for grouping visitors, the market can simply be split on the basis of these criteria. This approach is known as *a priori* (e.g., Mazanec, 2000) or commonsense (Dolničar, forthcoming) segmentation. It is implemented in four steps:

1. Splitting tourists into segments on the basis of characteristics known to be relevant. The relevance of characteristics depends on the purpose of the study and the context.
2. Testing whether resulting segments differ. This is typically done in tourism research by applying discriminant analysis to descriptive information (Dolničar, 2002) to determine with regard to which characteristics–other than the splitting criterion–the segments differ significantly.
3. Description of resulting segments in all available detail in order to be able to customize the entire strategic and operational marketing mix to best suit the needs of the target segment chosen.
4. Selection of the target segment best matching the destination strengths.

A few examples from published tourism research include the travel purpose (Kashyap & Bojanic, 2000) investigate differences between business and leisure tourists), age (Smith & MacKay, 2001), the level of intention to visit a destination (Court & Lupton, 1997).

If, however, destination management lacks prior knowledge of such kind, segments have to be determined first. Usually an empirical data set is the starting point. This approach is referred to as *a posteriori* (Mazanec, 2000), *post-hoc* (Wedel & Kamakura, 1998) or data-driven (Dolničar, forthcoming) segmentation. Data-driven segmentation requires six steps, the first three of which replace the first step in the *a priori* process:

1a. Selection of the segmentation base. The segmentation base is the block of questions from a survey that is used to find segments with similar answer patterns. Again, the relevance of the segmentation depends on the purpose of the study. Typical examples from tourism research include travel motivations (Formica & Uysal, 1998), benefits sought (Kastenholz, David & Paul, 1999) and travel behavior (Moscardo et al., 2000).

1b. Computation of groups which are as different from each other as possible while including maximally similar members.

1c. Splitting of tourists into segments on the basis of the partitioning process undertaken. The membership to the above groups is used as segmentation criterion.

2-4. see above

Typical examples from tourism research include travel motivations (Formica & Uysal, 1998), benefits sought (Kastenholz, David & Paul, 1999) and travel behavior (Moscardo et al., 2000).

A comprehensive study of data-driven segmentation studies in the area of tourism research was provided by Dolničar (2002) revealing a number of emerged standards in data-driven segmentation studies in tourism that undermine the quality of such studies. This includes unquestioned data-preprocessing, the use of inappropriate measures of association and clustering algorithms given the data format, computation of one single solution and thus ignorance of the exploratory nature of clustering techniques and use of too small sample sizes given the large numbers of variables chosen as segmentation base.

Austrian Destination Management

Austria has a very long tradition as a tourism destination and internationally ranks among the top tourist-receiving countries. Internally, the tourism industry makes a major contribution both to gross domestic product (7%) and to employment by directly or indirectly employing 14% of the Austrian workforce (Bundesministerium für Wirtschaft und Arbeit, Sektion Tourismus und Freizeitwirtschaft, www.bmwa.gv.at/ tourism, (last accessed on 6.10.2003).

The Austrian National Tourism Organisation (NTO) is located in the capital of Austria, Vienna. It was established in 1955 with the main goal of increasing the awareness of Austria as a tourist destination internationally as well as generating first time tourist visitors to Austria. Members of the organisation are the Republic of Austria, the nine provinces of Austria (see Figure 1) and the Austrian Chamber of Commerce.

The organisation was named "Österreich Werbung" in 1989. As a result of a major structural reform in 2001, the provinces withdrew from the association, which now consists of only two shareholders: the Republic of Austria (75%) and the Austrian Chamber of Commerce (25%). This information and further information about the Austrian NTO can be found at www.austria-tourism.at (last accessed on 6.10.2003).

The NTO is responsible for segment selection in Austria. An overview of responsibilities of NTOs and the specific responsibilities of the Austrian NTO and regional tourism organisations is provided by Dolničar and Schösser (2003). The two segmentation approaches to be compared in this article will be illustrated using the Guest Survey Austria data set and taking the perspective of a destination manager in Austria. This is a very realistic managerial situation, as the data resulting from this survey are used for precisely this purpose.

The Guest Survey Austria

The Guest Survey Austria (GSA) is an ongoing market research study that is repeated every 3 years and funded by the Austrian National Tourist Office, the Federal Ministry for Economic Affairs, the Chamber of Commerce Austria as well as the Austria regional tourism organisations. It is collected by drawing a quota random sample of tourists based on the region in Austria, the country of origin and type of accommodation. For this study, the summer data for the years 1994 and 1997 are used. These surveys were designed, administered and analysed by the Institute of Tourism and Leisure Studies at the Vienna University of Economics and Business Administration with the fieldwork having been conducted by the Austrian Society for Applied Tourism Science (ÖGAF) in co-operation with the Salzburg Institute for Basic Research. The design of the questions therefore could not be influenced by the authors of this study.

FIGURE 1. Austria and Its Provinces (Source: Österreich Werbung, Austrian NTO)

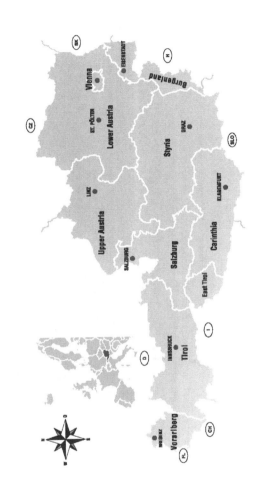

The survey is very rich in data. The information used for this particular comparison includes socio-demographic information about the respondents (country of origin, age, gender), travel related information (province in which the respondent is staying in Austria, number of overnight stays in Austria, kind of accommodation, star category of accommodation, travel group, travel expenditures), leisure activities and travel motives. Regarding leisure activities respondents stated which activities they engaged in during their vacation in Austria. The data includes the categories "often or sometimes" and "never." The summer vacation activities listed are playing tennis, cycling, riding, playing golf, swimming/bathing, sailing/surfing, boat-trips, going to a spa, using health-facilities, mountaineering, hiking, going for walks, participating in organized excursions, making excursions into the near surroundings (not organized), relaxing/doing nothing, going out for dinner, going to discos/bars, shopping, visiting sights, going to museums/exhibitions, going to the theatre/musical/opera, visiting a "Heurigen" (this is a typical Austrian wine tavern), visiting festivals/concerts and visiting Tyrolean evenings/amateur theatres.

Commonsense Segmentation –Geographical Segments

The typical approach of dividing tourists into market segments based on their country of origin is chosen. Regions of origin included in the survey are Vienna (916 respondents), Austria without Vienna (1090), Belgium (647), Denmark (515), France (621), Germany (3399), Hungary (442), Italy (690), Netherlands (913), Spain (234), Sweden (393), Switzerland (727), the UK (799), the USA (500) and other countries (387).

The entire survey data set is thus split into market segments based on one single variable, the country of origin. This results in 15 market segments. The Italian market segment is selected next for detailed description. From a managerial perspective, this decision clearly does make a lot of sense, as Italy can be targeted as one market using the same language and the same media structure all over the nation. However, the NTO (and this is probably the most typical segmentation approach used by NTOs worldwide) needs to gain as much understanding as possible into the Italian marketplace. This is done by describing the segment and testing for significant differences as compared to the other geographical target markets.

The results from the Guest Survey Austria provide management with the following descriptive insights of the Italian market: Italian visitors to Austria are younger than the other visitors, they spend fewer nights in

Austria, they spend more money per person per day in total during their vacation and have higher expenses for entry fees for cultural offers.

While Italian tourists have significantly less experience with Austria than visitors from other nations, no such differences could be detected with regard to the intention to return to Austria.

Italians more frequently visit Vienna and Carinthia, while less frequently spending their stay in Burgenland and Lower Austria. Also they are found camping very infrequently. The proportion of Italians in hotels, on the other hand, is higher than that of other visitors, with Italians favouring higher hotel star categories.

The profile of Italian visitors to Austria with regard to the vacation activities they engage in is provided in Figure 2, where the columns indicate the percentage of Italian tourists stating that they have engaged in each one of those vacation activities and the lines along the centre of each column indicated the percentage of tourist from all countries of origin undertaking these leisure pastimes. As can be seen, there are only minor deviations of Italian tourists to the total groups of holiday-makers to Austria. The differences are that Italian tourists spend less time swimming and bathing, relaxing, visiting spas and heath facilities, surfing and sailing, boating, mountaineering, participating in organised excursions and at so called "Heurigen," while engaging more in hiking, going out in the evenings, shopping, and participating in cultural activities.

From the managerial perspective the picture of the prototypical Italian tourist does not make it very easy to target the group, as there seems to be a substantial amount of heterogeneity within this common sense geographical segment.

If a message were designed based on the geographical segment profile, a NTO would probably choose to emphasize the cultural component, as the vacation profile shows above average interest in those activities. The product offer would probably feature a one-week stay in Vienna or Carinthia with up-market hotel accommodation and a lot of exhibitions and museums as well as some sports offers, especially cycling and hiking.

However, this advertising message and offer would be based on a heterogeneous group of visitors and would thus not provide a high quality product for all of the Italian tourists.

Data-Driven Segmentation–Behavioural Segments

The data-driven segmentation conducted for the case of Austrian destination management segment choice is based on vacation activities. The

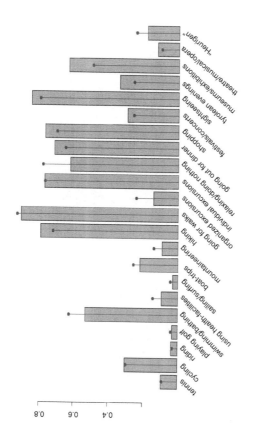

FIGURE 2. Vacation Activity Pattern for Italian Tourists in Austria

variables are coded in binary format, the partitioning algorithm used is k-means (e.g., Everitt, 1993). This algorithm is appropriate for large sample sizes and splits the respondents through an iterative process of (1) distance computation between each respondent and a centroid representing each segment, and (2) assignment of each respondent to the closest representant. The raw data was not pre-processed before the grouping (partitioning) into segments was undertaken. In order to determine if there exist natural clusters in the data and how many, market segmentation solutions with numbers of clusters from 1 to 14 (see horizontal axis in Figure 3) were computed and the development of inner variance (the sum of the distances of each respondent to the centre representing her or his segment) was plotted (see vertical axis in Figure 3).

As can be seen from the graph, no distinct drop in the inner variance measure can be detected, indicating that natural clusters are unlikely to exist. Therefore, deciding on the number of clusters becomes a manage-

FIGURE 3. Number of Clusters Plot

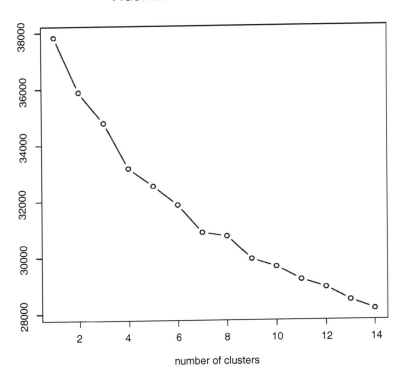

number of clusters

rial responsibility rather then being driven by numeric indices or criteria. This is not a general finding. The general rule with regard to the selection of clusters and numbers of clusters is to first explore the data. Only if no structure can be determined, is it up to the manager to choose the solution that is most useful. Solutions from 4 to 9 clusters were visually inspected and the six-cluster solution was chosen as managerially most useful. The six-cluster solution contains two answer tendency clusters. This is a typical phenomenon that occurs in clustering if the question format in the survey is susceptible to answer tendencies. Therefore these two clusters are not taken into consideration in choosing possible target segments: one of them is characterised by all segment members undertaking all activities more often than this is the case among the total of visitors to Austria (2096 respondents), and the second one showing the precise opposite behaviour (1787). The remaining four clusters can be named "cultural tourists" (1976), "summer relaxation visitors" (1513), "hiking and excursion holiday-makers" (2123) and "mainstream mix guests" (2778). Note that the numbers given in brackets are absolute number of respondents and would need to be multiplied by appropriate weights to get proportions of the total population, this is omitted for simplicity.

For the purpose of this example, the culture tourists are chosen as a segment for Austria. These tourists can be described in the following way: with regard to age, they are neither among the oldest, nor among the youngest segment. With regard to the duration of stay, the culture tourists spend by far the fewest nights in Austria: 8.6 nights on average. They spend almost twice as much money on entry fees for cultural offers than the behavioural segment with the second highest expenditures and nearly five times as much as the segment with the lowest entry fee expenditures per person per day. Even in terms of total expenditures per person per day, the cultural tourists spend the highest amount of all segment in Austria (82 Euros). This is 30 percent more than the amount of the second highest spending segment. Furthermore, three quarters of those tourists stay in hotels and they have an above average choice of high hotel star graded hotels, with one third staying in five star accommodation. All these pieces of information make the cultural tourist a highly attractive and very distinct segment to choose as a marketing target. However, there are some drawbacks that are just as distinct but not commercially attractive: Cultural tourists have a very low intention to return to Austria, with one fifth stating that that they can hardly imagine to return. They also have little prior experience with Austria, which paints a picture of tourists who come for the once in a lifetime cultural tour to Austria.

The activity profile for the cultural tourist is provided in Figure 4. As can be seen, the proportion of members of this segment that visits museums is far higher than the sample average (indicated by the line). Also sightseeing and the other cultural activities are engaged in more often than this is the case for all visitors to Austria. All sporting activities, however, are far below average.

All in all, the cultural tourist segment is a distinct and homogeneous segment. Figure 5 visualizes the contingency table cross-tabulating country of origin and *a posteriori* segment membership. Columns higher than the horizontal line indicate that citizens of a particular country of origin are over-represented in particular behavioural segments, columns lower than the line represent the contrary; the darker the column the stronger the deviation. In the cultural segment (marked with number 3 on the horizontal axis in Figure 5[1]) the number of Austrian, German, Dutch and Swiss tourists is extremely low, whereas French, Italian, Spanish, British and American tourists are highly over-represented. With regard to Italy, it becomes clear that the only significant overrepresentation is in the cultural segment, indicating a strong association of the commonsense geographic segment and the behavioural segment.

An advertising message for cultural tourists would clearly emphasize the cultural component. The product offer would include high star category accommodation and as much cultural offers as possible. The target group is distinct and homogeneous with regard to the profile which would lead to a higher probability of satisfying customer's needs and thus provide high quality of service to the tourists.

Comparing Segmentation Approaches from the Managerial Perspective

Two different approaches of market segmentation for purposes of destination management were illustrated using real data. Both approaches are used in practise, with the geographical technique dominating the market, however. This is not mirrored in the academic tourism research literature as much as by the reality of NTO structures and marketing programmes which are usually country-of-origin centred (see www.tourism-austria.atfor an example). The Italian market and the behavioural segment of culture tourists were chosen because of the strong association of the two markets that eases comparison from a managerial and customer service quality delivery perspective.

FIGURE 4. The Culture Tourist

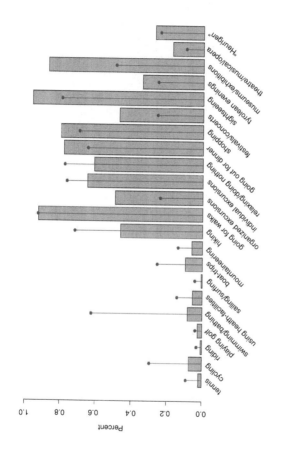

FIGURE 5. Association Plot of Geographical and Behavioural Segments

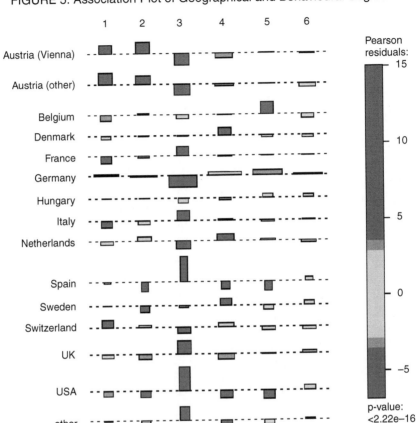

The advantages of the geographic approach include:

- *Simple concept that is easily understood by all employees of the NTO.*

The concept of targeting potential visitors from certain countries of origin is easily understood. It is unlikely that any misunderstandings among employees would occur. In the empirical example, for instance, it is trivial to understand that potential tourists from Italy are targeted and that this group has certain characteristics that have to be accounted for.

- *Straightforward possibility of targeting.*

The targeting procedure itself, the communication with the target market is easy, as all activity is limited to one country. The market can be reached very easily. For instance, in the Austrian example, the promotional effort is invested in Italy. The NTO only needs Italian versions of the promotional material and expertise in the media infrastructure of this one country.

The disadvantages include:

- *Danger of insufficient consideration of the heterogeneity of geographical target markets.*

In the case of Austria, the segment of Italian tourists, for instance, did not seem to be strongly dominated either by cultural or any other specific interests. The market is far more heterogeneous with regard to both the activity profile as well as descriptive information as it is the case for the cultural tourists derived from the data-driven segmentation approach. A product or promotional campaign designed for the Italian market would thus emphasize a mix of sports and cultural activities which might run the risk of attracting neither the sports-interested Italians, not the culture-interested ones.

On the other hand, behavioural segments–or data-driven segments in general–have the following advantages:

- *Relevant segments.*

Segments are identified or constructed on the basis of multiple variables that are assumed to be most relevant to the destination choice. It is assumed that an advertising appeal emphasizing those relevant pieces of information would be stronger than using a commonsense grouping criterion as the country of origin. In the example illustrated above, vacation activities were chosen as relevant segmentation base. Therefore the resulting segments are highly homogeneous with regard to the activity pattern. As vacation activities form a central part of the tourist service, encounter homogeneity in this respect might be the stronger concept than homogeneity with regard to the country of origin. The behavioural segments derived from the activity information would probably render more relevant groupings in the empirical example, as the segment turn out to be highly homogeneous not only with regard to the vacation activities, but also with respect to descriptive information.

- *Homogeneous segments.*

With regard to the selected segmentation base the tourist groups resulting from partitioning are more homogeneous than simple commonsense segments. In the illustration above even the descriptive information, that was in no way optimised to be maximally homogeneous, rendered a highly distinct profile.

- *General applicability.*

Data-driven segments are typically crossing the border of demographics. They are therefore more generally applicable. For instance, the Italian market is clearly larger than the market of Italian cultural tourists, but the market of cultural tourists extends over national borders (see Figure 5). An intelligent concept of targeting the cultural segment can thus easily be used on a broader scale than nationally customized messages or product offers.

The disadvantages of this approach include:

- *Data-driven segments are not simple to identify or construct properly.*

There are many possible pitfalls when data-driven segmentation solutions are computed (Punj & Stewart, 1983; Dolničar, 2002). These must be avoided in order to provide a solid decision basis for management and consequently a high quality service for the target segment chosen. However, there is a lack of expertise in this area among both NTOs and commercial market research companies. In the last consequence, this disadvantage leads to the conclusion that a wrong data-driven segmentation solution can never be useful. Unless the segments are derived in a methodologically clean manner, the entire solution is of doubtful value.

- *Data-driven segments are more complex to understand.*

Data-driven segments are more complex constructs. They are defined by certain common traits, but could be very heterogeneous with regard to the most obvious classification criteria of tourists, like age or country of origin. For instance, the term "cultural tourist" itself is very endangered by simplification. It is defined by a multidimensional activity pattern, whereas it might be tempting to assume that tourists were simply asked what kind of tourists they are and then classified themselves accordingly.

- *Higher complexity in implementation.*

The task of communication with the Italian market is not difficult to implement. Standard marketing media planning procedures can be applied. In the case of data-driven segments that exist in various geographical regions, cultures and language groups, the task of optimally allocating the marketing budget, modifying the single messages to suit each particular cultural background and translate them becomes far more complex to implement. Figure 5 indicated clearly that a number of geographical markets would have to be addressed in order to exploit the maximum potential of the cultural tourist segment.

CONCLUSIONS

The aim of this paper was to illustrate the usefulness of different kinds of segmentation studies for destination management and optimising the match between tourists' needs and destination offers to ultimately increase the quality of the tourist experience while maximizing profit as a destination. The managerial relevance of the study rests with the fact that the fundamentally different segmentation approaches are rarely compared. Typically, both in tourism industry and academic publications, one of the approaches is chosen and different solutions following the same technique are compared. This illustration provided an argument to compare *a priori* and *a posteriori* approaches before choosing the final target segment. This was achieved by explaining the theory of both approaches, the common sense segmentation approach and the data-driven approach, and illustrating possible resulting segment solutions for the case of the tourist destination Austria on the basis of survey data actually used for this particular purpose by the Austrian National Tourism Organisation.

A typical geographical segmentation was conducted based on the country of origin information and the segment of Italian travellers was chosen for detailed description. The data-driven segmentation was based on a set of vacation activities. Segments were constructed that can be described by similar vacation activity patterns. Among six behavioural segments derived, the cultural tourists were chosen as potentially interesting target segment and described in detail.

With both approaches having their advantages and drawbacks, the general recommendation emerging from this paper is as follows: the optimal results will be achieved by considering both segmentation approaches and empirically compare the appropriateness and usefulness for the managerial problem at hand. While no general superiority of one of the concepts can be claimed, the particular managerial usefulness can be evaluated in a context-independent manner. However, considering the fundamental and long-term nature of market segmentation decisions, it seems particularly important to be aware of the strengths and weaknesses of both procedures. In the best case it is advisable to compute multiple solutions and gain in-depth understanding by exploring those alternatives, and investigating the associations between them.

Future work includes operationalising criteria for the comparative evaluation of the two segmentation approaches and developing a methodological toolbox to support management in the selection process of the appropriate segmentation technique. Another important step is bridging the gap between state of the art statistical methodology and the heuristics widely used in practise. This process can be eased by supporting easy to use data analysis software and methodological support.

NOTE

1. Pearson residuals are computed as $(o-e)^2/e$ where o is the observed number of individuals and e is the expected number of individuals for the null hypothesis of independence. The p-value corresponds to the usual Chi-square test of independence in contingency tables.

REFERENCES

Court, B., & Lupton, R.A. (1997). Customer Portfolio Development: Modeling Destination Adopters, Inactives, and Rejecters. *Journal of Travel Research.* 36(1), 35-43.
Dolničar, S. (2002). Review of Data-Driven Market Segmentation in Tourism. *Journal of Travel & Tourism Marketing.* 12(1), 1-22.

Dolničar, S. (forthcoming). Beyond "Commonsense Segmentation" – a Systematics of Segmentation Approaches in Tourism. *Journal of Travel Research.*

Dolničar, S., & Grabler, K. (2003). Evaluating Geographical Target Markets–an Aggregated Portfolio Approach for Improved Managerial Decision-Making. *CD Proceedings of the APTA Conference,* July 6th-9th, 2003, Sydney, Australia.

Dolničar, S., & Schösser, Ch.M. (2003). Market Research in Austrian NTO and RTOs: Is the Research Homework Done Before Spending Marketing Millions? *CD Proceedings of the 13th International Research Conference of the Council for Australian University Tourism and Hospitality Education (CAUTHE).*

Everitt, B.S. (1993). *Cluster Analysis.* New York: Halsted Press.

Formica, S., & Uysal, M. (1998). Market Segmentation of an International Cultural-Historical Event in Italy. *Journal of Travel Research.* 36(4), 16-24.

Heath, E., & Wall, G. (1992). *Marketing Tourism Destinations–a Strategic Planning Approach.* John Wiley & Sons.

Kashyap, R., & Bojanic, D.C. (2000). A Structural Analysis of Value, Quality, and Price Perceptions of Business and Leisure Travelers. *Journal of Travel Research.* 39(1), 45-51.

Kastenholz, E., Davis, D., & Paul, G. (1999). Segmenting Tourism in Rural Areas: The Case of North and Central Portugal. *Journal of Travel Research.* 37(4), 353-63.

Mazanec, J. (1986a). A Decision Support System for Optimising Advertising Policy of a National Tourist Office: Model Outline and Case Study. *International Journal of Research in Marketing.* 3(2), 63-77.

Mazanec, J. (1986b). Allocating an Advertising Budget to International Travel Markets. *Annals of Tourism Research.* 13(4), 609-634.

Mazanec, J. (2000). *Market Segmentation.* In Encyclopedia of Tourism edited by Jafar Jafari, London: Routledge.

McDonald, M. (1984). *Marketing Planning–How to prepare them, how to use them.* London: Heinemann.

Morrison, A. M., Braunlich, C. G., Kamaruddin, N., & Cai, L. A. (1995). National tourist offices in North Amerika: An analysis. *Tourism Management.* 16(8), 605-617.

Moscardo, G., Pearce, Ph, Morrison, A., Green, D., & O'Leary, J.T. (2000). Developing a Typology for Understanding Visiting Friends and Relatives Markets. *Journal of Travel Research.* 38(3), 251-59.

Moutinho, L., Rita, P., & Curry, B. (1996). *Expert Systems in Tourism Marketing,* New York: Routledge.

Punj, G., & Stewart, D.W. (1983). Cluster Analysis in Marketing Research: Review and Suggestions for Application. *Journal of Marketing Research.* 20, 134-148.

Smith, M.C., & MacKay, K.J. (2001). The Organization of Information in Memory for Pictures of Tourist Destinations: Are There Age-Related Differences? *Journal of Travel Research.* 39(3), 261-66.

Wedel, M., & Kamakura, W.A. (1998). *Market Segmentation–Conceptual and Methodological Foundations,* Boston: Kluwer Academic Publishers.

Seasonal Trading and Lifestyle Motivation: Experiences of Small Tourism Businesses in Scotland

Philip J. Goulding
Tom G. Baum
Alison J. Morrison

SUMMARY. This article explores relationships between tourism seasonality and the lifestyle motivations of small tourism businesses, fundamentally a supply-side perspective of seasonality. Seasonal trading decisions are subject to a number of influences, not all of which are in the operator's control. Drawing from exploratory research undertaken in Scotland, the article argues that for some operators, especially located in rural and peripheral destination areas, lifestyle enterprise can confer a range of benefits, some of which are afforded by operating the business on a seasonal basis. Moreover, seasonal trading was seen to assume a

Philip J. Goulding (E-mail: philip.goulding@strath.ac.uk) is Research Student, Tom G. Baum (E-mail: t.g.baum@strath.ac.uk) is Head of School, and Alison J. Morrison (Email: a.j.morrison@strath.ac.uk) is Reader/Director of Research, all at The Scottish Hotel School, University of Strathclyde, 94, Cathedral Street, Glasgow G4 0LG, Scotland/UK.

[Haworth co-indexing entry note]: "Seasonal Trading and Lifestyle Motivation: Experiences of Small Tourism Businesses in Scotland." Co-published simultaneously in *Journal of Quality Assurance in Hospitality & Tourism* (Haworth Hospitality Press, an imprint of The Haworth Press, Inc.) Vol. 5, No. 2/3/4, 2004, pp. 209-238; and: *Hospitality, Tourism, and Lifestyle Concepts: Implications for Quality Management and Customer Satisfaction* (ed: Maree Thyne and Eric Laws) Haworth Hospitality Press, an imprint of The Haworth Press, Inc., 2004, pp. 209-238. Single or multiple copies of this article are available for a fee from The Haworth Document Delivery Service [1-800-HAWORTH, 9:00 a.m. - 5:00 p.m. (EST). E-mail address: docdelivery@haworthpress.com].

number of distinct roles, reflecting various characteristics of lifestyle operators. Accordingly, public policies that seek to promote seasonal extension based on the premise of local economic development or destination objectives are not necessarily destined to work. This is particularly pertinent if such policies do not recognise the wider supply-side dynamics of seasonal trading and fail to engage with the lifestyle aspirations of the operators themselves. *[Article copies available for a fee from The Haworth Document Delivery Service: 1-800-HAWORTH. E-mail address: <docdelivery@haworthpress.com> Website: <http://www.HaworthPress.com> © 2004 by The Haworth Press, Inc. All rights reserved.]*

KEYWORDS. Seasonality, seasonal trading, small businesses, lifestyle, rural areas, destination policy

INTRODUCTION

The emotiveness of tourism seasonality as an issue for economic policy makers and destination management organisations has been widely articulated over a long time period (for example Bar On, 1975; Baum and Hagen, 1999; Blass-Nogueira et al., 1968; Butler, 2001; European Commission, 1993). As an endemic market phenomenon in many tourism destinations (Allcock, 1995; Butler, 2001), seasonality is commonly held to characterise sub-optimal utilisation of economic resources over a part of the year, to discourage inward investment in an area's tourism superstructures, to limit operators' propensity to upgrade their facilities and in certain cases can act as an impediment to labour force recruitment, retention and development (Krakover, 2000; Lundtorp et al., 2001) either in tourism or in other economic sectors competing with tourism (Bull, 1995) such as agriculture (D'Amore, 1976). These and other economic symptoms of a seasonally defined tourism economy, such as external costs arising from peak season demand, generally provide a policy rationale for public sector intervention in combating seasonality. This is especially so in economically peripheral areas which have few productive opportunities, as illustrated by Baum and Hagen (1999) and Wanhill (1997) in northwest Europe and the North Atlantic margins. In such cases, public sector intervention may specifically address seasonality derived problems as part of a wider remit of improving the performance or contribution of the tourism economy *per se*, or it may be designed to contribute towards wider policy objectives such as rural development, small business enterprise, employment, community cohesion and so on.

Furthermore, for individual tourism businesses, structural seasonality within their destination area is an emotive issue if it impacts on their own desired level of performance. Goulding and Gunn (2000) for example, noted the importance proprietors in the Scottish Borders attach to public agency involvement in what they consider to be a wider 'problem'. In essence, the operators were articulating a rationale for public policy intervention to help combat seasonality, based on the perceived market failure of tourism in a peripheral, rural area and the viability of small and micro-scale tourism related businesses therein. Initiatives by Scotland's public sector tourism and economic development agencies over the years to tackle seasonality have stressed the 'common interest' among businesses to alleviate the condition. For example, the 1994-2000 Scottish Tourism Strategic Plan articulated the industry's concerns that seasonality led to the state of affairs whereby ". . . those who provide high standards of facilities and service feel let down by their weaker counterparts" (STCG, 1994: 9). In contrast, the New Strategy for Scottish Tourism (2000) does not make explicit any link between service quality and seasonal operation. Rather, seasonality is still expressed as a concern, linked particularly to the need to increase the benefits of tourism in rural areas (Scottish Executive, 2000).

However, there is a growing body of empirical work (for example Flognfeldt, 1988, 2001; Baum and Hagen, 1999) questioning the inevitable desirability of a year round tourism economy. The counterview is especially pertinent to locations where the environmental resources are deemed to be fragile and in need of 'post-season recovery' or where much of the local community itself appreciates a period of post-seasonal recuperation (Jordan, 1980; Mathieson and Wall, 1982). This clearly depends on the nature of the tourism product and its temporal characteristics within any destination area. As yet, however, there is little evidence to suggest that, in the UK at least, the weight of public policy regarding seasonal tourism has shifted away from the primacy of combating what is perceived as a clear symptom of market failure. In other words, the economic rationale of year round tourism activity still seems to predominate over the seasonal optimisation of tourism on environmental or social grounds.

Tourism and broader local economic development strategies in Scotland (for example Fife, 1997; SBTB, 1999; Scottish Executive, 2000) continue to give priority to lengthening the season and encouraging 'out of season' activities as key policy goals. This also reflects destination management priorities in many other regions and countries where tourism seasonality persists, such as in Ireland (Kennedy and Deegan,

2001), Turkey (Soybali, 1994) and even Singapore (Hui and Yuen, 2002). In the case of Otago in southern New Zealand, sports policy has been used to impact on seasonal tourism patterns (Higham and Hinch, 2002). The restructuring and extension of that area's rugby union fixtures season since the late 1990s has resulted in a variety of positive outcomes for the area's tourism economy, including the generation of additional domestic trips and excursions, the emergence of new niche markets and greater linkages between tourism and the area's broader tourism product. Such benefits have been recognised by the economic development agencies in the area (Higham and Hinch, 2002: 182). In North Wales, conference extension has recently been used as a key seasonal extension strategy (North Wales Economic Forum, 1998), while Iceland's capital city has pursued a joint policy of product and market extension (Baum and Hagen, 1999) respectively developing a New Year festival and weekend breaks for youth 'clubbers'. Thus, a variety of options are available to destination management organisations in pursuit of market-led seasonality strategies.

There is though, another factor in the debate over living with or combating seasonally defined tourism. During the past two decades there has been a gradual growth of research into the motivations of small tourism business entrepreneurs, highlighting the diversity of reasons for business start-ups and the goals or aspirations of such operators. Out of this has emerged the now widely used concept of 'lifestyle' business to describe a scenario in which proprietors either balance their economic and non-economic goals, or indeed are primarily motivated by a set of 'lifestyle' aspirations (Lynch, 1998; Morrison, 2002; Morrison and Teixeira, 2003; Thomas, 2000; Williams et al., 1989) which take priority over economic objectives. Though disparate in nature, lifestyle aspirations emphasise quality of life attributes such as personal relationships, personal development, benefiting from a slower pace of life, showcasing the domestic and local environment to visitors and compartmentalising work and leisure, among others. These benefits are typically pursued by balancing the business with other aspirational priorities throughout the trading year. However, some operators achieve their lifestyle aspirations through the seasonal trading opportunities and choices afforded by the market structure of tourism in their chosen area (Andrew et al., 2001).

The following sections go on to examine the broader context and range of supply-side determinants and influences on tourism seasonality relating to small business operators. The role of 'lifestyle' motivations is then assessed in relation to operators' trading behaviours and finally findings from an exploratory study undertaken in the Scottish

Borders in 1999-2000 are discussed in respect of evidence of linkages between seasonal trading and proprietors' lifestyle aspirations.

SUPPLY-SIDE FACTORS IN TOURISM SEASONALITY

Relatively few attempts have been made to develop a holistic understanding of supply-related aspects of seasonality. In particular, little exists in the way of empirical evidence to validate the role of tourism related enterprises in influencing the level of temporal variation in tourism through their operating practices, underlying motivations and aspirations.

Historically, much of the literature and empirical research on temporal variation and trends in tourism has concentrated on establishing *causal factors* and *policy responses* to tourism seasonality. Chief among the former group are a variety of *institutional, natural and social* categorisations of causal factors, as discussed by Bar-On (1975), Hartmann (1986), Allcock (1995), Baum and Hagen (1999), Butler (2001) and Frechtling (2001) among others. Often a push-and-pull framework of analysis is constructed to aid understanding of the dynamic of causal variables (Baum, 1997; Lundtorp et al., 2001). Climatic conditions in origin and destination areas, public and religious holidays, the structure of the academic year, tradition or inertia in holiday taking patterns and consumers' changing tastes have long been at the heart of the seasonality debate.

In their study of cold temperate peripheral North Atlantic areas, Baum and Hagen (1999) have articulated a framework of possible actions to extend the tourism season, embracing market diversification, product diversification, events and festivals strategies and environmental and structural responses. The latter extends to public-private initiatives to maintain out-of-season service levels in tourism related amenities such as public transport, leisure and entertainment centres, and initiatives to encourage labour market flexibility, such as relaxing the restrictions on importing temporary workers during shoulder or low season periods. Indeed, seasonal labour force issues give rise to a number of human resource related concerns, to which small tourism businesses are particularly susceptible. These include the disproportionate cost of recruiting seasonal staff, which in turn may inhibit the development of progressive remuneration packages for such employees (Goulding, 2003), lack of training and development opportunities provided by seasonal businesses, loss of skills and experience at the end of the season, the implications of this on service quality consistency from season to season (Baum and Hagen, 1999) and commitment from seasonal workers to the operation.

Causation and 'corrective' policy responses merely constitute parts of a wider understanding of tourism seasonality (Allcock, 1995; Butler, 1994 and 2001; Goulding and Hay, 2001) in which the trading influences and decisions of its service providers are largely ignored.

The role of supply-side factors in influencing tourism's temporal patterns is misunderstood for a number of reasons. First, the parameters of what constitutes the 'supply-side' are indistinct. Butler's (2001) conceptualisation of influences on seasonality encompasses a broad range of 'supply attributes' including climatic conditions (Figure 1), which in turn are modified by a range of 'actions' such as pricing, taxation and investment. To these, Baum and Hagen (1999) add competition from other economic sectors and the alternative use of touristic resources as supply-side constraints. In addition, wider distributional and infrastructural elements such as transport and travel trade components clearly must be included as supply-side influences on tourism seasonality. The recent trend in the ex-

FIGURE 1. Influences on Patterns of Tourism Seasonality

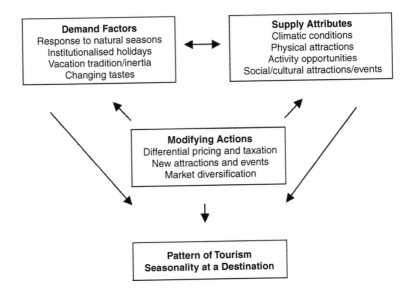

Source: Butler 2001:9

pansion of low cost airlines in opening up areas served by regional airports is a case in point.

The provenance of the 'modifying actions' that Butler refers to can of course include both individual business as well as collective business 'actions', for example destination marketing networks, as well as public agency interventions. This reflects Goulding and Hay's (2001) framework of supply-side responses to seasonality (Figure 2), in which business responses and public policy measures are seen as distinct from each another, though in both cases responses might reflect either a prevailing acceptance of the seasonal 'status quo' or the need to 'do something about it'.

Secondly, analysis of supply-side influences tends to concentrate on the 'macro' dimension of the destination area or region as a whole. A limitation of this is that there is an implicit assumption that 'places' and their communities may share a common experience and a common meaning of 'the season', 'peak season', 'seasonal downtime' and other temporally defined states. While there is a logic that a destination's seasonal patterns impact on its commercial tourism products in general, there may be less logic in the counter view that individual destination businesses and service suppliers' trading patterns tend not to impact on the destination's aggregate seasonal patterns, unless there is a monopolistic local operator. However, in much of cool temperate northern Eu-

FIGURE 2. Supply-Side Responses to Seasonality

Business Responses	Public Sector Policy Measures
to boost off-season demand : - *seasonal pricing* - *market diversification* - *product diversification* - *promotional activity* - *distribution mix* - *service level differentiation*	*to boost off-season tourism :* - *labour force incentives (eg. training)* - *staggering academic holidays* - *business support services such as marketing, financial planning* - *participation in seasonal extension programmes–* *(eg. destination events strategy)* - *fiscal incentives* - *subsidisation of transport services*
Acceptance of seasonality - *offer reduced capacity* - *full seasonal closure* - *temporary seasonal closure* *(eg. during lowest revenue period)*	*Acceptance of seasonality* - *enviromental regeneration initiative* - *focus business support on existing seasonal trading pattern* - *support off-season community initiatives (eg local arts festivals)*

Adapted from Goulding and Hay (2001:18)

rope, rural, peripheral and seaside destinations comprising mainly small scale independent businesses tend to have more seasonally defined patterns of tourism, and higher ratios of seasonally closing businesses (Baum and Hagen, 1999; Lundtorp et al., 2001) than in urban areas or warm temperate climes. This is particularly apparent in Scotland as exhibited in the contrast between seasonality and tourism structures in Edinburgh and the Scottish Borders. Both have adopted year round events strategies as the basis for combating seasonality, with success. However, the broader infrastructural base and wider market spread afforded by Scotland's capital city has provided more opportunities for local businesses to capitalise on traditionally 'low season' markets than is the case in many parts of the Borders (Goulding and Hay, 2001). Hence the importance of appreciating the structure and dynamics of destination areas' small tourism businesses, since 'macro' analysis is meaningless without a profound understanding of the behaviour and motivations of the actors.

Finally, at a 'micro' or individual business level, the range of supply-side factors influencing seasonal trading patterns is wide. For example, it was noted above how local labour conditions can affect seasonal trading. Baum and Hagen (1999) highlighted the degree to which the Swedish island of Gotland's tourism economy largely shuts down at the start of the academic year because of its dependence on seasonal student labour. Meanwhile Goulding and Gunn's (2000) exploratory study of seasonal trading of tourism businesses in the Scottish Borders revealed a number of other influencing factors. The findings revealed in that study are summarised and discussed in section 6 of this paper. Several such influences were noted to have distinct linkages with 'lifestyle entrepreneurship'.

SMALL TOURISM BUSINESSES :
LIFESTYLE CONSIDERATIONS

Part of the difficulty in evaluating the role of lifestyle in the seasonal trading patterns of small tourism businesses lies in the very breadth of small-scale tourism service provision. Thomas (2000) argues that as an analytical category, 'small tourism firms' is too broad a concept for any meaningful comparative analysis of the subjects or for public policy provision directed at the sector. There is the basic argument of definition through size arising from the characteristics of 'micro-businesses' compared with 'small' or 'medium' sized businesses. This is pertinent in an industry that more often than not comprises seasonal, part time, voluntary and non-remunerated family employment. Another difficulty is the different operational characteristics and financial considerations between the various types of service provider, such as comparative start-up and operating costs, specialist skills requirements and the nature of host-guest interaction. Such complexities add to the methodological problems inherent in conducting research in the field.

Despite the above definitional issues, a growing body of literature and empirical studies into small tourism business entrepreneurship and motivations enables a degree of insight into the 'lifestyle' considerations of proprietors. A valid starting point is to examine the meaning and context of 'lifestyle' within tourism proprietorship.

As a business-related concept 'lifestyle' can be considered as the consequence of a set of values and expectations which are self-selected by the business operators (Andrew et al., 2001). The hope of personal happiness and improved quality of life override social convention (Heelas and Morris, 1992) and conformity to an economic rationale in decision making. Motivations attributed to 'lifestyle proprietorship' include 'autonomy, control, independence' (Kuratko and Hodgetts 1998: 2), intrinsic satisfaction (Andrew et al., 2001) and social relationships (Lynch, 1998; Williams et al., 1989). Gray (1986: 16) refers to the common aspiration of 'lifestyle entrepreneurs' in gaining the 'trappings of the good life' without the encumbrance of 'extensive financial or time commitments'.

Other motivational aspects often attributed to small tourism proprietors include the desire to escape from the 'rat-race' of urban, city-scale living; to move up the housing ladder through investing in larger property which has the potential to generate some income from visitors (Williams et al., 1989) and the opportunity to act in a host capacity (Lynch, 1998). Importantly, the attractiveness of seasonal trading *per se* as a 'lifestyle motivation' may be explicitly articulated (Andrew et al., 2001; Lynch, 1998; Baum, 1997).

Subjective configurations such as family background, the internal dynamic of the business and other facets of the proprietors' social world can be explanatory in understanding the formation and performance of small firms (Gorton, 2000). For example, Lynch's (1998) study of female micro-entrepreneurs in the host family sector identified the ability to combine child-care with a commercial income activity in the domestic environment, the education needs of children and socialisation in the locality of the business to be important lifestyle factors. Blackburn (1999) notes the importance of the family as a productive unit in the domestic economy, a fact that is well represented in the tourist accommodation sector in rural Scotland. Clearly for many such operators, the tourism enterprise may provide a secondary income source, especially within an extended family, a cross-generational business or in a dual income based domestic environment (Birley and Rosewell, 1998).

An emotional attachment to the physical space, often the family home (Lynch, 1998; Morrison and Teixeira, 2003) can be a crucial factor in the various accommodation sectors. Seasonal trading represents a key strategem for achieving this, allowing proprietors to have control over the balance between showcasing their domestic environment to visitors for a certain period during the year and the intrinsic benefits achievable through closure of the business for parts of the financial year. Bed and breakfast, guest house and self catering operators are afforded significant flexibility in this respect. A similar rationale may also apply for small, independent visitor attraction or museum owner/operators for whom the periodic display of their collection combines intrinsic satisfactions and recognition within the local tourism community along with a marginal income source. Furthermore, Morrison and Teixeira's (2003) cross-cultural study of small accommodation businesses found evidence of a prevailing ethos of protecting the 'status quo' of a small market size. Smallness is also equated with 'distinctiveness' whereby, for example, getting to know their clients and providing a distinctive environment compared against the standardised branded hotel fit well into the adopted 'lifestyle'.

Thus it is important to appreciate that economic performance measures are not necessarily over-riding in small tourism related business operations. Indeed Morrison and Teixeira (ibid.) argue that small firm performance in the tourist accommodation sector is only partially explainable by conventional economic rationality. A recurring theme in 'lifestyle' business generically, and in tourism businesses specifically, is the idea that non-economic attributes including lifestyle values, motivations and aspirations are balanced with and sometimes take precedence over economic goals. Accordingly, achieving a desired 'quality of life' may be seen to represent a proprietor's personal utility evaluation of the various lifestyle attributes of operating the business, as determined by both economic and non-economic criteria. This would suggest that a value can be ascribed to factors such as 'playing the host,' the tranquil location of the amenity or the pleasure gained from guiding visitors, for example. The theme of 'balance' between economic and non-economic motives has been much debated in the tourism and hospitality literature over the years. Shaw and Williams' (1997) study of

English seaside resorts encapsulates many of its inherent themes, including ownership and business size attributes, in-migration motivations by entrepreneurs and those relating to their past employment history (escape, redundancy, dissatisfaction), improved living environments and less specific family or personal reasons. Their findings echo previous generic studies by Scase and Goffee (1984) and Storey (1994) on the breadth and complexity of entrepreneurial vs. lifestyle motivations.

However, Morrison (2002: 1-2) observes that many small tourism business proprietors have multiple sets of goals, wherein the notion of 'satisficing' financial returns to support lifestyle ideals is prevalent. She refers to 'survival' and *"securing sufficient income to. . . . [provide] . . . a satisfactory level of funds to sustain enjoyment in their chosen lifestyle"* as epitomising this 'balance' of personal utility, a view similarly echoed by Beaver (2002). Business growth and profitability may be two such goals, though both will be sub-optimal because of the importance attached to non-economic lifestyle motivations and aspirations as discussed above. Nevertheless, the debate is real. Thomas (2000) claims that the bulk of small tourism firms do not aspire to grow, whereas Buick et al. (2000) have recorded the opposite finding from their study of small, independent Scottish hotels. Holmengen and Bredvold (2003) add yet another dimension by suggesting that lifestyle motivations of small tourism enterprises are adjustable, according to what is economically achievable for the business.

Negative aspects of lifestyle trading tend to be given less emphasis in the literature than the perceived positive aspects, long working hours notwithstanding. Two levels of argument are characteristic, also reflecting a 'macro' versus 'micro' perspective of the issues. Firstly, at a 'macro' level, lifestyle proprietorship may be deemed 'problematic' within destination areas. For example, in their discussion of the phenomenon within the Scottish tourism industry, Andrew et al. (2001) attribute the 'resource poverty' of lifestyle businesses with a number of concerns relative to inward investment, quality standards, marketing and business development. These include creating a market situation in which commercial profit maximising operations are unable to compete in terms of service quality and pricing. Therefore, it is assumed their widespread presence effectively retards the development of international standards at the local destination level. Though not explicitly directed against lifestyle businesses, such a sentiment nevertheless found expression in the 1994-2000 Scottish Tourism Strategic Plan (STCG, 1994).

It is customarily at the destination level that negative linkages between seasonal trading and lifestyle businesses are articulated. Andrew et al. (2001: 13) propose that temporal operation reduces the propensity of the business to invest in marketing, training and quality upgrading, particularly where it is an 'accessory' to the lifestyle of the operator. However, such assertions could be equally directed at seasonal operators in urban areas which have less seasonally defined markets. In peripheral rural areas it is held that this may impact negatively on the total marketing effort at the destination level. Moreover, seasonal lifestyle operators are less likely to participate in seasonal extension destination marketing initiatives, should these be perceived to conflict with personal lifestyle objectives. 'Micro' level analysis of the negative aspects of lifestyle trading remains a largely unexplored area. The extended work hours and temporal unpredictability of passing trade and guests' service requirements in the hospitality sectors are readily observed (Lovelock, 1991; Morrison and Teixeira, 2003), however they may apply to all businesses irrespective of the proprietors' motivations.

The above provides a brief and partial overview of the literature pertaining to lifestyle motivations and small tourism businesses. The nature and extent to which any of these elements were evidenced in the exploratory study of seasonal tourism in the Scottish Borders forms the focus of the next section of this paper.

AN EXPLORATORY STUDY OF SMALL TOURISM BUSINESSES IN THE SCOTTISH BORDERS, 1999-2000

The prominence accorded to seasonality as a major policy issue in Scottish tourism provided the research impetus for a study of tourism businesses in the Scottish Borders. A consequent review of the literature and discussions with destination management personnel revealed that there was an 'understanding-gap' in the influences of tourism business operators' temporal trading decisions. Some initiatives were undertaken during the currency of the 1994-2000 Scottish Tourism Strategic Plan by destination management organisations (DMOs) representing rural and geographically peripheral areas, to determine 'best practice' in seasonal extension and the opinions of operators on that subject (SQW, 1997; Lowland; 1998a and 1998b; STB, 2000). The resulting investigation was designed to examine the relevance of a range of supply-side factors within the knowledge domains of seasonality and public policy. By framing the research as an exploratory study of businesses in a specific DMO area, the methodological approach, if proven sufficiently robust, might be repeated and/or tested comparatively for potential transfer to other areas and serve to facilitate theory building.

A particular objective was to explore the possibility of disaggregating demand-side influences from other factors in the trading decisions of tourism related businesses. For example, the non-participation of some enterprises in DMO-led seasonal extension initiatives might have little to do with the perceived costs or benefits resulting from an extended operating period (Andrew et al., 2001). Relationships between lifestyle factors and seasonal trading decisions were not explicitly articulated as an objective of the original research design. However, initial findings from the study indicated the presence of a range of linkages, and these are discussed in the findings below.

CONTEXT OF THE CASE STUDY AREA

The study was conducted in the Scottish Borders, one of 14 Area Tourist Board regions within Scotland. It is an intensely rural region in the south-east of Scotland, adjoining the English border region of Northumbria, yet only an hour by road from Edinburgh to the heart of the region (Figure 3). The area was chosen as a case study for logistical reasons, though also because it exhibits a number of characteristics, both in broad economic terms and in its tourism structures. Symptoms of peripherality were apparent, including limited access by public transport, declining traditional agriculture and an industrial sector based on agricultural output, a low value-added tourism economy and a predominance of micro-businesses, fragmented in market terms and uncompetitive to firms located within more central regions (Byron, 1995; Wanhill, 1997). The region accounts for around 2.5 per cent of Scotland's tourism earnings from domestic markets and around 1.5 per cent of the country's earnings from overseas visitors (STB, 1999) and has demonstrated a higher than average seasonal concentration of visitors and tourism earnings, compared with Scottish norms (Goulding and Hay, 2001). During the late 1990s, the Borders economy was badly hit by the combined effects of the BSE ('mad cow') crisis, the disinvestment of major electronics firms and the general decline in agricultural earnings for farmers.

The basis of the region's tourism is its outstanding natural landscape including the River Tweed and part of the Southern Upland hills, important coastal wildlife reserves and a concentration of historic houses, all

FIGURE 3. Map of the Scottish Borders

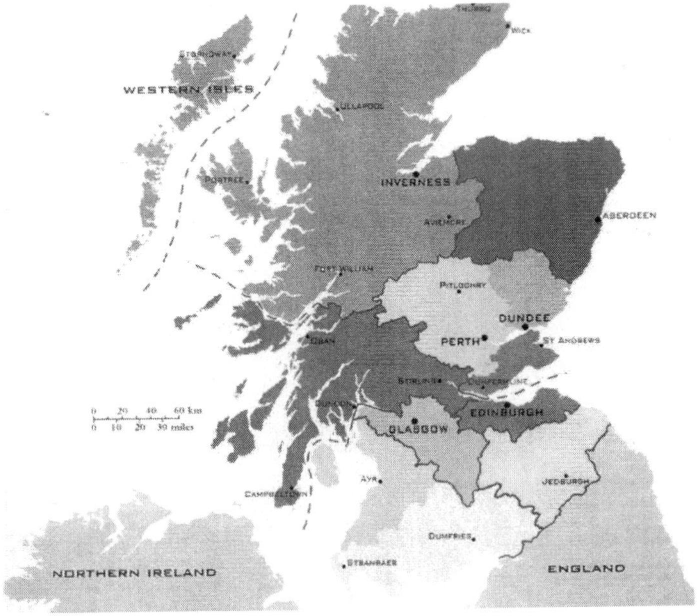

Source: Visit Scotland

of which operate seasonally (Goulding, 2003). There are no major urban centres, though clusters of attractive small market towns such as Kelso, Melrose, Selkirk, Jedburgh and outlying villages add to the appeal and identity of the region. In recent years the Scottish Borders Tourist Board priority has been given to the development of short break markets and activity based pursuits, including hill walking, cycling, fishing, golf, horse riding, appealing to high discretionary spend visitor markets (Goulding, 2003; SBTB, 1999).

METHODOLOGY

The methodological design mixed quantitative and qualitative approaches in the form of two inter-dependent stages, as detailed below. The first stage was designed to address the quantification and characterisation of seasonal operations in the study area (Goulding and Gunn, 2000), hence the use of a questionnaire mail shot as a data gathering tool.

For the purposes of narrative analysis of respondents' experiences and opinions, qualitative analysis was deemed appropriate (Flick, 1998).

(i) Stage 1: a structured postal questionnaire to a stratified sample of 311 businesses drawn from a database of around 1,050 tourism related businesses. The construction was *a priori* determined (Flick, 1998) using a statistical sampling approach (Oppenheim, 1992), based on different types of tourism-related operation, location within the Borders and whether the operation was year round or seasonal. The sample reflected geographical clustering within the study area, the sectoral spread of businesses, their status as members or non-members of the area's destination management organisation, and all known seasonal tourism-related traders in the area supplemented with a core of year round traders. The pattern of trading was determined by listings in promotional materials and through telephone contact with operators confirming their listing details. Inclusion of year round traders was designed to test the validity of individual supply variables through maximal variation (Flick, 1998).

After a piloting process, issues addressed in the questionnaire covered the age of the business, its period of operation and temporal variations throughout the year, trends in the length of the trading season, the importance of the market and of a variety of operational factors in influencing the temporal trading decision; proprietors' views on seasonality within the region and participation in the tourist board's seasonal extension initiatives. Variable ranking was used to ascertain importance measures, for example of selected trading influences, while questions probing proprietors' opinions mainly used simple semantic differentiation. In one case (views on the subject of seasonality) a 5 point Likert scale was applied to four separate statements. The high response rate to the questionnaire (57%) demonstrated the degree of emotiveness of the issues of seasonality. This is contextualised by the importance of tourism to the Borders' economy, the relative seasonal concentration of tourism in the region and the wider economic difficulties surrounding tourism, as previously described (Goulding and Hay, 2001).

(ii) Stage 2: semi-structured, in-depth site interviews with 19 operators also representing a cross-section of geographically spread, sectoral, seasonal and year-round businesses, though drawn purposively from the questionnaire respondents (Flick, 1998; Sommer and Sommer, 2002). These included proprietors of small family run hotels, country inns, holiday caravan parks, activity operators, several bed and breakfast establishments, self-catering operators, a gallery/shop, tea room, roadside restaurant, private museum, private country houses and a garden. The personal experience and unique perspectives of operators across the range of service

suppliers was sought above other considerations (Sommer and Sommer, 2002). This stage was designed to probe the relevance and relative importance of supply-side factors in determining the length and structure of trading patterns. Each interview lasted between 30-60 minutes and broadly followed the three main themes of the questionnaires, namely:

a. *'About the business,'* in which proprietors were prompted to expand on the nature of their service, the markets they served and the temporal characteristics of these markets; also the background to and development of the business, which included the nature of ownership and participation in the operation.
b. *Influences on the trading patterns,* including market, economic and non-economic factors in the decision-making process and their relative weight. A list of variables drawn from the questionnaire results was shown to the interviewees for comment. The construction of a supply-side framework as expounded in the findings (see Figure 4) derived from the discussions arising from these.
c. *'Your Views on Seasonality;'* in which interviewees were probed on their opinions of causation in the area's seasonality, whether or not they considered seasonality to be a problem and other observations pertinent to the operation of the business.

In analysing the questionnaire returns, Chi-square testing revealed some significant relationships in a number of the variables tested, including the incidence of variation in trading periods on the one hand, and on the other, the types of businesses, locations and length of trading. The transcribed interviews were initially limited to a straightforward content approach. Subsequently, thematic analysis was undertaken (Higham and Hinch, 2002) to detect where the narratives might indicate linkages between seasonal trading and lifestyle considerations. A wealth of data was generated from the two stages, though connections pertaining to seasonal trading and lifestyle associations were more evident from the interview narratives, given the purpose and design of the questionnaire, as described above.

FINDINGS

Discussion of the findings falls into three areas, including some primary results pertaining to the characteristics and incidence of seasonal trading, formative conceptualisations of supply-side influences) and the linkages between seasonal trading and lifestyle which emerged from these.

Characteristics of Temporal Trading

The degree of seasonal trading in the study area was significant, at 61.9% of the total questionnaire respondents sampled (Table 1). Around half of serviced accommodation and activity operators and 80% of self-catering and visitor attraction operators indicated seasonal closure, varying between a temporary closedown over the Christmas and New Year period to extended closure spanning over half the year, typically October till Easter. Businesses combining touristic facilities with local amenities, such as tea shops, retail outlets or craft centres, indicated much less propensity for seasonal closure (c15%). Furthermore, reported variations from the normal pattern of business hours and days during the course of the year indicated a more complex temporal trading pattern than simply one of extended periodic closure (Table 2). In some cases, 'year round' operators reported temporal variation in their trading patterns through adjustments in the days and hours of opening at different times of the year. Visitor attractions and shops/craft centres/small food and beverage outlets were most likely to adjust trading times and days during the course of the year. Issues of disaggregation of market influences and proprietorial discretion were thus considered to be pertinent areas of further investigation.

Market Influences on Trading Patterns

Given the seasonally-weighted composition of the sample and the level and variations of seasonal trading reported, it was not unexpected

TABLE 1. Frequency of Seasonal Operating Among Borders' Tourism Businesses

Sample Characteristics	
N = 176	
	Valid %
Seasonal Operating (< 12 months pa.)	61.9
Year Round Operating (full 12 months pa)	38.1
Seasonal Operators by Sector :	
Serviced Accommodation	51.4
Self-catering	80.0
Visitor Attractions	79.0
Activity centres and operators	50.0
Shops/retail/restaurants/craft centres	14.3

TABLE 2. Variation in Times and Days of Opening/Closure During the Year

	Valid %
Variation in the Hours of Opening	26.9
Later opening times during off-peak months	9.0
Earlier closing times during off-peak months	17.9
Other variation (eg. part closure of building)	8.4
Variation in the Days of Opening or Closure during off-peak months	25.6
Business closes on one or more weekdays during off-peak months	7.1
Business closes at weekends during some months of the year	11.0
Business closes down over the Christmas and/or New Year period	16.0
Other variation in daily opening/closing period during the year	11.6

to find that a degree of temporal business closure was claimed to be un-related to prevailing market conditions. However, over a third of the seasonally trading respondents rated the level of customer demand to be of little or no importance to their opening and closure patterns, com-pared with just over 50% of year round operators, many of whom clearly appear to commit to year round trading per se. Perhaps more sig-nificant in public policy terms was that only 35.8% of seasonal traders claimed customer demand levels to be the most important factor influ-encing opening and closure. However, some caution is required in inter-preting this finding, given the variation in the roles and context of businesses. For example, country inns and some hotels in rural areas of-ten fulfil a local community role beside that of a tourism resource, while a significant level of respondents reported other means of income. Nev-ertheless, such a significant finding provided a fertile basis for explor-ing individual case and sectoral experiences in the interviews.

Supply-Side Influences on Trading Patterns

A number of variables were 'tested' in this section of the question-naire, and followed up in the semi-structured interviews, which in turn revealed further influences through the narratives. Participants were asked which factors influence when and for how long the business trades during the year. Principal among the questionnaire responses from seasonal traders were the weather (mentioned by 55.9%), trading patterns of other tourism businesses in the area (44.1%), maintenance and repair work (41.2%) and significantly 'our own holidays' (36.8%) (Table 3). The surprisingly high incidence of other tourism businesses' trading patterns as influences reflects the local dominance of the historic houses throughout the study area. All of them operate seasonally and act as considerable magnets to both day trip and short break visitor markets (Goulding, 2003).

As stated earlier, the in-depth interviews were designed to draw out the significance of some of the data generated from the questionnaires. Influencing factors may have different meanings and significance across the spectrum of tourism operations. As an example, the role of the weather as a trading determinant was expressed in different terms by interviewees from different trading sectors. For some operators of activity pursuits, adverse weather may be a trading constraint from a health and safety perspective (e.g., diving schools, horse-back trekking). A few bed and breakfast operators, on the other hand, expressed the view that it was not worth taking bookings during 'empty' periods in adverse weather.

Analysis of open ended comments and transcripts of the interviews therefore suggested different decision making frames regarding opening and closure policy. These fell into two broad categories: *endogenous*, defined as decisions within the business' control, or *exogenous*, where the decision to close may be beyond the control of the operator. As can be seen from Figure 4, the range of factors within both classifications is wide.

TABLE 3. Importance of Supply-Side Variables on Seasonal Operators' Trading Decisions

Variable	Most Important Influence % of Respondents Ranking 1st	Frequency of all Rankings within Total Responses Given Frequency	%
The Weather	25.0	38	55.9
Trading Patterns of Other Businesses	17.6	30	44.1
Maintenance and Repair Work	7.4	28	14.2
Our Own Holidays	5.9	25	36.8
Rest and Relaxation	1.5	21	31.9
Other Businesses We Own	5.9	18	26.5
Business Planning & Development	2.9	18	26.5
Staff Training	-	14	20.6
Other Non-Commercial Interests	2.9	8	11.8

Moreover, the sample reflects a mixed tourism economy in a rural context, comprising an element of public sector provision (museums, leisure centres) and voluntary (not-for-profit) sector provision (National Trust for Scotland and local trust properties) in addition to the predominant small independent business presence based particularly in the hospitality sectors. Accordingly, operating objectives vary beyond those of economic maximisation, with conservation, preservation, education and local amenity provision occupying important roles in some instances, especially for visitor attractions.

In the case of small business operations within the bed and breakfast, guest house, self-catering, small hotel and guiding/local sightseeing tour sectors, a significant element of operational choice was revealed, though varying in the degree of trading flexibility. These sectors also demonstrated a higher than average propensity for seasonal closure compared with the total sample (Goulding and Gunn, 2000). The closure of other tourism businesses in the area and adverse climate conditions are considered to cross the boundaries of endogenous or exogenous influences given the degree of trading discretion that such factors afford.

The range of personal objectives, trading patterns and influences elicited from the fieldwork also suggests an apparent element of 'lifestyle' trading within the Scottish Borders' seasonal tourism sector.

FIGURE 4. Endogenous and Exogenous Supply Factors Influencing Seasonal Closure in Scottish Borders' Tourism Businesses

Endogenous Factors	*Exogenous Factors*
tourism business operated as a secondary business/source of income	licensing restriction–health and safety examples: holiday home park; diving school
recuperation of the resource: examples: botanic garden, historic house and garden	licensing restriction–environmental: examples: permit for fishing, hunting
adverse climatic conditions: examples: walking tour, sightseeing, pony trekking	
maintenance and repair example: owner occupied historic house	maintenance and repair: statutory order examples: leisure centre, museum
closure of other tourist business(es) in the area	
personal/family commitment overrides need to operate–eg. owner-managers	personal/family commitment, serious health problem–unforeseen eg. owner-manager
operator's rest/relaxation/holiday inc. observance of secular holiday examples: B&B operator, activity operator	operating season is determined externally examples: heritage agency, local authority (inc. dual use of amenity for non-touristic purposes)

Seasonality and Lifestyle Trading

While the postal questionnaire aimed primarily to quantify and characterise seasonal trading and operators' views of seasonality, the semi-structured interviews afforded the opportunity to probe selected respondents on their trading influences. This in turn yielded interesting narrative regarding the business and life circumstances of those operators.

The interview transcripts suggested a broad range of motivations underlying the trading patterns of some of the interviewees. Some reinforcement of the findings of other empirical works (Lynch, 1998 and 1999; Williams et al., 1989) was apparent in terms of the importance of the home environment and physical locality of the business. A small family hotel owner in a central Borders market town stated his emotional attachment to his surroundings accordingly:

> *I stood in the High Street today . . . looked down and could see all the hills there. . . . everything here is a living history.*

Meanwhile, a country house owner-operator saw his seven month operating season as contributing

> *another dimension to the land, which is beautiful. I make more money out of letting the land for grouse, for sheep. . . . .*

Echoing Shaw and Williams' (1997) findings regarding in-migration as a factor in Cornish small tourism businesses, a seasonal owner-manager of a traditional inn in a remote location in the west Borders emphasised the location of the property as important in the business start-up decision:

> *we were looking for a small country house in the middle of nowhere but we didn't expect this. It's really special, adding the caveat . . . we haven't made any money in the ten years we've been here.*

The relative prevalence of various non-economic influences (for example, proprietors' holidays, rest and relaxation, family commitments) alongside market and financial factors on trading decisions was more clearly articulated by those businesses operating to a defined season. Flexibility was a recurrent theme in the narratives:

we are private, therefore to a certain extent we have been able to do what we like,

from an independent visitor attraction operator, and

the season I now have is what I choose to fit in with my life,

from a bed and breakfast operator in a farming environment.

The incidence of seasonal closure for taking holidays, rest and relaxation crossed a number of types of tourism business operation.

At the end of six months you've got to have a holiday. . . . you're becoming too stale, you get short tempered. . . and . . . the staff can't wait for the end of the season so they can have a rest. . . .

talking to B&B places . . . a lot seem to have the impression that they work hard enough during the summer . . . that they earn the rest at the end of the season,

from respectively an independent attraction operator and an activity operator.

Meanwhile, the notion of the business as 'hobby' was evident to an extent in the country house and visitor attractions sector, exemplified by

the business is supported and subsidised by my other work–and hobby

from an independent gallery operator.

A range of 'lifestyle-oriented' aspirations and motivations was apparent, in some cases irrespective of seasonal trading patterns. Though based on a small sample of interviewees (19), the interviews did seem to support the argument that for some small tourism related businesses, operational and growth motivations cannot always be explained from a purely economic rationale (Andrew et al., 2001; Holmengen and Bredvold, 2003; Morrison, 2002; Williams et al., 1989), when their motivational equation encompasses physical and psychological comfort, personal health, socialisation and even environmental awareness, alongside revenue generation.

Manual narrative analysis of themes in the taped transcripts identified a number of distinct *roles* attributed to seasonal trading among the cross-section of interviewed proprietors. In some cases these roles were established through a process of sensitivity probing (Oppenheim, 1992) of specific variables such as family commitments or holiday taking, while elsewhere such roles emerged through unprompted discourse. Figure 5 provides a summary of such 'seasonal related lifestyle themes' from the interview transcripts.

Indicative Lifestyle-Related Seasonal Trading Roles

There are clear inter-linkages between some of the roles identified in Figure 5, each of which is the interviewer's own interpretation derived from the context of the individual narrative. For example, attributes of stability and control afforded to operators by seasonal trading may be

FIGURE 5. Roles of Seasonal Trading Discerned from the Interview Transcripts

Role of Seasonal Trading	Statement Examples from Interviewees
1. as an inherent motivation for entering the tourism/hospitality trades	"we decided to give it up [former trade] and bought the [holiday home park] which became a family home for all of us. We only operate seven months a year."
2. provides a framework for living-eg. stability, predictability, control	"we are private, therefore to a certain extent we have been able to do what we like…"
3. complements other business interests	"the season I now have is what I choose to fit in with my life"
4. complements time related lifestyle goals	"normally our holidays are taking groups …away on trips abroad…so we're not actually on our holidays…"
5. enhances emotional attachment to physical space, the home, material possessions, hobby	"out of season the house becomes ours again"
6. balances proprietor's environmental concerns/ values	"you don't want the place swarming with tourists [all year round]..it detracts from the beauty of living…"
7. fulfils social roles/allows family commitments	"…nor do we think it's environmentally sound…if you're cycling on that you're damaging that"… [referring to off-road cycling in the winter months]
8. 'downtime' allows physical and mental rest and recovery	"at Christmas and the New Year you have the family here, grandchildren here, that's important"
	"the staff can't wait for the end of the season so they can have a rest"
	"at the end of six months you've got to have a holiday….you're becoming stale, you get short tempered"

prerequisites for enabling proprietors or their partners to undertake other remunerated work. Moreover, it is acknowledged that specific attributes of seasonal trading vary according to individual proprietors' personal circumstances and thus will assume different ethnographic meanings and validity (De Laine, 2000).

Most, though not all interview subjects expressed lifestyle related motivations for temporal trading. A variety of personal circumstances was also apparent among seasonal operators, including cross-generationally operated businesses,

> *family businesses [like ours are] relatively satisfied with what they've got and are quite happy to see it handed to the family* (a holiday park operator),

sole proprietorship in single households and in partnership arrangements.

Therefore the nature of social roles afforded by seasonal trading can be expected to vary from business to business. Accounts by owner-managers of having entered the tourism sector with the intention of trading for several months of the year support the argument (Morrison, 2002; Alexander and McKenna, 1999) that access to lifestyle benefits is associated with having sufficient financial reserves. Also, a high incidence of dual income sources was reported by interviewees,

> *'it's our business but I just do the bed and breakfast bit on my own'* (a combined B&B and guiding operator) while in some cases the issue of seasonal complementarity between the tourism business and the other principal income source (agriculture) was articulated.

Connections between temporal trading and the home environment were observed on two levels. First, there was the aspect of emotional attachment to the physical space as 'home'. Several proprietors offered the opinion that temporal trading allows a sense of peace and ownership to be restored at the end of 'the season'. Secondly, a small minority of interviewees expressed sentiments relating the benefits of seasonal tourism to the state of the physical environment. Such views add support to the debate on the role of post-seasonal recovery as described by Baum and Hagen (1999), Butler (2001) and Flognfeldt (1988). Moreover they provide an interesting perspective on Morrison's (2002) assertion that small tourism and hospitality business owner-managers can be committed to sustaining the local environment and community for a range of moral and lifestyle, as well as commercial motivations. Examples include local sourcing (such as the Isle of Skye Food Initiative in which local accommodation operators buy local produce to serve their guests) and incorporating rural bank branches and post offices in small hospitality businesses (Morrison, 2002).

Finally, a range of attributes were raised pertaining to mental health and personal welfare, both of the proprietor and his/her family, and relating to employees. Articulation of the need for 'escape' or rest at the end of the season echoed other previous empirical studies of seasonality and destination communities, such as Jordan's (1980) work in Vermont and more recently Flognfeldt's (2001) study of Jotunheimen, Norway, in which the author noted the incidence of seasonal employees and employers taking long holidays during low seasons.

CONCLUSIONS

It is acknowledged that the realities of seasonal trading patterns in a destination locale transcend 'lifestyle' motivations of small tourism related businesses for a number of reasons. Tourism provides a complex mix of variables, such as the differing size and scale of enterprises, even within the categories of small and micro-businesses (Thomas, 2000), their pattern of ownership and involvement, the varying operational and personal objectives of operators (Andrew et al., 2001; Morrison, 2002) and the often disparate nature of services provided within the local tourism sector. Moreover, the tourism proprietor is operating in a unique physical environment, geographical context and economic structure. Yet seasonal traders are still pervasive within Scotland, especially in rural, peripheral areas (Baum and Hagen, 1999; Butler, 2001; Goulding and Hay, 2001). Where the incidence of seasonal trading is significant, they are part of the economic landscape of tourism. As such, they continue to attract the attention of DMOs and local economic development agencies who view seasonality as a challenge, a phenomenon of 'overcome'.

Accordingly, a clearer understanding of the nature and related influences affecting supply-side factors generally, and such destination management organisations and local economic development specifically, would be advantageous.

agencies. A number of issues underlie this need for greater understanding, especially in light of the increasing profile of tourism in the Scottish economy and the need to revitalise the rural economies (Scottish Executive, 2000).

Firstly, the range of reasons accounting for seasonal trading is broad. Operating on a temporal basis may provide a number of advantages to its proponents, which are unrelated to the nature of the market(s) they serve. The formative results of the exploratory study revealed the prevalence of both endogenous and exogenous factors in the seasonal trading decision frame. In the case of the latter, the influence of other seasonal businesses on the temporal trading decisions appeared to be a significant factor in the seasonal trading decision for some operators. On the other hand, a number of 'controllable' factors such as closure for holidays, rest and relaxation and personal/family commitments, were noted to wield some influence in small business proprietors' trading pattern decisions. Acknowledging the impact of such factors may help DMOs understand the apparent reluctance some operators may have in engaging in seasonally based market planning and development. Indeed, public and private-sector co-funded seasonal extension marketing initiatives may fail to achieve an optimal level of take-up by businesses within the destination area, if there is a significant attachment to seasonal trading (Andrew et al., 2001).

Secondly, seasonal trading by small business proprietors may be to the overall advantage of the local economy as a whole, especially where tourism complements other activities (Baum and Hagen, 1999; Flognfeldt, 2001). Increasing policy and product linkages between tourism and other economic sectors (Scottish Executive, 2000) such as agriculture and manufacturing are apparent throughout many of Scotland's tourism areas. Understanding the competing and complementary seasonal demands of tourism and other sectoral economies may contribute to the process of wider local economic development planning.

The exploratory study also suggested that seasonal trading can assume a variety of lifestyle-related roles for individual business operators, a number of which were elicited from the interview narratives. Although there is much scope to test the strength and validity of such roles through further study, the potential implications arising from them may provide useful input to such areas as the dynamic of the local tourism economy, local and network participation, individual business growth and turnover and, all, the motivational influences of private tourism operators.

tent a limited empirical scale, the study revealed a wealth of potential business directions and foci within the realm of small tourism proprietors' seasonal trading decisions. It is clear that there are linkages between market and non-market forces, exogenous and endogenous supply-factors and the role of lifestyle motivations and aspirations at play. Seasonal trading may be a desired modus operandi, attributable to the business motivations and aspirations of such operators, which are not always expressed in economic terms. However, the degree of potency of 'lifestyle' as an influence on seasonal trading and vice versa remains largely unexplored, empirically and conceptually, and a fertile area of enquiry towards greater understanding of the dynamics of tourism, especially within the rural Scottish context.

ACKNOWLEDGEMENTS

Acknowledgement and thanks are extended to personnel in the two key destination management organisations, the Scottish Borders Tourist Board and Visit Scotland (formerly the Scottish Tourist Board) for their kind help and resources offered in facilitating the design and implementation of the fieldwork.

REFERENCES

Alexander, N. and McKenna, A., (1999). Rural Tourism in the Heart of England. International Contemporary Hospitality Management, Vol. 10, No. 5, pp. 203-207.

Allcock, J. (1995) Seasonality. In Witt, S., Moutinho, L. (eds.), Tourism Marketing and Management Handbook, Student Edition., Hemel Hempstead: Prentice Hall International.

Andrew, R. Morrison, A. and Baum, T. (2001) The Lifestyle Economics of Small Tourism Businesses. Journal of Travel and Tourism Research, Vol. 1, June 2001, http://www.stad.adu.edu.tr. pp.16-25.

Bar On, R.R.V. (1975) Seasonality in Tourism: A Guide to the Analysis of Seasonality and trends for Policy Making. EIU Technical Series No. 2. London: The Economist Intelligence Unit.

Baum, T. (1997) Managing People at the Periphery: Implications for the tourism and hospitality industry. Proceedings of the 6th CHME Hospitality Research Conference. Oxford Brookes University, pp. 86-97.

Baum, T. and Hagen, L. (1999) Responses to Seasonality: The experiences of peripheral destinations. International Journal of Tourism Research, Vol. 1, pp. 299-312.

Beaver, G. (2002) Small Business, Entrepreneurship and Enterprise Development. London: Prentice Hall.

Birley, S. and Rosewell, B. (1998) Family businesses in Britain. Iin Family Businesses: How Directors Can Manage Key issues in a Family Firm. London: Director Publications Ltd.

Blackburn, R.M. (1999) Is Housework Unpaid Work? International Journal of Sociology and Social Policy, Vol. 19, No. 7/8, pp. 1-20.

Blass-Nogueira, M., Casamayor-Lagarda, J,, Diaz-Mier, M. and Eusebio-Rivas, P. (1968) La Estacionalidad en el Turismo y sus Posibles Correctivos. Cuadernos Monograficos. Madrid: Instituto de Estudios Turisticos.

Buick, I., Halcro, K. and Lynch, P. (2000) Death of the Lifestyle Entrepreneur: A Study of Scottish Hotel Proprietors. Praxis, Fall 1999/Winter 2000, pp 114-125.

Butler, R.W. (1994) Seasonality in Tourism: issues and problems. In Seaton AV et al. (eds.), Tourism-the State of the Art. Chichester: Wiley.

Butler, R.W. (2001) Seasonality in Tourism: Issues and Implications. In Baum, T. and Lundtorp, S. (eds.), Seasonality in Tourism. Amsterdam: Pergamon,

Byron, R. (1995) Economic Futures on the North Atlantic Margin. Aldershot: Avebury

De Laine, M. (2000) Fieldwork, Participation and Practice: Ethics and Dilemmas in Qualitative Research. London: Sage.

European Commission. (1993) All Season Tourism: Analysis of Experience, Suitable Products and Clientele. Brussels: Commission of the European Communities DG XXIII–Tourism Unit and Fitzpatrick Associates.

Fife Council, Kingdom of Fife Tourist Board and Scottish Enterprise Fife. (1997) Fife Tourism Strategy 1998-2001. St. Andrews: KFTB.

Flick, U. (1998) An Introduction to Qualitative Research. London: Sage.

Flognfeldt, T. (1988) The Employment Paradox of Seasonal Tourism. Paper presented at a pre-congress meeting of the International Geographical Union, Christchurch, New Zealand, 13-20 August 1988 (unpublished).

Flognfeldt, T. (2001) Long-Term Positive Adjustments to Seasonality: Consequences of Summer Tourism in the Jotunheimen Area, Norway. In Baum, T. and Lundtorp, S. (eds.), Seasonality in Tourism. Amsterdam: Pergamon.

Frechtling, D. (2001) Forecasting Tourism Demand: methods and strategies. Oxford: Butterwoth-Heinemann.

Gorton, M. (2000) Overcoming the structure-agency divide in small business research. International Journal of Entrepreneurial Behaviour and Research, Vol. 6, No. 5, pp. 276-293.

Goulding, P. (2003) Seasonality: The perennial challenge for visitor attractions. In Fyall, A., Garrod, B. and Leask, A. (eds.), Managing Visitor Attractions: New Directions. Oxford: Butterworth-Heinemann.

Goulding, P. and Gunn, G. (2000) A Supply Side Study of Tourism Seasonality: a case study of tourism businesses in the Scottish Borders. Proceedings of the 9th Annual CHME Hospitality Research Conference. University of Huddersfield, April 2000, pp. 361-369.

Goulding, P. and Hay, B. (2001) Tourism Seasonality in Edinburgh an the Scottish Borders: North-south or core-periphery relationship? Proceedings of the 7th ATLAS International Conference, June 2000, Discussion and Working Papers Series No. 3. ATLAS and Finnish University Network for Tourism Studies, pp. 16-33.

Gray, D. (1986) The Entrepreneur's Complete Self-Assessment Guide. London: Keegan Page.

Hartmann, R. (1986) Tourism, seasonality and social change. Leisure Studies, Vol. 5, No. 1, pp. 25-33.

Heelas, P. and Morris, P. (1992) The Values of the Enterprise Culture. London: Routledge.

Higham, J. and Hinch, T. (2002) Tourism, sport and seasons: The challenges and potential of overcoming seasonality in the sport and tourism sectors. Tourism Management, Vol. 23, pp. 175-185.

Holmengen, H. and Bredvold, R. (2003) Motives–the driving forces in achieving preferenced goals in tourism enterprises. In Quality of Life ATLAS Reflections 2003. Arnhem: ATLAS.

Hui, T-K. and Yuen, C.C. (2002) A study in the seasonal variation of Japanese tourist arrivals in Singapore. Tourism Management, Vol. 23, pp. 127-131.

Jordan, J.W. (1980) The summer people and the natives: Some effects of tourism in a Vermont vacation village. Annals of Tourism Research, Vol. 7, pp. 34-55.

Kennedy, E. and Deegan, J. (2001) Seasonality in Irish Tourism 1973-1995. In Baum, T. and Lundtorp, S. (eds.), Seasonality in Tourism. Amsterdam: Pergamon.

Krakover, S. (2000) Partitioning seasonal employment in the hospitality industry. Tourism Management Vol. 21, pp. 461-471.

Kuratko, D. and Hodgetts, R. (1998) Entrepreneurship: A contemporary approach. New York: Dryden Press.

Lovelock, C. (1991) Services Marketing. Englewood Cliffs: Prentice Hall.

Lowland Market Research. (1998a) Scottish Borders Tourist Board Seasonality Research: Findings from a programmes of SBTB members' research. Selkirk: SBTB.

Lowland Market Research. (1998b) Scottish Borders Tourist Board Seasonality Research: Findings from a programme of visitor research. Selkirk: SBTB.

Lundtorp, S. Rassing, C. and Wanhill, S. (2001) Off-Season is No Season: the Case of Bornholm. In Baum, T. and Lundtorp, S. (eds.), Seasonality in Tourism Amsterdam: Pergamon.

Lynch, P. (1998) Female microentrepreneurs in the host family sector: Key motivations and socio-economic variables. International Journal of Hospitality Management Vol. 17, pp. 319-342.

Lynch, P. (1999) Host attitudes towards guests in the homestay sector. Tourism and Hospitality Research, Vol. 1, No. 2, pp. 119-144.

Mathieson, A. and Wall, G. (1982) Tourism: Economic, physical and social impacts. Harlow: Longman.

Morrison, A. (2002) Small Hospitality Businesses: Enduring or Endangered? Journal of Hospitality and Tourism Management, Vol. 9, No. 1, pp. 1-11.

Morrison, A. and Teixeira, R.M. (2003) Small Firm Performance in the Context of Agent and Structure: A cross cultural comparison in the tourism accommodation sector. In Thomas, R. (ed.), Small Firms in Tourism: International Perspectives. London: Elsevier.

North Wales Economic Forum. (1998) Co-operating to Compete. North Wales Regional Tourism Strategy, 1998-2005.

Oppenheim, A.N. (1992) Questionnaire Design, Interviewing and Attitude Measurement. London: Pinter.

Scase, R. and Goffee, R. (1989) The Real World of the Small Business Owner. London: Routledge.

Scottish Borders Tourist Board. (1999) Scottish Borders Tourism Strategy 1999-2004. Selkirk: SBTB.

Scottish Executive. (2000) A New Strategy for Scottish Tourism. Edinburgh: HMSO.

Scottish Tourism Co-ordinating Group. (1994) Scottish Tourism Strategic Plan. Edinburgh: STB.

Scottish Tourist Board. (1999) Tourism in Scotland 1998. Edinburgh: Scottish Tourist Board

Scottish Tourist Board. (2000) Seasonality Solutions. Edinburgh: STB.

Segal Quince Wicksteed. (1997) Tourism as a Year Round Activity for Business: A report for Highlands and Islands Enterprise. Inverness: HIE.

Shaw, G. and Williams, A. (1997) The private sector: tourism entrepreneurship–a constraint or resource? In Shaw, G. and Williams, A. (eds.), The Rise and Fall of British Coastal Resorts: Cultural and Economic Perspectives. London: Mansell.

Sommer, R. and Sommer, B. (2002) A Practical Guide to Behavioural Research: Tools and Techniques. Oxford: Oxford University Press.

Soybali, H. (1994) Seasonality in Tourism: a case study of Turkey. 3rd Annual CHME Hospitality Research Conference, Napier University. Edinburgh.

Storey, D.J. (1994) Understanding the Small Business Sector. London: International Thomson Business Press.

Thomas, R. (2000) Small Firms in the Tourism Industry: Some Conceptual Issues. International Journal of Tourism Research, Vol. 2, pp. 345-353.

Wanhill, S. (1997) Peripheral area tourism: a European perspective. Progress in Tourism and Hospitality Research, Vol. 3, No. 1, pp. 47-70.

Williams, A. Shaw, G. and Greenwood, J. (1989) From consumption to production, from tourist to entrepreneur: tourism development in Cornwall. Environment and Planning A, Vol. 21, pp. 1639-1653.

Index

In this index, page numbers in *italics* designate figures; page numbers followed by the letter "t" designate tables.